Confronting Power and Sex in the Catholic Church

RECLAIMING THE SPIRIT OF JESUS

BISHOP GEOFFREY ROBINSON

johngarrattpublishing

Published in Australia by
John Garratt Publishing
32 Glenvale Crescent
Mulgrave Victoria 3170

Text: Geoffrey Robinson Copyright © 2007
Design and typesetting by Lynne Muir
Cover photograph by Alberto Incrocci, Getty Images
Edited by Cathy Oliver
Printed by Openbook Australia

First published August 2007
Second and third print September 2007
Fourth print November 2007

The National Library of Australia Cataloguing-in-Publication data:

Robinson, Geoffrey.
Confronting power and sex in the Catholic Church :
reclaiming the spirit of Jesus.

Bibliography.
ISBN 978 1 920721 47 3 (pbk.).

1. Catholic Church - Controversial literature. I. Title.

282

CONTENTS

Introduction 7

The More Immediate Causes of Abuse 9

The Wider Focus of this Book 19

A Personal History 20

1 Healthy People in A Healthy Relationship with a Healthy God 25

A Healthy God 26

Healthy People 30

A Healthy Relationship 40

Meditation 45

2 The Two Books of God 49

The Bible 50

The World Around and Within Us 57

Meditation 61

3 Spiritual Discernment 65

Tradition 65

The Tool of Discernment 73

Meditation 75

4 An Eternal Plan, a Sharing of Life and the Reign of God 77

God's Eternal Plan 77

A Sharing Of Life 78

The Reign of God 79

The Church 80

Meditation 84

5 'Like His Brothers and Sisters in Every Respect' 87

The Knowledge of Jesus 88

'Notification on the Works of Fr. Jon Sobrino S.J.' 93

Meditation 96

6 In Service of God's People 99

The Bible 99

What Has Been Handed On to Us 105

The Present Situation 116

Learning From the World Around Us 129

Meditation 132

7 The Authority of 'the Church' 137

A Peter-Figure 139

The Middle Level 144

The Faith of the Whole Church 145

Meditation 149

8 Free and Responsible 153

The Bible 153

Religious Liberty 158

Conscience 158

Assisting Conscience 164
Meditation   172

9 A Turbulence and a Whirlpool   175

The Bible   177
What Has Been Handed on to Us   193
Meditation 195

10 The Return to an Original Sexual Ethic   201

Origins of Current Catholic Teaching   201
An Ethic Based on Persons   204
The Major Questions   210
Meditation   214

11 A Dark Grace, A Severe Mercy   217

Spiritual Harm and Spiritual Healing   217
Forgiveness   220
A New Assignment to Ministry? 225
Meditation   231

12 The Prison of the Past   235

The Freedom to be Wrong   235
Truths Essential to Identity   237
One Authority Changing Another   241
Particular Issues   250
The Certainty of Faith   258
Meditation   260

13 A Government in which All Participate   265

Three Levels of Government   265

The First Level: the Peter-Figure 268
The Second Level: The Bishops 271
The Third Level: The Mind of the Whole Church 282
Meditation 287

14 A Change of Heart and Mind 289
Accountability and Professionalism 290
The Laity: Citizens or Civilians? 293
Renewing the Theological Conversation 296
Putting Our Own House in Order 297
A Church in the World 300
Conclusion 302
Meditation 304

Introduction

Sexual abuse of minors by a significant number of priests and religious, together with the attempts by many church authorities to conceal the abuse, constitute one of the ugliest stories ever to emerge from the Catholic Church. It is hard to imagine a more total contradiction of everything Jesus Christ stood for, and it would be difficult to overestimate the pervasive and lasting harm it has done to the Church.

This book is not directly about that abuse, but about the better church these revelations absolutely demand. In order to clear the way to speak about this better church, however, I believe that I must devote this introduction to the specific question of abuse.

In 1994 I was appointed by the Australian bishops to a position of leadership in responding to revelations of abuse, and for the following nine years I was at the heart of this storm within my country. I felt sick to the stomach at the stories that victims told me, I spent many sleepless nights and I lived at a constantly high level of stress. Those years left an indelible mark on me, for they led me to a sense of profound disillusionment with many things within my church, typified by the manner in which, I was convinced, a number of people, at every level, were seeking to 'manage' the problem and make it 'go away', rather than truly confront and eradicate it.

Through all of this I came to the unshakeable conviction that within the Catholic Church there absolutely must be profound and enduring change. In particular, there must be change on the two subjects of *power* and *sex*.

That we should look at sex is obvious, but there are two reasons why it is equally essential that we look at all aspects of power. The first is that all sexual abuse is first and foremost an abuse of power in a sexual form. The second is that within the Catholic Church there is a constant insistence that on all important matters Catholic people must look to the pope for guidance and direction. When a major matter arises, therefore, and there is a notable and extraordinary absence of guidance or direction from the pope - as was certainly the case in relation to the sexual abuse of minors - it is inevitable that many will react according to older values rather than with a new mind to meet a new problem. Those older values have for a thousand years included secrecy, the covering over of problems and the protection of the good name of the church.

In fact and in practice, there was a wide variety of responses to abuse within each nation, ranging all the way from the very good to the very bad. This very variety, however, was a symptom of the lack of leadership from the centre in a highly centralised church.

I am convinced that if the pope had spoken clearly at the beginning of the revelations, inviting victims to come forward so that the whole truth, however terrible, might be known and confronted, and firmly directing that all members of the church should respond with openess, humility, honesty and compassion, consistently putting victims before the good name of the church, the entire response of the church would have been far better.[1] With power go responsibilities. The pope has many times claimed the power, and must accept the corresponding responsibilities. Within the present structures of the Catholic Church, it is the pope alone who has the power to make the changes that are necessary.

Even now I cannot see evidence that a true confrontation of the problem is occurring. The staff of those clinical facilities specially set up for the treatment of priests and religious who have offended against minors have not been asked by Roman authorities for their findings on the causes of abuse. The bishops of the world have not been asked to coordinate research and study within their own territories. Until basic steps such as these are taken, I find it impossible to believe that church authorities are determined to confront rather than simply manage the problem.

The More Immediate Causes of Abuse

Under this heading I want to indicate areas where immediate study is needed and where the whole church should be involved.

Celibacy is not the sole cause of sexual abuse by priests and religious. It would actually be good if it were, for then, by the simple expedient of abolishing celibacy, one could abolish all abuse. But even if celibacy were abolished tomorrow, there is every reason to believe that the problem would not disappear. As I hope to show a little later, celibacy is a factor in a number of cases of abuse, but it is far from being the sole cause of all abuse.

The presence among the ranks of priests and religious of a number of persons with homosexual inclinations is also not the sole cause, or even a significant cause. Homosexual adults are attracted to other homosexual adults, and an attraction to minors, male or female, is a quite different phenomenon. A homosexual adult is not more likely to offend against minors than is a heterosexual adult. Screening out all homosexuals from the priesthood and religious life will not make the problem of child abuse disappear.

Offenders are not monsters who can be recognised as monsters at first glance. On the contrary, in order to offend, they need to be able to charm potential victims and win their confidence. Far from looking like monsters, they usually look like a very kind relative or friend, and they can be model priests or religious in all other aspects of their lives.

This is one of the difficulties in discovering them.

In short, there is no simple, one-cause explanation of child abuse by priests or religious. If we try to seize on any one single cause or give one simple explanation, we are avoiding the depth and complexity of the problem and we will fail to overcome it.

The best statement I have encountered concerning the causes of abuse, the one with the greatest promise of showing us the way forward, is that child abuse, by priests, religious or, for that matter, anyone else in the community, is most likely to occur when three factors come together: an unhealthy psychological state, unhealthy ideas concerning power and sex, and an unhealthy environment or community in which a person lives.[2]

Psychologists will admit that there is much about the phenomenon of sexual abuse that is still not understood. Despite this, there are many psychological studies on the subject. If I have a reservation concerning them, it is that they concentrate on the psychological state of the individual offender and look at unhealthy ideas and environment only in terms of contributing factors to this individual's psychological state. I suggest that each of the three factors in the lives of all priests and religious – psychological state, ideas and environment - deserves a complete study on its own, followed by the way in which they can interact on each other to produce the murky world out of which abuse arises.

An Unhealthy Psychological State

In this field I claim no special expertise, so I refer readers to studies that have been published,[3] and add only a few points.

There are two types of paedophile: the fixated and the regressive paedophile. The fixated paedophile is the person whose sole or at least overwhelming sexual attraction is towards minors,[4] and who is consequently not attracted towards adults of either sex. Just as there are no known means by which a homosexual can be turned into a heterosexual, so there are no known means by which a fixated attraction to minors can be turned into a sexual attraction towards adults.

The regressive paedophile is more common and most priest and religious offenders fit into this category. Such a person is basically either heterosexual or homosexual, but for a variety of reasons is tempted to offend with minors.

One of the problems in overcoming sexual abuse of minors is that there is no one single psychological profile of regressive paedophiles. As a consequence, there are no practical tests that can be applied to the general population that will tell us which persons will later offend in this field and which will not, so it is not possible to screen out all future offenders in advance.

There are what one writer has called 'red flags' of abuse[5], that is, signs that should alert others to the possibility of abuse, e.g. childish interests and behaviour, lack of relationships with one's own peers or a history of being abused oneself. It must be added, however, that the presence of such a red flag does not of itself mean that the person is an abuser, while the absence of all such signs is not proof that a person will not abuse others.

The regressive paedophile begins with free choice but eventually lives somewhere on the border between free choice and compulsion. In almost every case there is evidence of careful selection and 'grooming' of a victim, of planning of the circumstances, and of care taken to ensure that the victim does not speak to others of what has happened, so it is impossible to dismiss paedophile activity as the result of a 'sickness' for which the offender is not responsible. In most cases, there is clear evidence that offenders knew what they were doing and were responsible for their actions. On the other hand, there is also much evidence that even those offenders who most sincerely do not want to offend again can feel an urge to do so that is so powerful that, without outside help, they are unlikely to resist it. As in so many other fields, the truly important thing is never to commit the first crime, for there appears to be far more choice in that first offence than there is once the urge to repeat has become powerful.

Other than this, three general conclusions seem to be in order.

i) A wide variety of psychological problems within the person can be contributing factors when placed together with false ideas and an unhealthy environment.

ii) There are dangers if professional people, including priests and religious, are not equipped to deal with the high emotional demands of their calling.

iii) Professional people must have both the external and

internal resources to manage responsibly the authority with which they have been invested. To give great authority to a person who is incapable of handling it in a responsible manner is to invite problems.

UNHEALTHY IDEAS CONCERNING POWER AND SEXUALITY

POWER

All sexual abuse is first and foremost an abuse of power. It is an abuse of power in a sexual form. Unhealthy ideas concerning power and its exercise are always relevant to the question of abuse.

Spiritual power is arguably the most dangerous power of all. In the wrong hands it gives the power to make judgements even about the eternal fate of another person. It needs a sign on it at all times saying, 'Handle with extreme care'. The greater the power a person exercises, the more need there is for checks and balances before it is used and accountability after it is used.

If the governing image of how to act as a priest or religious is tied to the ideas of lordship and control, then, no matter how benevolently ministry is carried out, an unhealthy domination and subservience will be present. The worst case is that of the 'messiah complex', where a person believes that God is calling him or her to be, as it were, a messiah, a chosen one who is called to some special mission and is, therefore, above the rules that apply to ordinary mortals, including the moral rules. In such cases, if sexual abuse does not occur, some other form of abusive behaviour will.

There is an issue here that applies mainly to priests and only to a lesser extent to religious. In my years of training to become a priest, there was a phrase from the Letter to the Hebrews that was much quoted:

> 'Every high priest chosen from among human beings is put in charge of things pertaining to God on their behalf, to offer gifts and sacrifices for sins.' (5:1)

The Greek word (*lambano*) here translated as 'chosen' means simply 'taken', but the Latin text that was always quoted said *assumptus*, which means 'taken up'. The implication was that the priest was 'taken up' from among human beings to some higher level. This is not what the Letter to the Hebrews meant, for the next words are,

> 'He is able to deal gently with the ignorant and wayward, since he himself is subject to weakness, and because of this he must offer sacrifice for his own sins as well as for those of the people.' (5:2-3)

Despite this, the idea of being 'taken up' was part of the culture and it brought some reflection of the 'messiah complex' into that culture. It was not a healthy idea and it must now be confronted.

This in turn led to a 'mystique' of the priesthood, a permanent state of being 'taken up'. And this meant that a priest could not simply be sacked for an offence, as another worker might be. It was this 'mystique' that was in large part responsible for the practice of transferring offending priests to new appointments in a way that, say, a lay teacher in a Catholic school would not have been treated.

Closely allied to this can be an inability to accept failure and vulnerability. Priests and religious can be made to feel that, because they have been 'taken up', they must be perfect. When they realise that they cannot achieve this, they can feel that they must at least appear to be perfect. Perfectionism is dangerous in most fields, and it is particularly dangerous in a field as vast as the spiritual and the moral, where perfection is simply not possible for a human being. Feeling that one must appear to be perfect even when one knows that one is not, being unable to admit to failure and weakness, is an unhealthy attitude. Inherent in it is the covering up of faults that do occur. There must be room for a painful struggle towards maturity, with many mistakes along the way.

In priests and religious this attitude can be strengthened by the expectations of others. They can feel that religious superiors, people in their parish, the media and the community at large demand that they be perfect and will strongly criticise any lack of perfection. They can be made to feel that what would be described as an understandable failure in another person would be called 'sickening hypocrisy' in them. These expectations can cause them to show externally a level of perfection that they know they do not possess. In both priests and religious on the one hand, and in the community on the other hand, there needs to be change in the expectations that are present. Priests and religious are ordinary human beings, and if either they or the community forget this, one kind of problem or another will be caused.

SEXUALITY

In a later chapter I shall detail a number of unhealthy ideas concerning sex and sexuality in the teaching of the Catholic Church. Here I add only a few points that apply specifically to priests and religious.

Eros or desire is the source of passion, imagination and dreaming. It is associated with sensitivity, touch and vulnerability, and is at the heart of compassion. It is an important means by which a person participates in both social and religious life. For priests and religious, desire has often been denied or treated with suspicion. And yet the failure to cultivate desire can take away the natural warmth and spontaneity of love and leave goodwill a vague term not directed at anything in particular. Where *eros* is not given sufficient attention, chastity can become mere control and lovelessness. Given strong reasons, a young person might be prepared to contemplate a life without genital sex, but no young persons in their right mind should be prepared to give one second's thought to the idea of a life without an abundance of *eros* and love.

If *eros* is denied, it is inevitable that in male candidates for priesthood and religious life there will also be a denial of the feminine which nurtures and fashions its energy. If the masculine is not balanced by the feminine, there can be a growing danger of incapacity for interior reflection, an inability to relate with intimacy, a dependence on role and work for self-identification, and the loss of a humanising tenderness. The need for intimacy is particularly important, for it cannot be extinguished and, if unfulfilled, will seek expression in covert and distorted ways.

At the beginning of Chapter One I shall make the statement that in the past the spiritual life was often presented in the negative terms of self-denial, self-abasement and rejection of the 'world'. This negativity certainly extended to the management of one's sexuality and it contributed to the unhealthy world I am seeking to describe.

If some of the ideas of the church concerning sexuality have been unhealthy, I also consider the entire attitude that 'anything goes' to be unhealthy. When put together with other factors, it, too, can lead to one or other form of sexual abuse. Priests and religious who, in the name of breaking away from false ideas of the past, have dallied with this mentality have entered very dangerous territory.

AN UNHEALTHY ENVIRONMENT OR COMMUNITY

Traditional seminaries (for priests) and novitiates (for religious) can be unhealthy places in which to grow to maturity, especially when candidates are taken in as young as eleven or twelve years of age. There are many factors that do not contribute to healthy growth: the one-sex environment, the absence of parents and other nurturing figures, the other sex as a 'threat' to a vocation rather than as a positive and essential influence for adolescents, the absence of any positive preparation for a celibate lifestyle. At a time when adolescents and young adults need to develop their own identity, this is subsumed into a collective vision and expectation. The impersonal nature of the institution can cause a sense of emotional isolation, and this can be accentuated by an emphasis on the intellectual and spiritual at the expense of human development. Ordinary needs for intimacy can seek their satisfaction covertly. While the situation varies greatly from one seminary or novitiate to the next, one must seriously question whether institutions are the place to form priests and religious.

Religious communities can also be unhealthy places in which to live. Most members are trying to live by Christian principles, but this can merely put a coat of paint over the lack of intimacy and the failure to meet profound needs that can be present. It cannot make up for emotional inadequacy and a covering over of conflicts rather than facing and resolving them. A single 'difficult' individual can disrupt a whole community. In a number of communities one must query how much effective communication takes place and at what level. Today it is likely that the members of the community go out to different jobs each day and there is often little opportunity for an effective 'debriefing' on the stresses that are met in these different jobs.

Priests in parishes, on the other hand, more and more live on their own. Today, with fewer and older priests and increasing demands, they feel stressed and overworked. Profound human needs are not being met. The revelations of sexual abuse have caused morale to plummet and have diminished the sense of satisfaction in the work they are doing.

There are few checks and balances on the exercise of power by priests and religious and there is quite inadequate accountability. I shall return to this in a later chapter.

The Sum: A Climate of Abuse

The three factors mentioned can come together to form a *climate*, a murky world in which abuse is more likely to occur. The church must look at the different ways in which this *climate* can be created within its institutions.

There must be a three-pronged attack, a study of the psychological state of priests and religious, a study of their attitudes towards power and sex, and a study of the environment or communities in which they live. In each study we must look at any and all elements that are unhealthy and that could in any way contribute towards creating the climate of abuse. Rather than wait for convincing proof that a particular element has actually caused abuse, we must change all elements that are seen to be unhealthy and could, therefore, contribute. There is no point in making changes in one of the three areas while leaving the other two untouched.

The end result of sexual abuse may occur in only some cases, but unhealthy elements have negative effects on all priests and need to be changed for that reason alone.

Celibacy

We must look well beyond celibacy if we are to find and eradicate the causes of abuse. Nevertheless, celibacy is all pervasive in the life of a priest or religious and needs to be looked at in a special way.

Among the many and complex causes of abuse, there are three categories in which celibacy appears to have made a direct contribution.

While the abuse of children has been the object of almost all attention, there has also been abuse of adults, especially women, and this, too, has caused great harm to the victims. It has not received attention because the police have normally responded that it appeared to be a consenting relationship and so no crime had been committed. In almost all cases, however, there has been the sexualising of a pastoral relationship, and in many cases an abuse of spiritual power to obtain sexual favours. It is hard not to see celibacy as contributing to these cases of abuse of adult women.

There have been cases where persons have been taken into a seminary or novitiate at too young an age and, because of the environment, their psychosexual development has not progressed beyond the age of about fifteen years, so that it is minors towards whom they are attracted. This is the explanation of only some cases of abuse, but they do exist.

In the third category, it is known that in an environment such as a prison, some heterosexual persons can become involved in homosexual sex, not by preference, but because it is all that is available. It would seem that there have been some priests and religious who abused minors, not by preference, but because minors were available, either physically or psychologically. Physically, they have been available in places such as orphanages or schools. Psychologically, it is known that some offenders against minors can claim that celibacy applies only to relations with adult women, so they claim in all seriousness that they have not broken their vow of celibacy. For some priests and religious, this may be the sense in which adult women are psychologically 'not available' but minors are. Once again, this applies only to some cases and it would be foolish to think that with these three categories we had now explained all abuse.

In most cases it is not celibacy itself that is the problem, but obligatory celibacy. There have been saints who were so madly in love with both God and people that the idea of marriage did not even occur to them, for there was so much to do in loving people and caring for them that there would have been no time for marriage. A celibacy freely chosen out of a burning love for people is unlikely to lead to abuse, for it is not unhealthy.

The problem occurs when young persons are attracted to priesthood or religious life but find that it comes wrapped in a package that contains many elements. Because priesthood or religious life can exert such a powerful call, some of the other elements of the package, e.g. celibacy, do not receive the attention they should. The system of removing the candidates from the world and from 'temptation' does not assist them in this. Some time after ordination or profession, they can find that priesthood or religious life still looks attractive, but celibacy does not. Sadly, many priests and religious fall into this category. If the pope were to ask for a disclosure 'before God alone' on this point from all priests and religious, in secret and without betraying their identity, there might be both surprise and alarm at just how large is the number of those who are genuinely dedicated to the priesthood or religious life but are living it in an unwanted, unassimilated and, therefore, unhealthy celibate state. Many of those who have left the priesthood or religious life in the last forty years have been in this category, but so are many of those who remain.

All of this points to the major problem with obligatory celibacy, namely, that it is the attempt to make a free gift of God obligatory, and one must seriously question whether this is possible.

The law of celibacy assumes that everyone who is called by God to priesthood is also called by God to celibacy and given the divine assistance necessary to lead a celibate life. But is this a mere assertion or a proven fact?   Is it a case of human beings making a human law and then demanding that God follow that law by giving special divine assistance to those bound by the law? If church authorities really wish to insist on obligatory celibacy as a requirement for priesthood, should they do far more than simply assume a call to celibacy in those interested in the priesthood?   Should they, for example, continue to take students into the seminary before they are adults and have an adult understanding of what celibacy means?   May they continue to assert that those thousands of priests who have left the priesthood in recent decades in order to marry were all called by God to celibacy and given every divine help they needed, but deliberately refused this assistance?

Celibacy can contribute to the unhealthy psychological state (e.g. depression), the unhealthy ideas (e.g. misogyny or homophobia) and the unhealthy environment (e.g. an unwanted and unassimilated celibacy) out of which abuse arises. If it is far from being the sole cause of abuse, it cannot be said that it makes no contribution. If the church is serious about overcoming abuse, then the contribution of celibacy must be most carefully considered.

There is one other way in which celibacy has contributed to abuse. A significant reason why the response of many church authorities has been poor is that many bishops and religious superiors, not being parents themselves, have not appreciated just how fiercely, and even ferociously, parents will act to defend their children from harm. If they had been parents, there would surely have been a more decisive response.

At least in the Western world, celibacy has come to be seen as the acid test of whether the church is truly serious about overcoming abuse. Much that is said can be simplistic and involve misconceptions, but this does not change the fact that, unless and until the church puts celibacy on the table for serious discussion, people will simply not believe it is serious about abuse. To start with the statement that the requirement of obligatory celibacy cannot and will not be changed or even examined, as both Pope John Paul II and Pope Benedict XVI have done, is to lose credibility before the discussion even begins. Some may speak all they wish of the benefits of this celibacy for the church, but others will not stop asking, 'How many abused children is celibacy worth?'

The Wider Focus of this Book

It is not my intention to delve further into the matters I have just raised, for they must be the subject of a broader study in which the expertise of many different people in different fields is brought together.

Instead of this, the present book will look at a wider picture, including many elements that may not at first sight appear directly connected with abuse. There are two reasons for this wider study. The first is that we must look at the very *foundations* of attitudes towards both power and sex in the church, for without changes in these foundations, any action taken would not touch the underlying problems. The second reason is that the fact of abuse has revealed a double problem, the abuse itself and the response of church authorities to that abuse, and the second problem has caused as much scandal as the first. It is only by studying the wider church that we can see some of the more fundamental issues involved in both of these questions. The rest of this book will, therefore, be about the wider church rather than directly about abuse.

It will never be possible to 'manage' the revelations, so that they go away and are not mentioned again. I have a serious fear that many church leaders are now feeling that the worst of the problem is behind them, that is has been successfully 'managed', and hence that they do not need to look at deeper issues. This attitude grossly under-estimates the negative effects the scandal has had and involves wishful thinking for the future. Yes, inroads have been made into the backlog of cases that had built up over several decades and some offenders have been deterred, if not by any moral reasons, then by the sheer terror of an offence being disclosed. But if we remain silent and hope the problem will go away, abuse will continue to occur. One day, sooner or later, the whole problem must be confronted. Granted the present structures of the church, what we must cry out for is a pope who will say publicly, 'Yes, I am genuinely serious about confronting both abuse and the response to abuse, and I will ruthlessly change whatever needs to be changed in order to overcome both of these problems. Please help me to identify all contributing causes.'

A Personal History

Before beginning the wider study, I must confess that I am not a purely objective student of this matter.

The years I spent working in the field of sexual abuse had such a profound effect on me because I had myself been sexually abused when I was young. The offender was not a priest or religious, nor anyone within the Catholic Church, nor was he a relative. I belonged to that five percent of cases where the offender was a stranger. Neither in my age at the time it happened nor in the duration of the abuse was it as serious as much of the abuse I have encountered in others, and yet, if the man had been caught in any one of his acts against me, he would have been sent to prison. It was never a repressed memory, but for most of my life it was, as it were, placed in the attic of my mind, that is, I always knew it was there, but I never took it down to look at it.

When, in 1994, I was appointed to an official position in the church's response to abuse, I passed through three stages. In the first stage I tried to act as a good human being, a good Christian, a good priest. I soon realised that this was not enough, so I quickly moved to a second stage of listening to as many victims as I could in order to learn from them. Somewhere in this process I moved to the third stage where what they were feeling and saying stirred strong echoes within my own mind and heart. It was only then, some two years after

I had been appointed, and some half a century after it had happened, that I finally took my own history down out of the attic, looked at it again and, for the first time in my life, named it as sexual abuse. With the help of counsellors, I became conscious of some of the effects it had had on me.

Flowing from all of this, my problems with the church's response to the revelations of sexual abuse ran deep and reached up to the highest levels of the church, for I was one of many people crying out for strong and compassionate leadership on this matter and trying to do my best without the support of that leadership. I felt that here was the perfect opportunity for the papacy to fulfill its most basic role of being the rock that holds the church together, but this did not happen, and the church fractured. I found it impossible to accept that I must give 'submission of mind and will' to most words written by a pope, but a failure to give leadership in a crisis seemed to count for little. I felt that the demand was being made that I give my submission to the silence as well as to the words, and I could not do this.

When, in front of several journalists at a public meeting, I answered a victim's question by saying that I was not happy with the level of support we were receiving from 'Rome', I received an official letter (7 August 1996) expressing 'the ongoing concern of the Congregation for Bishops that you have in recent months expressed views that are seriously critical of the magisterial teaching and discipline of the Church.' I was told that 'in a recent audience, the Holy Father has been fully apprised of your public position on these issues and He has shown 'serious preoccupation in your regard.' Two months later (16 October 1996) I received a further letter informing me that 'The relevant documentation will be forwarded, for its information and review, to the Congregation for the Doctrine of the Faith', implying that I was suspected of some form of heresy.

I admit that I felt personally hurt by this criticism of the only truthful reply I could have given to a room full of victims, but it also led me to the conclusion that an authority that had to be defended in a manner as heavy as this must have had serious doubts about its own response to abuse.

There has never been a perfect church and there never will be. I must always work within an imperfect church, and must never forget that I am myself an imperfect member of that imperfect church, contributing my problems and failures as well as my assistance. Sometimes, however, circumstances can arise where there is only a fine line between accepting that I must work within an imperfect church and becoming complicit in the harm that those imperfections are causing to people.

I eventually came to the point where I felt that, with the thoughts that were running through my head, I could not continue to be a bishop of a church about which I had such profound reservations. I resigned my office as Auxiliary Bishop in Sydney and began to write this book about the very foundations of power and sex within the church.

I believe that in this book I describe a better church, a church that is not contrary to the mind of Jesus Christ. How others will react to the book is up to them, but the case for reform must be most seriously considered, for we must confront all factors that have in any way contributed either to abuse or to the inadequate response to abuse.

THANKS

I acknowledge the assistance of a number of people who have read all or part of a draft of this book and offered valuable comments that saved me from errors and gave greater depth to the book. It says much about the need for change that, in the atmosphere that prevails within the church, I would be creating difficulties for them if I gave their names. They know who I mean, and to each one of them I offer my sincere thanks for their comments and support.

FOOTNOTES

[1] The document that is always referred to as the response of the pope to abuse is a letter to the bishops of the USA of 11 June 1993. This letter, however, highlights the problems, for it is addressed to the bishops, not to victims; it makes no call to the church like the one I have just outlined; it spends almost a third of its length decrying 'sensationalism', i.e. blaming the media; and the only solution it offers is that of prayer. Needless to say, I am in favour of prayer, but I would hate to limit my response to victims to saying, 'I will pray for you.'

[2] See David Ranson, of the Catholic Institute of Sydney, in his article 'The Climate of Sexual Abuse', *The Furrow*, 53 (July/August 2002), pp.387-397. In much of what follows I am indebted to this article.

[3] For an excellent summary of the point psychology has reached and for nineteen pages of bibliography on the subject, see *Child Sexual Abuse: A Review of the Literature*, The John Jay College Research Team, Karen J Terry, principal investigator and Jennifer Tallon, primary researcher. See also *The Nature and Scope of the Problem of Sexual Abuse of Minors by Catholic Priests and Deacons in the United States*, a Research Study conducted by the John Jay College of Criminal Justice. Both documents may be found on the website of the United States Conference of Catholic Bishops at *http:/www.usccb.org/ocyp/webstudy.shtml.*

[4] In much of the literature there is a distinction between paedophiles, who are attracted to children under the age of twelve, and ephebophiles, who are attracted to minors over the age of twelve.

[5] Stephen J. Rossetti, *A Tragic Grace, The Catholic Church and Child Sexual Abuse*, The Liturgical Press, Collegeville, Minnesota, 1996, Chapter Four, *Red Flags for Child Sexual Abuse, pp.64-79.*

CHAPTER ONE

Healthy People in a Healthy Relationship with a Healthy God

U nhealthy ideas lead to unhealthy actions, and in any religion the most important ideas are those that concern the kind of god who is being worshipped and the kind of relationship we should have with that god. In describing a better church in which abuse will not happen, this is where we must start. Indeed, if we do not get this right, most other changes would be a waste of time. Studying this topic will also show us how God has exercised power over us, and this must surely be the model for how all authorities in the church should exercise power.

In the past much of the spiritual life was presented to people in the negative terms of self-denial, self-abasement and rejection of the 'world' and this constant negativity played its part in creating the murky world out of which sexual abuse arises. In our own day we have seen a reaction against this attitude, but it has too often gone to the opposite extreme of being a quest for personal self-fulfilment that is not always sensitive to others. There is need for a middle ground, and I suggest that it can be summed up in the idea of 'healthy people in a healthy relationship with a healthy God'. By the word 'healthy' I intend ideas and attitudes that give people the freedom to grow to become all they are capable of being.

A HEALTHY GOD

In any religion, everything without exception depends on the kind of god that is worshipped, and in practice this means that everything depends on the human ideas that people impose onto their god. For those who believe in one God, the danger is that, unable to grasp this infinite God, they so impose their own ideas onto the god they believe in that they create their own god within their own mind and worship this 'god'. It is just as easy for Christians to do this as it is for the members of any other religion. There is only one God, but an endless variety of human misunderstandings of God.

If we cannot have adequate ideas of God, we can at least seek to agree on ideas that are basically healthy rather than unhealthy.

There is no human being who does not have profound fears and there is no human being who does not have almost infinite longings. Over the millennia the fears have caused people to think of God as angry, while the longings have caused them to think of God as loving. Because we all have fears and longings, we are never free from the danger of imposing both our fears and our longings onto the god we believe in.

As a consequence, human beings have always had problems in combining the two ideas of justice and mercy in the one god. We have difficulty in finding the right balance between mercy and justice in all aspects of our lives, and we have reflected this difficulty in our attitudes towards our god. There have been many examples of gods who appeared to veer from angry justice to loving mercy and back again in a quite contradictory manner. It must be said that the Hebrew bible, often called the Old or First Testament, contains many such contradictions.

During the last millennium the Catholic Church reflected far too much of the angry god. At its worst people were ordered to perform the impossible task of loving a most unlovable god under pain of damnation. Millions of people were affected by these ideas and their lives were, to a lesser or greater degree, made sadder and poorer. Many of the worst pages in church history came out of belief in an angry god, emphasising that the question of the kind of god we worship is a crucially important question.

In recent decades there has been a strong reaction against the angry god. It has been a good reaction in so far as it has rejected the false idea of a jealous god who is greatly concerned with power and majesty and quick to take offence. It has been good in rejecting the idea of life as walking through a minefield of 'mortal sins' that are likely to explode at any second.

Like most reactions, however, it has tended to go to an opposite extreme. If I may use an analogy with parents, this movement has gone all the way from parents who beat their child into submission to parents who spoil their child. It has created the idea of a god of soft and indulgent love, a god so 'loving' that nothing is asked of people and they are challenged to nothing. Under such a god it is just as certain that people will not grow as it is that spoiled children will not grow as they should. The followers of this god can go so far as to deny the very existence of right and wrong, personal responsibility or standards of conduct.

Healthy ideas of God must be found in the middle between these two extremes, and we can take our start from our understanding of what makes people good parents and good teachers. The best parents and teachers love children, but with an intelligent love that knows when to give a child a big hug and when to challenge a child to further effort. Their overriding desire in all they do is that the child should grow to become all he or she is capable of being. There is a place for obedience, but it is never an end in itself. Obedience is a means and growth is the end it must serve. So parents and teachers will seek to inspire children to want to grow and they will place before them challenges that are appropriate to their age and level of development, for it is in large part by meeting these challenges that they grow.

In a similar way, there is a place for obedience in our relationship with God, but it is only a means to an end. God's glory is not to be found in our obedience as an end in itself, but in our growth. We cannot grow under an angry god and we will not grow under a god of soft, indulgent love. We will have a true freedom to grow only under a god who loves us and, because of this love, wants us to grow to become all we are capable of being, and so is not afraid to challenge us to grow. It is my profound belief that this is the idea of God that Jesus consistently presented to us.

In relation to one of the central points of this chapter, God has exercised power over us, not by control and the demand for obedience, but by constant love and by loving challenge, always seeking our growth and our co-operation in that growth. This must be the model for church authorities.

We will never be free from profound fears, so the angry god has deep roots within us and it is never easy to leave this god behind. In fact, no amount of willpower will achieve it, but only the *experience* of the God of love.

A GOD BEYOND OUR GRASPING

The theologian Paul Tillich has written, 'It is not easy to preach Sunday after Sunday without convincing ourselves and others that we *have* God and can dispose of him.... I am convinced that much of the rebellion against Christianity is due to the overt or veiled claim of the Christians to possess God.'[1]

This has been true in a particular way in the Western half of the Christian world. There has been a passion to analyse God, to set out lists of the attributes of God, to attempt to penetrate even the mystery of the Trinity, and in general to fill books with our human comments about God. The Orthodox Churches have been more aware of the need for silence, wonder and awe before the mystery of God. In the Jewish tradition, too, when Moses asked God for a name, the mysterious reply was that of JHWH. Western Christians have constantly spoken this name out loud as either Jehovah or Yahweh, but the Jewish people have understood it better by treating it as too sacred and too mysterious to be spoken at all.

Among the many traps the Christian religion has fallen into through this passion to say things about God is that of presenting an exclusively masculine god. We are constantly reminded that Jesus spoke of God as his father, but rarely that he also used the language of a hen gathering her chickens under her wings or that, in many stories in the gospels, he saw powerful reflections of God in the women he met. When we present a masculine god, we limit God; and whenever we limit God, we turn God into a very large human being rather than a true god. All such limitations involve the setting up of an unhealthy god who will prevent our true growth. Only a god who is above our human concepts of masculine and feminine, and above all the words we use, can be an explanation of the world we live in and an answer to our deepest longings.

If this is true of God, it is true also of all the things that flow from God. The constant search for truth and the constant openness to truth are more important than the possession of truth. The constant and genuine search to find moral goodness is more important than the possession of particular moral truths. The search for answers to questions of evil and suffering is more important than any answers we come to. And the search for God is more important than any ideas of God we may have. The bible is a search, morality is a search, the spiritual life is a search, life itself is a search, love is a search and God is a search. There will never be a time in this life when we can stop searching because we are in possession of all that we need to find. We must move from a god we can possess to a god of infinite surprise. We must never forget the necessity for a profound humility.

A God Who Comes to Meet Us

There are two aspects of the angry god that can remain even when we feel that we have embraced the God of love. The first idea is that God sits still and waits for us to do all the work of bridging the gap between us, and the second is that, if we do all the right things, we can earn the love of God. In both of these cases the relationship with God would remain an unhealthy one that would prevent our growth.

In relation to the first idea, if the life, death and resurrection of Jesus Christ have any meaning at all, they mean that God did not sit still and wait for us to do all the work, but came to meet us. Jesus was God born as we are born, feeling hungry and thirsty, tired and sad as we do, meeting fear and suffering as we meet them, and dying as we must die. In any relationship between God and ourselves God always takes the first step and every single thing we do is a response to God's invitation. God is always the first to say, 'I love you'.

In relation to the second idea, a couple cannot earn each other's love, for their love is a free gift or it is nothing. In a similar way, everything we possess and are is a pure gift from God. We did not earn our life with all its possibilities, we did not earn the talents and abilities we possess, we cannot earn God's infinite love, and we cannot earn an eternity of happiness with God. There can be immense relief in learning that we do not have to earn God's love, for it is there already in abundance.

Healthy People
Self-Denial and Self-Love

Jesus said, 'If any want to be followers of mine, let them deny themselves and take up their cross and follow me.'[2] It is obvious that Jesus lived these words in his own life, so no Christian can ignore them. To be a Christian involves denying or renouncing ourselves and following Jesus to some form of Calvary.

On the other hand, today there is a wealth of material telling us that a basic self-love and self-esteem are essential to our freedom to grow. It has been pointed out that being self-centred is far more often the result of self-hating than of self-liking. The self-hating person feels an emptiness within and must fill this void by constantly thinking about self, while the self-liking person can forget self and go out to help others.[3]

It has also been said that, while giving oneself for others is good, sacrificing one's own deepest good for others is not, for all true love must benefit two people, the lover and the one loved.[4] I can deny myself any unnecessary material goods, I can deny my comfort, advantage or convenience, but I must not deny my own deepest good or my own spiritual growth. I must love my inmost self and my love for others must be a love than gives both them and myself the freedom to grow.

The Christian Context

There are two extremes that the Christian must avoid. One extreme speaks only of personal self-fulfilment and denies the example and words of Jesus about taking up a cross. The other extreme speaks only the negative language of denial and renunciation and does not allow for the proper self-love without which true growth is not possible. There is a middle ground and it may be found only when we reject both extremes and try to combine into one the two ideas of renunciation and self-love.

Imagine that I go to a symphony concert where the orchestra and a soloist play Tchaikovsky's piano concerto. If the pianist is very good, there can come a moment when everything around me fades away and I am taken up into direct contact with Tchaikovsky alone, who speaks to me through his music. At that moment the pianist could paraphrase the words of St. Paul in his letter to the Galatians, 'I live now, not I, but Tchaikovsky lives in me'.[5]

It is Tchaikovsky alone who can support and continue this moment, for it is his music alone that contains the inspiration, the genius, the divine spark that no one else in that hall possesses. Take this away and the music would come to an abrupt halt, for no one else can supply it.

At the same time, it is at this moment when we have forgotten the very existence of the pianist that the pianist is most fully alive, most fully all he or she is capable of being. There will have been a vast amount of hard work, and, therefore, of self-denial and renunciation, before this moment became possible, and it would never have been possible if the person had had a narrow and indulgent idea of self-fulfilment. On the other hand, there would also have to have been a basic self-love, self-esteem and self-confidence, or the pianist would never have had the courage to begin the long journey to this moment, let alone complete it.

I have chosen Tchaikovsky deliberately, for he was homosexual at a time when it was not possible to be open about this fact and he suffered greatly from this tension in his life. This suffering is so much part of the music he composed that I do not believe any pianist who knew nothing of suffering could really take me to that moment when I was in direct contact with Tchaikovsky himself. The pianist would not need to have had exactly the same experiences as Tchaikovsky, but would need to have known anguish, helplessness, fear and anger.

In a similar way, people could be in a position to say the words of Paul, 'I live now, not I, but Christ lives in me' only when they had combined these different elements in their lives. Jesus alone would supply the spiritual inspiration and genius and they would have to be constantly connected to this source of spiritual energy. They would need to have a basic love of self and belief in self, as Jesus certainly did, for without this growth would not be possible. They would have to make every effort to become all they were capable of being, with all the renunciation and self-denial this would involve. And, like Jesus, they would have to open themselves to the full pain and tragedy of the world around them and seek to enter the depths of its mystery. They would need to experience their own brokenness.

There is a long history behind the few thoughts I have expressed here. Much of that history was negative and went too far with the idea of denying oneself. In recent decades the reaction has gone too far in the opposite direction. For the next millennium it is essential that the church find and articulate that middle ground that gives the only true freedom to grow.

THE SEARCH FOR MEANING

There are certain fundamental questions about life that all people are constantly asking themselves: Who am I? Where do I come from? Where am I going? What is the purpose and meaning of my existence?

Whether people are consciously aware of these questions or not, they are in fact giving some answer to them. The answers they give might be complete or partial, they might be satisfying or unsatisfying, they might include a divine being or they might not, but whatever they are, they express the spiritual dimension of their lives.

In this broad sense the word 'spiritual' indicates that which links all the different facets of our life into one whole and gives a sense of meaning to that whole.[6]

We constantly ask these big questions about life because they reflect one of the most profound drives within human beings, the search for meaning. Meaning is of the greatest importance to people. When they become bored with their marriage or their job or their lot in life, they begin to feel that their life is going nowhere, that it lacks meaning. And there are few things that so eat away at a person's sense of dignity and self-worth as a loss of a sense of meaning in life.

Not long ago there was a top-level meeting in the city where I live on the subject of illegal drugs. Different people saw drugs as a health problem, a social problem, a law and order problem or an education problem, but there was no public mention of the fact that it might also be a spiritual problem in the sense in which I have used the word here. And yet, it is when people have no sense of meaning in life, no satisfying answers to the big questions, nothing that links the various parts of their lives into one whole, that things like drugs and even suicide can begin to seem attractive. We will not make serious progress against drugs and suicide until we confront the spiritual dimension of the problem. Our society has been good at destroying many of the spiritual values of the past, but it has not been good at replacing them with other values that young people might find truly satisfying.

Love

So where do we look for meaning? Modern psychology agrees with every major religion the world has known in saying that there is only one source of meaning in the world: love.

Love is the deepest longing of the human heart and comes from the very centre of our being. All other desires and longings within us can be traced back to this source and are different expressions of this one fundamental longing. It is so deep that nothing on this earth can satisfy it, not even all the loves of our life put together.

Whenever we try to say anything about this longing in words, however, we find that we ask too much of the poor little word 'love'. The ancient Greeks at least came closer by having three words to express three different aspects of love: *eros* (desire), *philia* (affection) and *agape* (self-giving love).[7]

Since the time of Freud, *eros* and its adjective 'erotic' have been largely restricted to sexual desire, but in earlier times the word included all desire. *Eros* or desire is the unquiet aspect of love: the fire within, the restlessness, the loneliness and nostalgia for better times, the wildness and ache at the centre of our being. It can be felt as a pain, dissatisfaction and frustration, but it can also be felt as an energy and pull towards beauty and creativity. It is a subject of eternal fascination, and we love stories about desire, sexual attraction, journeys into the unknown, tragic loss and triumphant regaining.[8] We can desire something with all our being and yet, when we achieve it, find that it has done little to assuage the deepest desires of our heart. Ultimately, all desire, no matter what form it takes, is a desire for love.

Philia is the affection that we feel for those close to us. We want them to be an important part of our life, we want all that is good for them, and we want these things so much that strong feelings are spontaneously engaged. *Philia* can include all the feelings of romantic love and all the tenderness of true friendship.

Agape goes out to others without looking for anything for oneself. It is the genuine love one might feel for people on the far side of the world who are dying of hunger. It does not exclude affection (e.g. the self-giving love of parents), but it extends even to people for whom one has no feelings of love. It is the type of love that can be known only from the actions it prompts and, if it prompts no actions, one must query its existence. It exists within all people who have not totally hardened themselves to others. If some self-sacrifice would prevent a war between two countries, most individuals would be willing to make that sacrifice. Even if the condition were attached that no one would ever learn of the sacrifice, most people would still act.

All true love starts as desire, leads to affection, and culminates in self-giving love. For example, a couple desire a child (*eros*), are overwhelmed by feelings of affection and tenderness when they first hold their baby in their arms (*philia*), but quickly discover that this love involves immense self-giving (*agape*).[9] It is important that self-giving should not leave desire and affection behind, but be constantly strengthened and renewed by them.

Our whole life is a response to this multi-faceted longing for love within the depths of our being.

To take a simple example, a young person might come to love the violin and work hard to learn to play it. This love will give the person three things. Firstly, it will give a sense of achievement in doing something worthwhile and through this a sense of deeper love, and hence of *meaning*. Secondly, because it gives a sense of meaning, it will also give the *energy* to keep on pursuing the love, so that the person will continue to work hard to master the instrument. Thirdly, at a later point the love can actually create a significant part of the person's very *identity*, so that, if you asked another person 'Who is that?', the answer might well be, 'Oh, that's the violinist.' The love has then become at least part of the person's answer to the big questions of life, a feeling that part of the reason for the person's very existence is to be a carrier of the beauty that violin music can contain. It has then become one part, and perhaps even a significant part, of the spiritual dimension of this person's life, that which brings all the different facets of life into one whole.

In the same way, other people become lovers of husband/wife and children, lovers of nature, science, literature, animals, sports or an almost infinite variety of other things.

The object of our love can be:

i) any *person* such as a husband or wife, a child or a friend,

ii) any *object* such as a flower, a painting or a gemstone,

iii) any *activity* such as playing or listening to music, walking by the sea or studying history,

iv) any *idea* such as a passion for justice or a search for perfect beauty.

Our sense of meaning in life then comes from the *sum total* of the loves of our life. The more love there is, the more meaning there is. And there is no other source from which meaning can come. There can never be too much love and there can never be too much meaning.

Three Conditions of Love

There are three conditions for healthy love. Firstly, the love must give people and things the freedom to grow. It must not be the possessive love that suffocates, the conditional love that manipulates, the selfish love that seeks only its own good, or the mistaken love that denies one's own deepest good. Love is not an ability but a capacity, for it consists in creating space in which people and things are free to grow.[10] If love does not create the freedom to grow, it is not true love.

Secondly, if it is to give meaning and energy, the love must in some manner be returned.[11] Flowers return our love, just by being beautiful, even though they will wither and die. Activities can return the love we give them, though they can also give us bad days when we feel that our love is not returned. A passion for justice can bring much frustration, but it can also bring a powerful return of love. Persons are by far the most satisfying, for no object or activity can return love in the way they can, but they are also the most dangerous, for no object or activity can hurt in the way they can.

Thirdly, there must be some balance and proportion among the things we love. If the young person I mentioned earlier spent so much time practising the violin that there was no time left over for people, the love would have become an obsession that would suffocate rather than allow to grow.

There are many paradoxes in love. If we want to see our love returned, we should give without thought of return. Love is not bought or sold, it is always gift. It is fallen into rather than planned. The more we love another person, or even a thing, the more we must make ourselves vulnerable to be hurt by that person or thing. And yet, despite these paradoxes, it is love alone that gives meaning to our lives.

Divine Love

Every time we experience love for anything at all, we feel some satisfaction and sense of meaning in our lives, but we also know that we long for a deeper and fuller love and meaning. We feel that we are somehow prisoners within our bodies and we long to escape and fly beyond the stars. We feel something infinite within ourselves and long for the infinite. Ultimately we long for perfect love and perfect meaning. Any way of life that does not even attempt to answer this infinite longing will not satisfy us. So God is an essential part of our meaning-making at its deepest level.

On the other hand, religion can make the mistake of speaking as though infinite, divine love were the only love that mattered, and this is not true. Indeed, if I were told that a certain person had a burning love for God, but loved nothing and no one else, I would instantly know that something was radically wrong. Jesus insisted that love of God cannot exist without love of neighbour, and there is a psychological as well as a religious truth to this statement. If a religious body presents some contradiction between love of God and love of the world God created, it is failing its people. There is much wisdom in the words of a Jewish writer, 'People will be called to account by God for all the legitimate pleasures they failed to enjoy.' All genuine love is a sharing in divine love and leads to God.

My sense of meaning in life, therefore, comes from my relationships with people and from the many ways in which those relationships are expressed. It comes from flowers and music, from colour and perfume. It comes from the marvellous complexity of nature, from stars and planets and from atoms and particles. It comes from the fluid grace of a horse or cheetah or eagle or dolphin. It comes from a passion for justice for the poorest people in the world and a desire for reconciliation with the dispossessed. It comes from all these things and many more, and even then it still leaves me with a profound sense that all these loves are not enough.

Divine love is, therefore, essential. Without divine love, there is always the danger that we will ask too much of objects and persons in this world. Music can express exquisite beauty, but we cannot demand total meaning of the whole of life from a violin. Romantic love can be overwhelmingly beautiful, but it is dangerous to demand total meaning in life forever from one other limited person. God alone can meet the bottomless depth of our longing for love.

The fragility of love reminds us that we should never take it for granted. On one occasion when I visited a refuge for homeless youths, there was a young man there who had had to appear in court that morning on a charge. I noticed something moving on his upper arm and asked what it was. He unzipped a pocket there and took out his pet mouse. I asked whether he had had the mouse with him in court and he said that he had. My first thought was that this was a dangerous thing to do, but I then thought that, if a pet mouse is one of the few things in life you love, if it is one of the very few reasons you have for getting up in the morning, then you will insist on keeping it with you in all circumstances. It was a reminder that, after all the talk, many people do not find love everywhere they look and have to take the little they can get.

The world we live in has destroyed many of the values of the past. At times it presents to us things so grossly superficial that they cannot possibly provide lasting satisfaction. The search for love and meaning is universal, profound and at times desperate. We can never take love for granted, and it is good to be grateful for the love that we have in our lives.

One of the great tasks of the church in the third millennium should be to help people to find the maximum amount of love and meaning in their lives from every possible source, human as well as divine. It must do this from its own spiritual resources and in dialogue with the world. This is one of the great crying needs of today and it will be present throughout the whole millennium.

TO BE FULLY ALIVE

St. Irenaeus once wrote, 'The glory of God is a human being fully alive'.[12] This is a marvellous statement that is as strong today as it was when it was first spoken eighteen hundred years ago. It means that God does not find glory in millions of human beings bowing down in obedience and fear. God's glory is to be found in human beings who are fully alive. What might be meant by this phrase?

Many parents see in their first baby a great composer or painter or writer or scientist, an Olympic athlete, a pope or president. Most of these dreams will not be realised, but they reflect the fact that every baby is at the beginning of a journey towards all it is capable of being.

The desired end to this journey is different for each individual. We live in an age when people have unrealistic ideas of perfection and consider themselves failures if they do not achieve them. The reality is that we all have disabilities. Indeed, those who are called disabled can often be the true realists, for they more frequently accept their disabilities and learn to live within them, while the rest of us can deny our limitations and seek an unrealistic perfection.

Some babies will be physically stronger, some will have higher intelligence, some will have greater artistic gifts. But none will have all possible gifts in all possible fields. Throughout their lives all will carry two packs on their back wherever they go. One pack will contain their cultural baggage, the limitations imposed by the time and country and culture into which they are born. The other will contain their psychological baggage, the limitations imposed by their genes, their upbringing and the events that have affected them. They can do something about lightening the load, but they can never be free of the packs.

Within these limitations, the task of each person is to advance as far as possible along the road towards all that particular individual is capable of being. This will involve the development of their whole persons – their physical, intellectual, emotional, social[13], artistic, moral and spiritual being.

According to their circumstances, most parents do all they can for the physical and intellectual health of their children. They are also concerned for emotional and social health, but these are so complex and subtle that the results are more varied. Artistic development is sometimes fostered and sometimes not. Moral and spiritual growth can sometimes be the first consideration and sometimes the last.

And yet all seven forms of growth are essential parts of our journey towards all we are capable of being. All can be used to help other people and to love God. None of them should be left out. It has been said, for example, that persons who work at being physically fit need only a small part of their energy to get through the day and have much energy left over to help other people, while persons who do not take care to be fit need much of their energy just to get through the day and have far less left over to help other people. Why, then, would a genuinely spiritual person who wants to help others not spend time keeping physically fit?

It is, of course, legitimate to emphasise one or the other form of growth. The manual labourer and the athlete will emphasise physical development. The teacher and the scientist will have spent much time in intellectual development. The psychiatrist will see the harm that can be caused by lack of emotional development. The painter or sculptor or musician will be concerned with artistic development. The person who seeks to inspire change in society will look to social development. The person with a passion for justice will want moral development and the person with a passion for wholeness will seek spiritual development.

And yet no one of these seven forms of development should so dominate that the other six are neglected. The person who is all muscle and no brain, the intellectual who cannot relate to people, the artist who uses and abuses people in the pursuit of art, the moral person who constantly judges others, the person who, in seeking the spiritual, despises human qualities — none of these persons represents the end of the journey towards all we are capable of being.

Spiritual Development and Human Development

The denial of human development in pursuit of the spiritual is a problem that runs deep in the church. The central Christian doctrines about this world are the Creation and the Redemption, and this error came close to denying the very goodness of God's creation and the very completeness of Christ's redemption. It created divisions between matter and spirit, body and soul, sacred and profane and church and world that should not have existed. The tragedy was that, when the human was ignored, people could not become 'fully alive'.

Even people who were physically weak or of low intelligence or without any seeming artistic talent have become saints. Indeed, even people who were quite neurotic have been canonised. But there has never been a true saint who was deliberately weak or ill or ignorant or neurotic. There has never been a true saint who could have overcome any of these difficulties and would not do so. The true saints all knew that talents are gifts from God that are meant to be developed to the fullest possible extent and used for the good of all people. They knew that denying the talents they had been given was not humility, but fear or laziness. Even in the seeming absence of all other talents, they knew that, at the very least, they had an immeasurable talent for love.

They did not develop their talents in a selfish manner, as though developing talents was an end in itself. They developed their talents through helping others and they developed them so that they could help others even more.

And so, to be 'fully alive' involves recognising our talents as God's gifts, greeting them with wonder and gratitude, developing every talent to its full potential and seeking to use it for the good of other people, recognising the talents of other people and being grateful for them too, avoiding the futile comparisons between others' talents and our own, and accepting that every talent is also a challenge and hence a responsibility.

After the creation of the man and woman, 'God saw *everything* that had been made, and indeed, it was *very* good' (Gen.1:31). Jesus added, 'I have come that they may have life and have it in all its fullness' (John 10:10).

A Healthy Relationship
A Person and a Story

Christian faith is first and foremost faith in a person and a story, the person of Jesus Christ and the story of his life, death and resurrection. From this story will flow many truths (for example, God created the world), many norms of living (for example, it is wrong to murder) and a worship of God (for example, going to church on Sundays), but the response to the person and the story comes first.

Without this personal relationship, the truths will become lifeless, the norms of living will be burdensome tasks and the worship will be empty. With the relationship, the truths will come alive, the norms of living will be the most natural things in the world and the worship will be life-giving. If we take the personal relationship out of religion, all that is left will be nothing more than empty formalism.

In the person of Jesus Christ and the story of his life God is constantly saying to each one of us, 'I love you'. It can never be enough to answer, 'I believe all the truths you have revealed' or 'I will obey all of your commands' or 'I will go to church every Sunday'. The only genuine answer is a response of love to love, and that means a response of our whole person – our minds, our hearts, our feelings, our very core.

If the relationship between ourselves and God is not a love relationship, it will inevitably be a commercial relationship, in which we are saying to God, 'I will believe all the truths you have revealed, I will obey all your moral rules and I will go to church on Sundays, and you in return will give me eternal happiness in heaven.' But a commercial relationship will never satisfy us, for it cannot reach the depths of our longings. In a commercial relationship we will forever be critical of the terms, we will seek to reduce what is required of us to a minimum, and we will always want to be in charge, determining exactly and in detail what part God shall have (and shall not have) in our lives.

There is a sad paradox in the fact that many people are afraid to commit themselves to a love relationship with God out of fear of what it might ask of them, and so limit themselves to truths, moral rules and worship, even though this ensures that their religious beliefs and practice will never satisfy them. Religious faith makes sense only as a love commitment of one's whole self, for it is only the response of love to love that can give the Christian religion its dynamism, its attractiveness and its power to satisfy the depths of the human soul.

Truths, norms of living and worship all have their legitimate and important place, but religious faith must never be reduced to intellectual assent to truths, external compliance with norms of living and physical attendance at public worship. Presenting faith as a series of propositions and moral rules to be learned by heart can never be a substitute for the passing on of a living faith in a person and a story.

At every moment of every day God is saying to each one of us, 'I love you. There are no conditions. I love you exactly as you are, with all your faults and weaknesses. I do not demand that you change into a better person before I will begin to love you.' This and nothing else is the foundation of all religious faith, and that faith is born when we can begin to answer, however timidly, 'I love you too'.

> 'I bless you, Father, Lord of heaven and earth, for hiding these
> things from the learned and the clever and revealing them to mere
> children.'[14]

PRAYER

In his book *The Brothers Karamazov* Dostoyevsky has a scene in which Ivan debates with the devil and says, 'Either God is or I am God'. There is a profound truth in these words, for we must all have a centre to our lives around which everything else revolves. It can for a time be another person, but in the long run the centre will be either God or myself.

Many people have made the clear decision that they want to have God as the centre around which their life revolves. They consequently want a closer relationship with God and so would like to pray more, but they feel that they are so busy with their duties that they cannot find time for prayer. Is there a solution to this common dilemma? I believe there is.

When we love other people, we desire all that is good for them and we desire that they be an important part of our life. Feelings flow from this, but the very essence of our love is in that double desire. Needless to say, it is important that we constantly meet with those we love, talk with them and do things for them, but these are simply natural expressions of our desire and are empty if they are not. In a similar way, when we respond to God's love with our own love, we want God's goodness and greatness to be known and we want God as an important part of our life. And the essence of prayer is in that double *desire for God*.

St. John Chrysostom said,

'You should not think of prayer as a matter of words. It is a desire for God.'[15]

And St. Augustine repeated the same message about prayer:

'This very desire of yours is your prayer. If your desire is continual, your prayer is continual too. It was not for nothing that the Apostle said: `Pray without ceasing.' Was it so that we should be continuously on our knees, or prostrating our bodies or raising our hands that he says: `Pray without ceasing.' If that is how we say our prayers, then my opinion is that we cannot do that without ceasing. But there is another and interior way of praying without ceasing, and that is the way of desire.'[16]

Prayer is anything that, by thought, word or action, expresses the desire that God be an important part of my life, the centre of my existence. It will always have to fight against the temptation to make myself the centre of my own existence, so I need to recommit myself to God each day.

It follows that we are praying whenever we desire God or when any work we are doing is an expression of our desire for God. We can be praying when we are sweeping a floor or running a country. We can be praying when we are not thinking about God or 'holy things'. We can even be praying while sleeping through the night if that sleep is part of our desire to be able to work the next day for God and our neighbour. We can quite literally pray twenty-four hours a day, for everything we do can be an expression of our desire for God. Yes, we also need to meet with God, listen to God and talk with God, and we need to make our desire for God explicit at frequent intervals, no matter how brief they may be, for without these things our desire for God will inevitably grow weak. But the essence of prayer is not in any words; it is in the desire for God.

Imagine a young couple with their first baby. One parent must go out to work each day and must concentrate on the work, and yet the desire for the other and for the baby will constantly be present just below the surface. Sometimes it will break into conscious thought, sometimes it must be firmly put aside to concentrate on work, and yet it is always there, always informing everything that is done. This is a good image of prayer as the desire for God.

In a marriage the crucial questions that a person must continually answer are: 'Just how important do I want my family to be in my life? Just how much do I desire their good?' And the essence of prayer lies in my considered answer to the question: 'How important a part of my life do I want God to be? How much do I desire God?'

If we have healthy ideas about God, ourselves and the relationship between us, we have a firm basis on which to build many other things in the church. If we do not establish this basis first, changes in other areas may achieve little. And if we take our model of how power should be exercised from God's exercise of power in fostering our growth, we have the best possible basis for a study of how power should be exercised in the church.

Meditation

There is only one God, but an endless variety of human misunderstandings of God. Our ideas of God will always be inadequate, but can at least be healthy, that is, enable us to grow. To achieve this health, we must move:

- from a god we can understand, possess and dispense to others to a god of infinite surprise
- from an elderly male god to a god who is above all our limitations
- from a religion in which beliefs, duties and worship hold first place to a religion in which a love relationship with God holds first place
- from a religion in which we must constantly abase ourselves before God to a religion in which self-denial and self-love work together to help us become "fully alive"
- from a commercial relationship with a god whose rewards can be earned by doing right things to a love relationship with a god who is pure gift
- from a relationship in which we determine exactly what part God shall be allowed in our lives to a love relationship of total giving
- from a god who demands that we bridge the gap between us to a god who always takes the first step and comes to us

- from a world in which meaning comes from fulfilling duties to a world in which meaning comes from the sum total of all the loves of our lives
- from a god greatly concerned with glory and majesty to a god not threatened by anything human beings can do, but caring passionately what they do to each other, to themselves and to their community
- from a god whose glory is to be found in our obedience to a god whose glory is to be found in our growth
- from an angry god, not to a god of soft love, but to a god who, out of love, is never afraid to challenge us to grow
- from prayer which consists solely in words to a prayer in which our whole lives seek to express our desire for God
- from a god about whom we use many words to a god whose greatness and mystery reduce us to silent wonder.

FOOTNOTES

[1] Paul Tillich, *The Shaking of the Foundations*, pp.151-52.

[2] Mt. 16:24.

[3] Cf. John Powell, *Happiness is an Inside Job*, Tabor Publishing, Valencia, California, 1989, p.14.

[4] cf. M Scott Peck, *The Road Less Travelled*, Arrow Books, London, 1990, pp.118-123.

[5] Gal.2:20

[6] The Macquarie Dictionary gives thirty separate meanings to the word 'spirit' and ten to the word 'spiritual'. Some are directly religious, but others give a broader meaning, e.g. 'an inspiring or animating principle such as pervades and tempers thought, feeling or action' or 'of or pertaining to the spirit as the seat of the moral or religious nature.'

[7] There is, in fact, considerable variety in the way the words are used in the Second Testament and what I say here is admittedly a simplification. See *Theological Dictionary of the New Testament*, edited by Gerhard Kittel and Gerhard Friedrich, translated and abridged in one volume by Geoffrey W. Bromley, William B Erdmans Publishing, Grand Rapids, 1985.

[8] See Ronald Rolheiser, *Seeking Spritualality*, Hodder and Stoughton, London, 1998, p.4.

[9] Much beautiful writing on this topic is found in Pope Benedict XVI's encyclical *Deus Caritas Est*, 25th December 2005.

[10] Gerald G. May M.D., *The Awakened Heart*, HarperCollins, San Francisco, 1991, p.10.

[11] '... man cannot live by oblative, descending love alone. He cannot always give, he must also receive. Anyone who wishes to give love must also receive love as a gift.' Pope Benedict XVI, *op.cit.*, no.7.

[12] *Adversus Haereses*, Book IV, chap.20, section 7.

[13] For the purposes of this presentation I understand 'emotional' to refer to harmony and balance within the individual, while 'social' refers to the ability to relate to other people. Needless to say, the two depend on each other.

[14] Luke 10:21

[15] Homily 6 on Prayer, from Friday after Ash Wednesday, *The Divine Office*.

[16] Discourse on Psalm 37:13-14, from Advent, Friday of Week Three, *The Divine Office*.

CHAPTER TWO

The
Two Books
of God

There are two sources of our knowledge of God: the bible and the world around and within us. They have sometimes been called "the two books of God". Human beings have had a significant role in the writing of both books, but both can also provide us with insights into divine wisdom.

The bible and the world around and within us are the only two *sources* of our knowledge of God. Reason is not a third source of knowledge, but a *tool* that we must use in studying the true sources. The study of religion has much in common with the study of art, so the full tool is not just reason, but also the very real, if less tangible, tools of both feelings and spiritual insight. I shall here put reason, feelings and spiritual insight together under the word "discernment".

Later in this book I shall argue that one of the major problems with power in the Catholic Church has been the confusion that has often been present between the sources and the tool, with the tool becoming something of a third source. So in this and the following chapter I need to set out my understanding of the true nature of the sources and the tool, and the proper relationship between them.

Furthermore, down through the centuries there has been a long line of preachers who, with a sense of absolute certainty, thundered "the word of God" from the pulpit and demanded obedience. Far too often a divine authority was claimed for human words. This was often the principal means by which false ideas about God, ourselves and the relationship between us were instilled in people. This fact reminds us that it is in the manner of reading, interpreting and presenting the very sources of our religious knowledge that attitudes to power within the church find their foundation. So in this chapter I shall look at the two sources.

THE BIBLE

The bible is one of the two great sources of our religious knowledge, containing abundant treasures of divine wisdom of great grandeur and beauty. There is a problem, however, in that the divine wisdom that is reflected there is inextricably mixed with the human wisdom (and lack of wisdom) of the human authors of the bible, and it is a most difficult task to separate the two.

Alongside the stories of good people, the bible contains stories of bad people as well.[1] Together with sublime religious thought, it contains many insights that were at best partial and much that is far from sublime. A poem that begins as a profound spiritual longing,

> By the rivers of Babylon–
>
> there we sat down and there we wept
>
> when we remembered Zion,

can end as a bloodthirsty call for revenge,

> Happy shall they be who take your little ones
>
> and dash them against the rock.[2]

It contains examples of good deeds we are meant to imitate, bad deeds we are meant to avoid, and mixed deeds where we must distinguish the good from the bad. It contains profound sayings that are reflections of divine wisdom,

> "Cease to do evil, learn to do good;
>
> seek justice, rescue the oppressed,
>
> defend the orphan, plead for the widow,"[3]

and sayings that reflect no more than human and even worldly wisdom,

> When you sit down to eat with a ruler,
>
> observe carefully what is before you,
>
> and put a knife to your throat if you have a big appetite.[4]

It contains abundant amounts of both racism and sexism. It takes for granted the existence of slavery and does not condemn it.

The bible is, therefore, a dangerous book on which to base claims of divine authority for human words, and the practice has done untold harm.

THE STORY OF A JOURNEY

God could have chosen a group of people who lived at an oasis in the desert, a people separated from all the movement of the times by the desert that surrounded them. Under the influence of divine inspiration, this group of people could have contemplated the grandeur of the heavens, plumbed the depths of human nature and written a book of sublime spiritual poetry. But God did not do this.

Instead, God led a particular group of people to a narrow strip of land, Israel, blocked by the sea on one side and the desert on the other. Because the desert blocked other routes, all land traffic between Asia and Africa, and Africa and Europe had to pass through this narrow funnel.[5] The inhabitants met a constant migration of peoples, armies, merchants, ideas and religious beliefs passing from one of those continents to another, making it one of the most turbulent places on earth. For almost all of their history they lived under foreign domination.

If God wanted a book that contained only pure divine wisdom, unmixed with any human ideas, God might have chosen the tribe at the oasis. But if God wanted a book containing a mixture of the divine and the human, and the story of a god who spoke to people, less by divine oracles from heaven, and more *in and through* the turbulence of the world around them, then Israel was the perfect place.

The bible is the *story* of a people's long and painful spiritual *journey* through a world of turmoil towards a deeper understanding and a higher morality. It does not present us only with the perfect end-product, but contains the beginning and the middle of the journey as well, the false paths as well as the true ones.

There are two aspects that we must look at briefly, that of the form in which much of the bible is written and that of the idea of inspiration in the bible.

"Talking in Pictures"

An Aboriginal leader in Australia, who in his youth had been thoroughly trained in European thought patterns, tells the story against himself that he was once addressing an Aboriginal community and that one of the elders sat on the ground beside him. After a while the elder became agitated and started constantly interrupting him with the advice, "Talk in pictures, talk in pictures."[6] This is the way of the Aboriginal people and of many other peoples, and it was the way of Jesus. Much Christian preaching on Sundays would vastly improve if preachers paid heed to this advice rather than spoke in abstract ideas.

Scholars of the bible believe that the people who fled from Egypt were utterly convinced that they had experienced a genuine action and presence of their god in their escape and in their coming into the land of Israel. Most scholars now believe that they then told the story of this escape, not literally, but in vivid, imaginative, powerful and highly effective stories. What we find in the bible, therefore, is neither a literal account of exactly what happened nor pure fantasy, for the authors told of a real and divinely-assisted escape from slavery, but they did so by "talking in pictures". The evidence we can gain from all sources supports this view and is so strong that it can no longer be sustained that Christians must believe that each one of these stories tells the literal truth of what happened. The ancient Hebrews, like many other peoples, told their factual history through pictorial stories, and many Christian problems began only when people began to reverse this process and take the stories as factual history.

THREE STAGES OF UNDERSTANDING

Most of us have gone through three stages in our understanding of the stories recounted in the bible.

The first stage occurred when we first heard the story as children and probably believed it literally. Thus I once actually believed that a prophet named Jonah was swallowed whole by a large fish and spewed up onto the shore three days later. Children have a good understanding of the word "story", and I would hope that in the future children will not be told anything that must later be contradicted.

The second stage occurred when we came to understand that the stories were not to be taken literally. Thus my increasing knowledge of science led me to understand that the presentation of the universe in the first chapter of Genesis is not intended to be scientific, e.g. that one cannot speak of "days" before there was even a sun. For many people this stage is experienced as liberation: "I no longer have to believe all that nonsense I was told. I'm free." As a result, many never reach the third stage.

The third stage occurs when we realise that the writers of these stories would have been quite disconcerted to think that anyone would take their stories as literal accounts of exactly what happened. They were always nothing more and nothing less than stories designed to tell important truths.

Thus I have come to understand that the person named Jonah in the book bearing his name was not a real flesh and blood person but a symbol, a personification, of the whole Jewish people of the time, and the book is a powerful message about the obligation of this people to hand on to other nations the message of God's love that had been given to them. In the story Jonah was told to go to the hated Assyrians and tell them of God's love for them. But he believed in a god in whom justice came before mercy, so he was convinced that the Assyrians should be punished, not loved. He took ship and headed in the opposite direction in order to avoid God's command. The storm, the fish and the later visit to Nineveh are a story, including deliberately comic elements (e.g. cattle repenting), about God bringing the people of Israel back to their obligation to reach out to other nations, even the most hated.

The inspired message of the book was that God loved all people and that the people of Israel were meant to share with others the gifts that God had given to them. The whale was nothing more than "talking in pictures", a story designed to convey this inspired message in a manner that was both powerful and easy to remember.

Because of the way in which the Western mind has been trained to think, there is the danger that some people will be unable to move to this third stage of understanding, where story and symbol reign. They will conclude that, because many bible stories are not "true", that is, accurate literal accounts of what happened, they are, therefore, "untrue" and can be ignored. We must always try to move to the third stage and ask why the story is contained in the bible and what the people who put that story there might be trying to say to us.

INSPIRATION

Christians have always believed that the bible is inspired. In many cases this was taken just as literally as were the bible stories and it was thought that the human writers were no more than hands holding a pen, while God moved the hand and wrote the words. The massive and quite overwhelming evidence of human imperfection in the bible means that this theory must be decisively abandoned.

For example, where did inspiration lie in the proverbs contained in chapters 10 to 31 of the Book of Proverbs? They are largely non-religious proverbs, some reflecting an openly worldly wisdom, and they were first coined over many centuries in many countries by many different individuals, Hebrews, Arabs, Persians and others. Only in an impossibly broad sense could it be claimed that God "chose" every single one of these persons and "acted in them and by them". Is it possible that the true inspiration, the true openness to God, belonged to that group of persons who, centuries after the first proverbs were coined, collected these proverbs together and decided to include this collection in the bible because, imperfect as the proverbs were, they were a significant part of the story of a journey?

To take another example, it has long been recognised that the books of the great prophets were not written by the prophets themselves, but by disciples of these prophets, sometimes a number of disciples. More recently it has been recognised that writers of later centuries, and even whole schools of writers, carried out an extensive re-editing of these books, adding and changing many phrases to adapt the book to the conditions of their own time. Scholars now query just how many different hands were involved in producing the books as we now know them and over how long a period of time. Are we to believe that God directly inspired every single one of these many people?

Should we not rather say that, in the first place, inspiration must mean that there was a genuine presence and action of God in the origin and story of the people of Israel, and that the many decisions by many individuals to tell the bible story were *inspired* by, that is, were a response to, this divine presence and action? If there had been no first action of God, there would have been no inspiration to tell the story.

In the second place, should we say that inspiration means that human beings worked with God, opened their minds and hearts to God, in some manner experienced God, and then sought to express as best they could that part of the story of the journey that they had within themselves?

If this is accepted, would it be logical to conclude that among the many human authors of the bible there were degrees of working with God, degrees of opening the mind and heart to God, degrees of experiencing God, degrees of human understanding, degrees of ability to put religious thoughts into words, degrees of ability to tell stories and paint word pictures, and hence degrees to which the human authors could allow God's inspiration to be expressed? Is this the only explanation that fits the mixed nature of the material we find in the bible?

Even if we admit these degrees of inspiration of the different authors, may we still claim that the whole bible is inspired, in the sense that God did not want a perfect book of unalloyed divine wisdom, but the *story of a journey* towards a deeper understanding and a higher morality? In that story was there room for the primitive as well as the sublime, and for every stage between them? While the words came from human authors, with all their limitations, is the bible as a whole exactly the bible God wanted: not a book of pure divine wisdom but the rich, vivid, graphic and very mixed story of a journey? Understood in this sense, may we continue to affirm that the entire bible is inspired, that is, that it is, in its entirety, a response to God's action and exactly the kind of bible God wanted?

The Essential Truth

What is the "essential truth" about the bible that we must believe if we are to call ourselves Christians? It is not whether history is told factually or through stories, and it is not whether every word was directly inspired by God. It is something more fundamental than either of these considerations. One writer has expressed it well:

> "For Christians, the status of the Bible as sacred scripture means that it is the most important collection of writings we know. These are the primary writings that define who we are in relation to God and who we are as a community and as individuals. This is the book that has shaped us and will continue to shape us."[7]

The bible is

> the constitution of the Christian world",[8] "the ground of the world in which Christians live"[9], "the primary collection of ancient documents with which Christians are to be in continuing dialogue. This continuing conversation is definitive and constitutive of Christian identity. If the dialogue ceases or becomes faint, then we cease to be Christian and become something else."[10]

> "To be Christian means to live within the world created by the Bible. We are to listen to it well and let its central stories shape our vision of God, our identity, and our sense of what faithfulness to God means. It is to shape our imagination, that part of our psyches in which our foundational images of reality and life reside. We are to be a community shaped by scripture."[11]

It is the story of a people's journey towards God, and it is through the bible that we make ourselves a part of that story.

There is no basis on which to claim that the "essential truth" of the bible is that it is a book of divine answers to every possible question, that every word is part of these divine answers, and that our only task is to read the bible and obey.

God's Exercise of Power

This brings me to my major focus in this chapter, namely, how God has exercised power and authority towards us. The contents of the bible strongly indicate that, while God did reveal powerful truths, God refused point-blank to do people's work for them. God wanted people to grow and it is only free response that brings growth, so God did everything possible to encourage free response. Obedience on its own does not bring growth, so God did not give the people of Israel specific orders on all possible subjects, God did not give them answers to all questions. Instead, they had to struggle through the surrounding turmoil in order to understand what they should do. They frequently had to make their decisions in the midst of uncertainty and in the absence of any divine revelation. There is much divine wisdom in the bible, but there is nothing there that excuses us from the hard work of separating that divine wisdom from all the faulty and misleading human ideas that the bible also contains. The very nature of the bible ties in closely with what was said about the spiritual life in the first chapter, that is, that God wants our growth rather than simply our obedience, and the way to growth is to be found in struggle, challenge, free decision and responsibility. At the heart of the story of a journey found in the bible is the freedom to grow.

In our reading of the bible, is there a danger that divine wisdom can be made subject to human wisdom? Yes, this can certainly happen but, if we look at the history of the last two thousand years, there is an equal danger that weak human wisdom can be mistaken for divine wisdom. It is wrong to seek to manufacture certainties for ourselves where God chose not to provide certainties. Instead of seeking to manufacture certainties, we must ask why God wished us to live in uncertainty. We must find a balance between the need to study and assess all the elements that make up the bible and the need to approach a divine mystery with humility and reverence.

THE WORLD AROUND AND WITHIN US

Any created thing tells us much about the person who created it, for all creation is revelation. The statues of Michelangelo reveal much about their sculptor and the plays of Shakespeare reveal much about their author. It was quite impossible for these artists to create what they did without revealing many truths about themselves. Even if we knew nothing more about them, we could learn most of the essential elements and values of their lives from their creations. And the world around us and within us reveals much about the God who created that world.

If it is an essential truth that we must be in constant dialogue with the story of a journey contained in the bible, it is an equally essential truth that we must be in constant dialogue with the story of the human race's journey to understand the world around and within us.

PARENTS

Our understanding of what makes a couple good parents has developed over the years. In the past the separate roles of father and mother tended to be emphasised. A major role of the father was seen to be that of authority, where obedience was demanded and discipline enforced. Thanks to a better understanding of the human sciences, we would today not separate the roles of father and mother in the same way. While we would still see a place for obedience in young children, we would not see it as an end in itself. We would see the holistic growth of the child as the end to which everything else is directed. We would stress the importance both of challenges appropriate to the age and ability of children and of their gradually learning to make decisions and take responsibility for their own actions. We would insist that the love of both parents is important for the child's growth and we would want their love to be constant and not dependent on the child's performance.

If our collective study of the world around and within us has led us to conclusions such as these about parenthood, will they not be in our minds as we read the bible? When we come to the process of applying our powers of discernment to the two sources of our religious knowledge, should we, or indeed could we, separate what we learn from the world around us from what we learn from the bible? Doesn't it follow that our newer understandings of parenthood must cause us to ask some questions about the many statements in the bible which seem to say that God's love is dependent on people being obedient?[12]

In the past, did the bible and popular ideas about parenthood influence each other, that is, did the bible's statements about God influence how people thought parents should behave, while popular ideas about parenthood influenced how they read the bible and thought about

God? In reading the bible, should we conclude that God is a poor parent with out-of-date ideas? Or must we ask whether many ideas about the parenthood of God in the bible did in fact come from God or have been merely attributed to God by limited human minds?

STRUCTURES IN THE CHURCH

Virtually the only forms of government known in the ancient world were those of absolute rulers. Jesus gave a model of a ruler that was radically different from that of the nations of his time, for he insisted that the sole reason authority is given to anyone is so that he or she may serve the community.[13] May we ask whether his followers were capable of thinking beyond the model of an absolute ruler who acted in a Christian manner? Because they had no other model, did they then conclude that this was what Jesus must have intended? Are we now free to think in different ways?

Is it conceivable that God would have imposed on the church permanent structures that were contrary to much that the best of the world around us is now telling us? Would that not put the bible and the world around us against each other? Would it not suggest that different gods were the authors of these two books? There have been genuine discoveries in relation to matters such as group climate and group dynamics, group motivation, leadership styles, the qualities of leadership, methods of decision making, conflict resolution and the managing of change. These matters have an important and direct influence on how well a community grows and how well the individual members of that community grow. Does it make sense to say that a church is above such matters and not subject to them? Must we not look again at some traditions and structures in the light of these factors?

Today, of course, we suffer from an overload of information on many subjects and we are constantly bombarded with new statements about the world around and within us. Some of these statements will stand the test of time, many will not. To race after the latest theory on every topic and claim that we must instantly reinterpret the bible in the light of it would be most imprudent. But to leave out altogether the wisdom of the world around and within us and to rely solely on the bible would be to deny everything that God's creation tells us about God.

There is much work to be done in studying how our knowledge of God that comes from the bible and our knowledge of God that comes from the world around and within us should interact on and complement each other.

Meditation

"Can a woman forget her nursing child,
or show no compassion for the child of her womb?
Even these may forget,
yet I will not forget you." *Is.49:15*

We can learn this truth about God from the bible, but only because we have first learned from the world around and within us the depth of a mother's love for her child.

"For God so loved the world that he gave his only Son."
Jn.3:16

This phrase speaks to our depths only because we have some understanding of the sacrifice that parents must make in giving their only child to some cause.

It is only through a dialogue between the bible and the world around us that we are led into a deeper understanding of both.

Without the world around and within us, the bible could not exist, for it would have no words to use, no images to express, no experiences to call on. We cannot separate what we learn from the bible from what we learn from the world around and within us.

Our first task is to immerse ourselves in the world of the bible and the story it tells, allowing our experience gained from the bible and our experience gained from the world around us to speak to each other.

Our second task is to use the collective intelligence, feelings and instinct for the spiritual of all people in discerning the truths for the sake of our salvation that God wishes to tell us through the story of the journey contained in the bible.

Our third task is to make this story part of our own story, so that our journey follows the same paths to the same goals.

Our fourth task is to allow the thoughts, images and stories of the bible to so permeate us that they become fundamental, not just to what we do or say, but also to who we are, our very being.

FOOTNOTES

[1] Among the best known would be e.g. Ahab and Jezebel, who opposed the prophet Elijah. See 1 Kings 16:29-22:40

[2] Ps.137

[3] Micah 6:8

[4] Prov.23:1-2

[5] The best example of the crucial geographical position of Israel is probably that of Alexander the Great. He was a European power who wished to attack Asia, but first he felt the need to pass through the narrow corridor of Israel in order to ensure that he did not have an African power behind his lines when he attacked Asia.

[6] Patrick Dodson told this story about himself in a newspaper article. I regret that I cannot give the reference.

[7] Marcus J Borg, *Reading the Bible Again for the First Time,* HarperSanFrancisco, 2001, p.29.

[8] *Ibid.* p.30

[9] *Ibid.* p.30

[10] *Ibid.* p.30

[11] *Ibid.* p.31.

[12] e.g. Lev.26:14-45, Deut.28.

[13] Mk.10:42-45

CHAPTER THREE

Spiritual Discernment

I n the last chapter we looked at the two *sources* of our religious knowledge. In this chapter we shall turn our attention to the *tool* of discernment, and the manner in which it, too, calls for struggle, responsibility and growth.

TRADITION

In popular understanding the word "tradition" is usually taken to mean a turning back to the beliefs, attitudes and customs of the past. But the basic meaning of the word expresses the more dynamic concept of the *process* of handing on the stories, values, insights and faith of the past to the future. The word "tradition" derives from the Latin word *tradere*, which means "to hand on".

The word has been a controversial one between different Christian churches since the time of the Reformation. This has been compounded by the fact that the word "tradition" means different things to different people. Indeed, in reading any book or article on the subject one must be constantly asking, "What does the author mean by the term here?" Articles that do not give a clear meaning to the term are automatically condemned to lack of clarity. We must start by going back to the beginning.

The Time after the Ascension

The disciples of Jesus experienced his life, death and resurrection as a personal saving event for themselves and as a definitive saving event for the whole of humankind. For this reason they were conscious of an obligation to "hand on" (*tradere*) to others everything that they had seen and heard - the words, actions and whole way of life of Jesus. Opening themselves to the Spirit, they sought to do this by means of their own words, actions and way of living. They were aware that they were not just passing on a memory of past events, but that through them the Spirit was transmitting the very presence of Jesus into the lives of the people they spoke to. In other words, what was handed on was a living faith and a way of living based on that faith.

As the original witnesses to the historical and unrepeatable events of the life of Jesus began to grow old and die, those remaining became acutely aware that it was essential to set down a written record of the original events so that they would remain accessible to the people of later ages. As part of their "tradition" or handing on of their faith, the followers of Jesus did this, and the writings of the Second Testament emerged.

The four gospels are central to the Second Testament. Modern studies have abundantly shown that the writers began their task by seeking to go back to the original events through the "tradition" or process of handing on that had already occurred. They sought not merely the details of the events, but also the meaning of the events, and in this they used the wisdom of different communities which had pondered the events, sought to understand the presence of the Spirit in those events, and gradually come to understand some of their deeper meanings. Thus the process of "tradition" or handing on was essential both before and during the writing of the Second Testament.

From the century after the death and resurrection of Jesus there is an extensive literature of "gospels".[1] It is possible that some of those not accepted by the community might contain traces of authentic incidents from the life of Jesus not recorded in any of the four we know. So why do we now have four gospels rather than one or ten? The answer is that the process of "tradition" or handing on was brought to bear here as well.

Three principles were adopted – antiquity, universality and authenticity. The question of antiquity asked whether a particular gospel was written while eyewitnesses were still alive or, if not, whether its contents could be traced back to eyewitnesses. The question of universality asked whether the particular gospel was read aloud in all the churches or only in a few. And the question of authenticity asked whether there was an internal coherence in the gospel. Was it in harmony with what could be known from other gospels? Did it lead to a deeper understanding of Jesus and of God?

Four alone passed all tests, so that the whole Christian community could come to the conclusion that they were, in their entirety, authentic expressions of the life and meaning of Jesus Christ and authentic means of "handing on" faith. It was also important to the early church that the diversity of four gospels could come closer to the full truth about Jesus Christ than any one gospel could on its own. The process was a long and gradual one. Though most major communities had agreed on the point by the end of the second century, it was only around the year 400 that there was universal agreement.

The Scriptures of the Second Testament are a product of "tradition" in this basic sense of "handing on". "Tradition" came before the Scriptures, they were created for no other reason than to assist the process of "tradition", and it was "tradition", the united voice of the whole community in its task of "handing on", that determined which writings were authentic and inspired. It is not possible to insist on "Scripture alone" in a manner that seeks to abolish all idea of tradition and tries to delete the very word itself. Without "tradition" we would have no Scriptures. No matter how many problems it may create, the word "tradition" refuses to go away.

Meanings of the Word "Tradition"

After the last direct witness to the life of Jesus had died, the process of "tradition" or handing on continued. The writings of the Second Testament were central to this process and the authenticity of any handing on always had to be tested against them. Gradually, however, other writings and sayings from great saints also began to be handed on, as people realised that these writings or sayings were valuable attempts to express the meaning of the life of Jesus (e.g. the saying of St. Irenaeus, "The glory of God is a human being fully alive"). They were not part of the bible and there were no claims of infallibility for their authors, but they were seen as part of the increasing treasury of Christian wisdom and acquired a valued place in the handing on.

Just as there had been an earlier need to set down the life of Jesus in writing in the gospels, so after a few centuries a profound need was felt to come to an agreement on and set down in writing some of the essential truths about Jesus and about God. In particular, there were the two questions of how Jesus could be both divine and human at the same time, and how one God could be spoken of as Father, Son and Holy Spirit. Between 325 and 787 seven Councils sought to give answers to these and other questions. They were councils of the whole Christian world before either of the major divisions (Catholic-Orthodox and Catholic-Protestant) had taken place and they have a special authority down to our own day.

After this the writings, sayings and councils continued, and a vast body of literature and teaching was built up. This led to four different meanings of the word "tradition":

i) The entire dynamic *process* of handing on the meaning and message of Jesus Christ, a process that began after the Ascension and continues to this day, then and always a work of the Spirit and human beings working together;

ii) "Tradition" over against Scripture, that is, those truths that the Catholic Church appeared to claim were handed down from Jesus but not included in the Second Testament[2] ;

iii) The whole vast body of wisdom and teaching that has been built up over two thousand years;

iv) Teaching seen as authoritative, that is, the teaching of the first seven councils plus the teaching given by general councils or other authorities within either the Catholic or Orthodox or Protestant world.

Of these four meanings, must we not reject the second because we can have no convincing proof that such verbal handing on of statements of Jesus occurred?[3] In this chapter I shall see the fourth (authoritative teaching) as part of the third, that is, as part of the whole vast literature that has come down to us. I shall speak of authoritative teaching in later chapters.

This would reduce the authentic meanings to two, and we can look at them in terms of the *process* of handing on and the *content* of what has been handed on.

THE GREAT TRADITION

Many writers speak of traditions and of the Great Tradition. The word "traditions" refers to the content of tradition, that is, particular truths that have been handed on, while the Great Tradition speaks of the process.

In the first chapter, I said that my faith is first and foremost faith in a person and a story, the person of Jesus Christ and the story of his life, death and resurrection. From this faith in a person flow truths, rules of living and worship, but the person and story come first. In this book I shall refer to the Great Tradition as the essential handing on of this person and story and the response of faith, hope and love that it evokes. It does not exclude particular truths, but the handing on of the person and story comes first.

There are two things to note about it. The first is that it is always the story of God reaching out to humanity through Jesus Christ in the power of the Spirit, so it is always the work of the Trinity before it is human work.

The second is that the Great Tradition cannot be contained in books and papal documents, or even in the bible. It exists only in so far as it is received, accepted, assimilated and lived by human beings, and then passed on to others. It is not words, but a living faith, that is, a way of living based on a person and a story.

The handing on is, therefore, a dynamic process in which those handing on must be faithful to the person and story (and, therefore, have a basic fidelity to the beliefs, rules of living and forms of worship), but they must also use their powers of discernment, their creativity and their imagination in adapting the story to their audience.

If I say that someone like Francis of Assisi was inspired by the Holy Spirit, I do not mean that every word he spoke is guaranteed to be true. I mean that the Holy Spirit was present in his choice to live a life of poverty, simplicity and closeness to nature, and that we can learn valuable lessons for our own lives from the way he lived. The lessons come from his fidelity to the past, but also from his creativity and imagination in the manner in which he handed on the person and story to others. In him the Great Tradition lived.

Some time ago I celebrated the sacrament of Confirmation for a group of people affected by Downs Syndrome. As I looked at the people in front of me I knew that, while remaining faithful to the sacrament, I would have to be creative and imaginative in the way I handed on this reality to them. If I did no more than recite the formulas from the book, I may have been faithful to the past, but I would not have been "handing on" to those present, so no genuine "tradition" would have occurred. Here, too, the Great Tradition had to come alive.

In the minds of those living the Great Tradition there might be errors concerning some truths, rules of living and worship, but these errors do not necessarily mean that the Great Tradition is not being handed on. Indeed, if only those who were perfect in their understanding could authentically hand on the Great Tradition, we would have serious problems.

I shall return to this idea of the Great Tradition later in this book.

HANDING ON VERSUS BETRAYAL

There is a caution that must be added. The Latin word from which we derive the word "tradition" is *tradere*, and it is no accident that the same word can equally be translated as "to hand on" or "to betray". In the creative and imaginative process of handing on what we have received it is always possible to betray what was handed on to us. Where does creative adaptation end and betrayal of the very substance of what has been handed on begin?

There were probably arguments in the communities of the writers of the gospels on this point. I know that people made this accusation against Francis of Assisi. On the other hand, I know of a priest years ago who, in an attempt to adapt to modern culture, celebrated Mass with a pizza and a can of beer rather than bread and wine, and the instinctive reaction both of myself and of many other people was to cry betrayal rather than creative adaptation.

Throughout history people have felt the need to be creative and imaginative in receiving, assimilating and handing on what was given to them in order to be truly faithful to it, and throughout the same history other people have accused them of betrayal of what was handed on. There is no clear line between creative adaptation and betrayal, and the argument will probably continue forever. It is a field where much tolerance and understanding are required.

THE CONTENT OF WHAT HAS BEEN HANDED ON

There are two *sources* of our knowledge of God, and there is one *tool* for understanding and interpreting both of these sources. The *tool* of discernment is not, and cannot be, a third *source* of our knowledge of God. Not even a consensus of Christian people or a constant belief over many centuries can turn the tool into a source. The tool can lead to insights into divine truth that have never been put into words before, but the *source* of the insights remains the bible and/or the world around us.

Over a period of time the insights gained by means of discernment have built up into a body of beliefs, attitudes and customs called "tradition" (with a small "t" and better expressed in the plural as "traditions"). These traditions are not a new *source*, but the *accumulated result of the use of the tool on the sources*.

More dynamically, they are the result of the ongoing interpretation of the bible and the world around and within us and the application of this interpretation to the concrete circumstances of the present.

When we seek to resolve a particular question, we may legitimately place this accumulated result alongside the bible and the world around us, not as a new source, but as a body of knowledge representing the wisdom of the past. It is not on the same level as the two sources, and yet we cannot ignore it without arrogantly dismissing the past.

In the long history of the Christian religion most of the problems we face today have occurred many times before and the people who faced those problems in earlier centuries struggled to find the best answers they could. It would be an intolerable arrogance on our part to think that we had nothing to learn from them. As the famous saying puts it, "Those who ignore the past are condemned to repeat its mistakes."

Though there are significant differences between what has been handed down in different churches, there is no Christian church that is in a position to deny the power of the past in forming what it is today. Even those churches that most loudly proclaim that they base themselves on "Scripture alone" have their own ways of interpreting the Scriptures and they have formed structures, customs and laws based on these interpretations. I have heard Christians from "Scripture alone" churches speaking passionately about the events of the Reformation as though they had happened yesterday, and it has been crystal clear to me that many words and events of that period are a powerful source of their beliefs, attitudes and customs today. If these are not "traditions", then they are simply using another word to describe the same reality.

If we must use our powers of discernment in understanding and assessing the bible and the world around us, however, we must even more use our powers of discernment in assessing the human interpretations of the bible and the world around us that have been handed down to us.

We must always look closely at the social and religious forces that were at work in the decisions that were made in the past, the level of knowledge on a particular topic at the time and the realistic choices that were presented to people. The mere fact of a long-standing tradition is not proof of its truth, for defective attitudes can persist for a very long time. We can point, for instance, to examples such as slavery and torture in Christian history, and we must confess that much that is called "tradition" has contained so pervasive and sustained a bias against women that it is the weakest of foundations on which to base our conclusions concerning the dignity and role of women today. It is here that the work of expert historians and theologians is of the greatest value.

Much wisdom and much humility will be required when applying our powers of discernment to what has been handed down to us, but it is impossible to deny its existence and it is impossible to deny its force.

The Tool of Discernment

Neither in the bible, nor in the world around and within us, nor in what has been handed down to us do we find certainty on all subjects and clear divine orders on all we are to believe and do. It would seem crystal clear that, while we have the certainty of faith on the most important subjects, God wishes us to struggle to discover the truth, for it is through this struggle that we grow.

In studying any particular question, it would seem wise to consider *together* the bible, the world around and within us, and what we can learn from the wisdom of the past. No decision the Christian church arrives at should ever contradict a genuine truth of the bible or a genuine insight into the world around and within us or a genuine insight of the past.

The problem, of course, is to determine which understandings of all three are genuine and which are not. Since this is often a very difficult task, the safest way to proceed is surely to use each of the three in interpreting and testing the other two, and to do all that is possible to harmonise the findings of all three. At all times we must use the powers of discernment God has given us.

We must also constantly test our findings against the Great Tradition, by asking whether particular truths are an authentic handing on of the person and story of Jesus Christ and of our response of faith, hope and love to that person and story.

Many may object that the bible must surely be seen as superior to the other two, for it expresses divine wisdom. In answer I certainly acknowledge divine wisdom as superior to human wisdom, and I acknowledge that the bible alone contains the defining story of the life, death and resurrection of Jesus, according to which a Christian should view everything else on this earth. This still leaves us with the problem of determining how to distinguish divine and human wisdom in the bible. It is not legitimate to use a literal reading of the bible to beat the other two around the head, just as it is not legitimate to use either of the other two to tell the bible what it may and may not say.

Furthermore, the weight we give to each of the three elements will depend on the question. For example, when we try to understand the nature and meaning of the Eucharist that Jesus left to us at the

Last Supper, the bible will be of first importance. On the other hand, when we look at the morality of holding stockpiles of nuclear weapons, the bible will be of only indirect assistance and we will have to place greater reliance on theories of a just war handed down to us since the time of Augustine and on the knowledge we can acquire today from the world around us and within us.

Within the Anglican Communion there are three branches that are sometimes called evangelical, catholic and liberal. All three have great respect for the bible, all three acknowledge that specifically Anglican ways of doing things have been handed down and all three would consider themselves reasonable and rational. Nevertheless, *relative to each other*, the evangelical branch gives more weight to the bible, the catholic branch gives more weight to what has been handed down, and the liberal branch gives more weight to the wisdom of the world around us and within us. The same preferences can be seen in other churches.

I mention this fact to stress the difficulty of finding the right balance between the wisdom of God contained in the bible, the wisdom of the present studying the world around and within us and the wisdom of the past embodied in what has been handed down. Much thought needs to be given to this matter and nothing less than the collective wisdom of the entire Christian world will be sufficient. The extremes of all three tendencies must be sternly resisted and we must work towards an understanding where each of these means of knowledge is properly balanced by the other two.

Meditation

I cannot hand on to others the person and story of Jesus Christ without at some point telling them about the many truths that flow from belief in Jesus, the many rules of living that are inherent in following him and the different forms of worship through which we might express our respect and love for him.

On the other hand, it is all too easy for the truths, rules of living and worship to take the dominant place. It is easier to judge the presence and authenticity of Christian faith by these clear and measurable goals than by the unmeasurable criterion of a response of one's whole being to a person and a story. Particular traditions can dominate the Great Tradition.

And yet it is the Great Tradition that contains all the dynamism of the church and its attractiveness to those outside it. The truths, rules of living and worship, separated from the Great Tradition or placed before it, will rarely attract people.

The need to maintain order and coherence within the Church can be in conflict with the need to reach out to the whole world through the person and story of Jesus Christ. Regaining the spirit of Jesus always involves reminding ourselves daily where the priorities lie.

FOOTNOTES

[1] E.g. the Gospel of James, the Gospel of Thomas, the Gospel of Peter, the Gospel of Nicodemus (the Acts of Pilate), the Secret Gospel of Mark, the Gospels of the Ebionites, the Hebrews and the Nazoreans, and many others.

[2] I shall say more about this in a later chapter.

[3] I refer further comment on this point to a later chapter.

CHAPTER FOUR

An Eternal Plan,
a Sharing of Life
and the
Reign of God

If we are to look at that better church that must arise as a response to abuse, we must next look at what our sources tell us about God's desires for the church, for surely in this matter it is God's desires rather than our own that we should be seeking to follow.

The gospels speak rarely about the church, and frequently about a greater reality, the 'kingdom of God'. The whole of the New or Second Testament then takes this idea further through three key terms, one used frequently in the gospels by Jesus himself, the other two belonging mainly to Paul.[1]

GOD'S ETERNAL PLAN

The first of the three key words is a Greek word used by Paul, *mysterion*, a word that means, not simply something mysterious, but God's eternal plan for the whole world, partly revealed in the First Testament, then more fully made known in Christ.[2] To place the accent on the 'mysterious', that is, the obscure and unknowable, is to miss the point made by Paul that in Christ God has revealed this eternal plan. The eternal plan of God, rather than being simply mysterious or unintelligible, can be said to be of 'inexhaustible intelligibility'[3], for our difficulty with the idea comes less from any inherent mystery and more from its sheer magnitude.

Paul sensed the groaning of all creation for fulfilment[4] and saw this as a reflection of God's eternal plan seeking its fulfilment.

> '..this grace was given to me ... to make everyone see what is the
> plan of the *mysterion* hidden for ages in God who created all things;
> so that through the church the wisdom of God in its rich variety
> might now be made known to the rulers and authorities in the
> heavenly places. This was in accordance with the eternal purpose
> that he has carried out in Christ Jesus our Lord.'[5]

We are easily lost in the problems of the present moment and can hardly conceive of a plan that extends over thousands, let alone billions, of years. We can be tempted to think that anything that takes that long has to be chance and that there cannot be an eternal plan for the world. The bible tells us the story of many people caught up in the turmoil of the present moment, but through and behind these stories it also gives us glimpses of nothing less than God's eternal plan for the whole world.

The church is meant to be a means by which this eternal plan becomes a reality in the world, and a sign of its presence, but it is not the only means and it can never be more than a sign; it can never be the total embodiment of the eternal plan.

A Sharing of Life

The term *koinonia*, used frequently by Paul, has been traditionally translated into English by Protestants as 'fellowship' and by Catholics as 'communion'. In other European languages 'communion' has been more common and it is the translation now used in ecumenical dialogue.

Koinos means 'common', and *koinonia* means a sharing in common or participation or fellowship in something. It means 'to make common to others what is personal to oneself'. It was Jesus who made common to us what was personal to God, and we were then invited to share this gift with others. What belonged to God alone and was then shared with us in Jesus Christ was 'life in all its fullness'.[6] At the heart of the eternal plan is God's desire to share with the whole human race the divine gift of life in all its fullness.

Just as the eternal plan is larger than the church, so is the sharing of life, for the whole world is called to share in this life in all its fullness that comes from God, and the church is not the sole or exclusive means by which people may do so.

THE REIGN OF GOD[7]

The Greek word *basileia* is usually translated as 'kingdom', but the translation can be misleading. On the lips of Jesus the word does not refer to a place but to an activity, not to a kingdom but to a reign or royal rule, for Jesus did not come to found a kingdom of this world, but to implement a reign within the human heart based on the values of justice and love.

In Mark's gospel Jesus first announced his presence with the words

'The time is fulfilled and the reign of God has come near.'[8]

In Jesus, God's reign was present in a new way and with a greater immediacy, but the fullness of that reign was still to come. The reign had 'come near', but it was not fully present because Jesus had not yet died and risen again, and because this reign exists only when it is accepted within the minds and hearts of human beings.

'Once Jesus was asked by the Pharisees when the reign of God was coming, and he answered, `The reign of God is not coming with things that can be observed; nor will they say, `Look, here it is!' or `There it is!' For the reign of God is within (*entos*) you.'[9]

God's reign can never exist on this earth as some sort of external reality outside the hearts of individuals. It follows that the growth of God's reign cannot simply be identified with the external growth of the church, both because it is something that exists within human hearts and because the reign of God is broader than the church and extends to the whole world and the whole of creation.

The Church

The word *ekklesia* (church) is used only three times in the gospels and does not appear to have a technical meaning, for it means only the gathering, the coming together, the communion or common-union of the followers of Jesus. In terms of the three words we have been considering, Jesus invited all those who came in contact with him to share in God's eternal plan of life in all its fullness through the acceptance of God's reign within their hearts. Acceptance of this invitation through baptism is the basis of membership of the church. For an adult, baptism is the conscious acceptance of and will to share in this sacred reality, and the church is the community of those who have taken this step. The three Greek terms, however, are all broader than the term 'church', and there are several conclusions that we must draw.

A Common Foundation

Firstly, Catholics, Orthodox and Protestants have all equally accepted the sacred realities of an eternal plan of life in all its fullness through the reign of God within their hearts. These terms can be the common foundation on which Christian unity may be built[10]. Without minimising the many and serious differences that still exist, an adequate notion of church must include all those who through the one baptism have accepted these sacred realities. In this sense the one church of Christ already exists and always has existed in a real but not complete communion (*koinonia*). As St. Augustine said,

> 'Whether they like it or not, they are our brothers and sisters, and they will only cease to be our brothers and sisters if they cease to say 'Our Father'.'[11]

THE CHURCH IN THE WORLD

Secondly, God's eternal plan, sharing of life and reign are for the whole world and the whole of creation. It follows that the church is not the goal of its own strivings; this goal is the reign of God in the whole world. It was this reign of God within the hearts of all people that Jesus wanted above all else and his whole message was directed towards this end. All of his parables concern this reign rather than the church ('The reign of God is like…'). The reign of God is the end and the church, or community of the followers of Jesus, is a means to this end and a sign pointing towards it. It can never be the end in itself. While it should always seek to become a better and better sign of the fact that the reign of God has already broken into this world, it can never claim to be the entire reality of that reign. If it ever becomes an end in itself or claims to be the reign of God on earth, the message of Jesus is being distorted. This would certainly happen if the two ideas of the reign of God and the church were treated as being one and the same thing.

Even today many Christians seem to reflect a dualism between church and world, and seek to defend the church against the world instead of reaching out to the world. The great Lutheran martyr of the Second World War, Dietrich Bonhoeffer, spoke strongly of the consequences of this dualism.

> 'The attack by Christian apologetic upon the adulthood of the world I consider to be in the first place pointless, in the second ignoble and in the third un-Christian[12].… The place of religion is taken by the Church… but the world is made to depend upon itself and left to its own devices, and that is all wrong.'[13]

Other writers speak of a 'churchianity'[14] that turns in upon itself and does not sufficiently look outwards. And yet the church exists for the sake of the world and is at the service of the world. As one writer has put it, God is concerned with the world, not really with the church as different from the world[15]. The church is not primarily an institution or an experience of ritual and worship or a belief system. It is primarily an offer of life to the whole world and the whole cosmos. If it is not this, it is failing in its task.

The Authority of Holiness

Thirdly, in seeking to bring about this one overriding goal, the external authority structures of the church will often be of only minor importance. Far more important will be the authority of the saints, the prophets, the contemplatives and all who seek to imitate them. These are the ones who most profoundly hand on the Great Tradition, who are most deeply in touch with the God whose eternal plan they serve, and who most authentically speak out of an inner experience of God. Just as the greatest moment of musicians occurs when their existence is forgotten and, through them, we are in direct contact with the composer, so the greatest moment of Christian people occurs when they put us in direct contact with God and could truly say, 'I live now, not I, but Christ lives in me.' The external authorities of the church must never seek to control and limit this deeper authority, for it claims a far more profound obedience than any external authority could ever claim. The authority of Jesus came from his inner experience of union with the One whom he named as Father, and the authority of anyone who speaks in the name of Jesus is directly proportional to the integrity and authenticity of his or her inner experience of God.

Anything and everything I shall say about external structures of the church in the rest of this book must be seen within this all-important context. External structures must be judged primarily according to how well they serve God's eternal plan of a sharing of life in all its fullness through the reign of God within the hearts and minds of the whole of humankind, for the church has no other purpose than this. The idea of the freedom to grow to become all we are capable of being is at the very heart of this plan, and external structures of the church may be judged by how well they enable this growth.

Service

Fourthly, the sole basis of power or authority within this community is to be that of service. The entire church was meant to serve the coming of the reign of God within the hearts of all people. If some were to be given authority within the community, this was solely so that they could serve the others and all could serve the reign of God. The model of the actions of Jesus would always be the rule.

RESPONDING TO GOD

Fifthly and finally, in all three terms the first action lies with God: it is God's eternal plan, God's sharing of life and God's reign. The church should always be responding to God's action rather than acting on its own and it must always be pondering over the wonder and inexhaustible intelligibility of God's eternal plan.

> 'To God who is able to strengthen you... according to the revelation of the mysterion that was kept secret for long ages but is now disclosed, ... to the only wise God, through Jesus Christ, be the glory forever. Amen.'[16]

Meditation

It is God's will that every single human being, regardless of age, gender, colour, race, caste, religion or sexual orientation, should grow to become all she or he is capable of being. In this way the human race as a whole can grow to become all it is capable of being.

In harmony and to the extent possible for each individual, we are called to develop our potential in seven areas: physical, intellectual, emotional, social, artistic, moral and spiritual. By doing this, we learn to use to the full all the gifts God has given us to help our world to grow.

To help us to do this, God invites us to share in an eternal plan of life in all its fullness through the reign of God within our hearts.

Which particular path we walk in seeking this eternal plan, Jewish or Christian or Muslim, Catholic or Orthodox or Protestant, is important, but the sincerity of our search is even more important.

We constantly live the tension that we must both walk humbly with others, and at the same time find our individual way to God by taking personal responsibility for the choices we make.

A path to God is authentic if it eventually forces us to find God in the very depths of our own being. Within the Christian community the real authority of any person is directly proportional to the integrity and authenticity of this experience of God within one's own depths.

It is persons, not religions, that God loves. God is happy when persons of any or no religion do things that help others, saddened when they do things that harm others, and loves all of them always, whatever they do.

War, terrorism, suicide, coercion, hatred or despising others, in the name of religious beliefs, is an abomination to God.

Footnotes

[1] In the presentation that follows I acknowledge my debt to Charles Hill, *Mystery of Life, A Theology of Church*, Collins Dove, Melbourne, 1990. I have, however, taken his ideas in my own directions and drawn my own conclusions, and so take responsibility for what I have written.

[2] As St. Paul uses the word, it is not simply a Greek word, but an inadequate Greek translation of Hebrew concepts and its meaning comes from the First Testament.

[3] John O'Grady, *Models of Jesus,* Image Books, Garden City, 1981, p.22.

[4] Rom.8:19-22

[5] Eph.3:8-11. cf. Rom. 16:25-27; 1 Cor 27-8; Col. 1:24-28, 22-4.

[6] Jn.10:10

[7] In the four gospels the term *mysterion* occurs only once (Mk.4:11) and the term *koinonia* does not occur at all. Instead we find on the lips of Jesus in the gospels the frequent use of the term *basilea*.

[8] 1:15

[9] Lk.17:20-21

[10] cf. *Church as Communion: an Agreed Statement by ARCICII*, Catholic Truth Society, 1991.

[11] St. Augustine, Commentary on Psalm 32, The Divine Office, Vol.III, Tuesday, Week 14.

[12] Dietrich Bonhoeffer, *Letters and Papers from Prison*, Fontana, London, 1953, p.108.

[13] ibid., p.95.

[14] cf. Edmund Flood, *Work and the Gospel* . The Tablet, 4 May 1991, pp.538-540.

[15] Johannes Metz, *Theology of the World*, Herder and Herder, New York. 1969, p.50, note 51.

[16] Rom. 16:25-27

CHAPTER FIVE

'Like His Brothers and Sisters in Every Respect'

In considering the nature of the community or church that originated in Jesus, and hence the exercise of power within it, it is important that we next consider the question of the knowledge that Jesus brought to his mission.

Christians believe that Jesus Christ was God, but they also believe that in Jesus certain divine privileges were freely surrendered so that he would be fully identified with humanity. For example, the divine privilege of not being able to suffer was surrendered, so that Jesus did not go through his passion pretending to suffer, while not really feeling any pain, but suffered exactly as any human being would in the same circumstances. The sufferings he endured throughout his life brought him far closer to us than a person who never experienced suffering, for they were an important part of becoming, not a pretend-human being, but a real human being like us.

The Knowledge of Jesus

In recent decades there has been much discussion concerning the knowledge of Jesus. He was God, but did he at all times possess the complete and perfect knowledge that God has or did he willingly surrender this privilege too, and have only limited knowledge such as all other human beings have?

Not possessing perfect knowledge would have had two major effects. Firstly, like us, Jesus would have had to struggle to know what to do and would have felt the same uncertainty that we constantly feel. He would have had to make decisions, but may then have been uncertain whether these decisions were the right ones.

Secondly, he would have been tempted to sin. For example, because his insights were so superior to those of others, he would have been tempted to pride. He would have been tempted to be uncharitable towards those who opposed him. He would have been strongly tempted to avoid his suffering on the cross and find some less painful way to carry out his mission.

It is obvious that such a lack of perfect knowledge would have made him far closer to us. He would be far more closely identified with our struggles, our ignorance and our temptation than a person who passed through this world possessing perfect knowledge at all times. Just as his suffering brought him closer to us, so his lack of perfect knowledge would make the incarnation far more real and we could identify far more closely with such a Jesus.

Despite the importance of the question, we have to say that a crystal clear answer does not emerge from the Second Testament.

THE GOSPEL OF MARK

The gospel of Mark appears to assume only limited knowledge. In its first chapter it speaks of Jesus sent out into the desert and there tempted by Satan[1], though it would hardly have been a real temptation if he had perfect knowledge. A particularly good example occurs in 1:29-39. Jesus entered the house of Peter and Andrew and found that Peter's mother-in-law was ill with a fever. Even for Jesus charity began
ne, so he cured her, and this one cure was enough to cause the

flood of human suffering from the whole town to be brought to him. In the scene that follows Mark uses the words 'all' or 'whole' four times, and in each case there is an emphasis on the word. On the first two occasions they brought *all* the sick to him and the *whole* town came to see what would happen. In the middle of these four words meaning 'all' we find one 'many', for 'he cured many'. In Hebrew the word 'many' can mean simply 'a large number', without specifying whether this means all or less than all. Here, however, if Mark had meant that he cured all, it would have been enough to say 'he cured them'. Instead, we have this contrast between the four 'alls' and the one 'many'. What might this mean?

I have no problem with the fact that Jesus cured all the obviously sick who were brought to him, but we must go further and think about what would have happened after these obviously sick people had been cured. Firstly, there were those who could not be simply 'cured'. For example, there were surely many elderly people in the town, even some close to death, and yet we never hear of Jesus reversing the ageing process. There may have been a young mother whose child had been tragically killed in an accident, and even Jesus could not take away the grief she would constantly feel whenever she thought of her child. Jesus could not change the past history of people, and that is often the source of their problems, e.g. a person who as a child had been abused.

Secondly, am I simply describing human nature if I suggest that, after he had cured the obviously sick persons, others in the crowd would have come forward with lesser but annoying and painful ailments in themselves (e.g. arthritis, gout, haemorrhoids)? Would the psychological problems have followed (e.g. anxiety, depression)? Would there have been a single person in that crowd who could not think of an ailment for which a cure was desirable? Would not the entire crowd have eventually come forward, concerned to find out just how far and deep this man's cures could go?

Thirdly and lastly, the next morning the Roman occupation was still there and the endemic poverty of the people was still present. Most important of all, the human condition itself was still there, for Jesus had to live within that human condition and could not take it away. So even after his 'many' cures, there was still a multitude of problems in the town. The statement of Mark that 'he cured many' does not limit the power of Jesus, but is a profound comment on the human condition.

The contrast between the 'all' and the 'many' is strengthened by what follows. Very early, before the sun rose, Jesus got up and went away to pray, asking his father to help him discern what to do next in light of the immensity of human suffering. Peter and his companions searched for him (the Greek word says 'hunted him down'), saying that *all* were looking for him, for by now all would have thought of more things Jesus could do. In prayer, however, he had found his answer and he told them that he could not stay in Capernaum forever, but must go elsewhere to proclaim the message of God's love, for this could reach further and deeper than his physical cures. He would still cure, but his priority would be the proclamation of God's message of love. So they went into the *whole* Galilee.

In the following scenes Jesus tried to keep to this priority,[2] though in the very next scene he had to make an exception when confronted with the special needs of the leper, and he would constantly encounter misunderstanding and opposition because the crowd's priorities were the opposite of his.

Mark also speaks of Jesus making a serious reassessment of his mission after the authorities, the crowd and the disciples themselves had failed him,[3] and he has Jesus saying that he did not know the time of the end of the world.[4] In the garden of Gethsemane he presents Jesus as afraid and tempted to avoid his passion.[5] In fact, through the device of the presence of the inner circle of Peter, James and John, he deliberately contrasts the transfiguration, when Jesus appeared at his most divine, and the garden of Gethsemane, when Jesus appeared at his most human. On the cross Jesus cried out, 'My God, my God, why have you abandoned me?'[6]

OTHER BOOKS OF THE SECOND TESTAMENT

The gospel of Matthew reflects that of Mark on this point, while the gospel of Luke says that the child Jesus 'increased in wisdom and in years and human favour'.[7] The letter to the Hebrews is explicit:

'Therefore he had to become like his brothers and sisters in every respect, so that he could be a compassionate and faithful high priest of God's religion, able to atone for human sins. Because he himself suffered temptation, he is able to help those who are tempted[8]......
For we do not have a high priest who is unable to sympathise with

our weaknesses, but we have one who in every respect has been tempted as we are, yet without sin'.[9]

It may be suggested that there were, in fact, five very human qualities which, by God's will, were inherent in the humanity of Jesus:

    i) he suffered;

    ii) he felt strong and changing emotions (e.g. in the scene of the leper);

    iii) he had a sense of humour;

    iv) he had limited knowledge;

    v) he was tempted.

On the other hand, the gospel of John appears to assume perfect knowledge at all times.

A COMPOSITE JESUS

Over the last two thousand years most Christians have believed in a composite Jesus, that is, they have taken passages from each of the four gospels and put them into one whole in a way that we would now realise is not legitimate. One classic example is that they have taken the idea of the perfect knowledge of Jesus from the gospel of John, but they have also included the scene in the garden of Gethsemane when Jesus prayed that he be spared the suffering of the cross. This scene appears in the three gospels of Mark, Matthew and Luke, where it sits easily with the idea of a Jesus who did not have perfect knowledge. And yet the scene does not appear in John's gospel, for the simple reason that the Jesus of that gospel is presented as so perfect and complete that he would not have made this very human prayer. We must accept that there are differences between the four gospels and that we cannot neatly reconcile them.

THE SECOND VATICAN COUNCIL

In commenting on the gospels, the Second Vatican Council insisted on the completeness of the humanity of Jesus.

'(Jesus Christ) worked with human hands, he thought with a

human mind. He acted with a human will, and with a human heart he loved.'[10]

POPE JOHN PAUL II

In a recent document Pope John Paul II referred to the question of the knowledge that Jesus possessed, and called it the 'frontier zone' of the mystery of Christ. He insisted that Jesus eventually came to the clear self-awareness that he was God, but he notably left open the question of whether he possessed perfect and complete knowledge.[11]

TWO OPPOSING TENDENCIES

For two thousand years there have been two strong and opposing tendencies in relation to Jesus: to make him too divine, and thereby take away his humanity, or to make him too human, and thereby take away his divinity. For many people he was either fully God or he was fully human, but they find it difficult to accept that he was both. And yet that Jesus was fully divine and fully human at one and the same time is at the centre of Christian belief. We are meant to see God suffering in the garden and God dying on the cross, and we are meant to see a human being, one like us, actually rising from the dead. A Jesus who was God but who had given up the two privileges of perfect knowledge and of not being able to suffer reflects this idea well.

PRACTICAL CONSEQUENCES

The question has very practical effects, for if Jesus possessed perfect knowledge of all things, even future events, there is a stronger argument for saying that he determined many aspects of the church he founded. If he possessed only limited knowledge and knew no more of the future than other human beings can know, there is a stronger argument for saying that he called followers and expressed a number of ideas concerning their community, but also left many practical decisions concerning the future to them, knowing that they would have to be guided by experience.

We cannot have certainty on the subject, but John wrote his gospel a number of years after the other three gospels, and it is certainly possible that by then some people were denying or downplaying the divinity of Jesus, so that John felt the need to stress it.

What appears certain is that we cannot say that it is proven fact that Jesus possessed perfect knowledge and, therefore, it is not proven fact that Jesus determined all details of his future church with perfect knowledge and divine authority.

It would follow that the divine origin of many elements in the church could not be simply assumed but would have to be proven. If their divine origin could not be proven, we would have to conclude that God deliberately left the choices to us and that we are free to decide whether such elements should or should not be part of the church of the future.

'NOTIFICATION ON THE WORKS OF FR. JON SOBRINO SJ'

This book was in its later editorial stages when a new document was issued by the Congregation for the Doctrine of the Faith, a Notification on the works of Father Jon Sobrino S.J. (signed on 26ʳNovember 2006 and to be published on 14 March 2007). In a covering letter addressed to all bishops it says that 'Bishops should remain vigilant that the present document serves as a normative reference point for confronting the problematic affirmations found in the work in question.'

No.V, para.8 deals with 'The Self-Consciousness of Jesus'. Father Sobrino is quoted as saying, 'With regard to faith, Jesus in his life is presented as a believer like ourselves, our brother in relation to God, since he was not spared having to pass through faith. But he is also presented as an elder brother because he lived faith as its 'pioneer and perfecter' (Heb.12:2). He is the model, the one on whom we have to keep our eyes fixed in order to live out our own faith.'

To this the Congregation replies, 'These citations do not clearly show the unique singularity of the filial relationship of Jesus with the Father; indeed they tend to exclude it. Considering the whole of the New Testament it is not possible to sustain that Jesus was 'a believer like ourselves'. The Gospel of John speaks of Jesus' 'vision' of the Father: 'Not that anyone has seen the Father except the one who is from the Father; he has seen the Father' (Jn.6:46; cf. also Jn.1:18). This unique and singular intimacy between Jesus and the Father is equally evident in the Synoptic Gospels (cf. Mt.11:25-27; Lk.10:21-22).'

I have already stated that the gospel of John clearly affirms the complete and perfect knowledge of Jesus at all times, but I cannot agree that this 'vision' of John is 'equally evident' in the other three gospels, for there is a marked difference between the viewpoint of John on this question and those of the other three gospels. I note that the Congregation does not quote the gospel of Mark at all, and quotes only the one saying in the other two gospels. It does not refer to the temptation of Jesus at the beginning of his ministry or to the story of the garden of Gethsemane in all three gospels. It does not quote the statement from the gospels of Mark and Matthew that the son of man does not know the time of the end of the world. While it quarrels with Sobrino's interpretation of Hebrews 12:2, it does not refer to any other passages from that letter. In other words, it makes no attempt to assess the totality of the biblical evidence, but tends to brush it aside with the statement that the vision of John is 'equally evident' in the other gospels.

The document then quotes from two popes and from the Catechism of the Catholic Church. Here, too, I have problems with the document, for it quotes a sentence from no.26[13] of Pope John Paul II's *Novo Millennio Ineunte*, but does not refer to the sentence two paragraphs earlier (no.24) that I quoted in this chapter naming this question of the self-knowledge of Jesus as 'the frontier zone' of Christology today. Surely one must assume that the pope did not wish to contradict in no.26 what he had just written in no.24, that no.26 must rather be interpreted in the light of no.24. It is surely disingenuous to quote no.26 as though it proved something contrary to the earlier, unquoted statement.

There are three possible conclusions from the biblical evidence. The first is that it is proven fact that Jesus had only limited knowledge, as Father Sobrino appears to affirm, and I cannot agree with this statement. The second is that it is proven fact that Jesus had complete and perfect knowledge at all times, as the Congregation maintains, and I cannot agree with this statement. The third conclusion is that the biblical evidence is conflicting and we cannot draw certain conclusions. I believe that this is the soundest conclusion, the one that best respects the conflict of the evidence and the humility that we should always have before the divine. We are, after all, speaking of exactly what went on within the mind of Jesus, an individual unlike any other who has ever walked on this earth, a person within whom the divine and the human were bound together in a singular manner. In the absence of crystal clear and consistent evidence from the bible, is it not dangerous for any mere human being to claim to have certain knowledge of what went on within the mind of Jesus? I have no problem with the statement that there was a 'unique and singular intimacy between Jesus and the Father', but I cannot agree that it is proven fact that this intimacy was that claimed by the Congregation.

I repeat my conclusion that it is not 'proven fact that Jesus possessed perfect knowledge and, therefore, it is not proven fact that Jesus determined all details of his future church with perfect knowledge and divine authority.'

Meditation

Is it possible that the following is the story of what actually happened?

The child Jesus "increased in wisdom and in years and human favour". Under the guidance of the Spirit, he gradually came to understand that he was called by God to a special mission, and he worked hard to develop within himself the knowledge and the qualities he would need for this mission. He read about and pondered the idea of the promised messiah and at some point came to the startling realisation that the hopes surrounding that messiah were vested in himself.

He felt a power within himself and eventually came to understand that this was a divine power and that God was actually saying to him, "You are my son, the beloved; with you I am well pleased". He began to think of God as his father and to speak to God in familiar terms (*abba*). Despite this, he quickly learned that he could not overcome all problems in the world. Ultimately, he could not overcome the limitations of the human condition itself, for he knew that, in order to fulfil God's eternal plan, he himself had to live within those limitations.

He came to realise that he was a key part of God's eternal plan for the world (what Paul would later call the *mysterion*). According to this plan he wanted to share (*koinonia*) with the whole world the fullness of life he found within himself, and he knew that the reign (*basileia*) of God within himself was the source of the fullness he discovered there, so he wanted to bring about this reign within the minds and hearts of all people. He attracted followers and formed them into a common-union (communion) or church so that these goals could be more readily available to all peoples of all times. Working with the same Holy Spirit as Jesus, they began to make the decisions that had to be made.

FOOTNOTES

[1] 1:13

[2] E.g. 2:2, 2:13, 4:1, 6:2, 6:6, 6:34.

[3] 8:22-38

[4] 13:32

[5] 14:32-42.

[6] 15:34.

[7] 2:52

[8] 2:17-18

[9] 4:15

[10] Pastoral Constitution on the Church in the Modern World, *Gaudium et Spes*, no.22.

[11] Apostolic Letter *Novo Millennio Ineunte*, 6 January 2001, no.24. 'In his self-awareness, Jesus has no doubts: 'The Father is in me and I am in the Father.' (Jn.10:38) However valid it may be to maintain that, because of the human condition which made him 'grow in wisdom and in stature and in favour with God and man' (Lk.2:52), his human awareness of his own mystery would also have progressed to its fullest expression in his glorified humanity, there is no doubt that already in his historical existence Jesus was aware of his identity as the Son of God.'

[12] Mk.1:11

[13] 'His (Jesus') eyes remain fixed on the Father. Precisely because of the knowledge and experience of the Father which he alone has, even at this moment of darkness he sees clearly the gravity of sin and suffers because of it. He alone, who sees the Father and rejoices fully in him, can understand completely what it means to resist the Father's love by sin.'

CHAPTER SIX

In Service of God's People

Against the background of the earlier chapters, we can now begin our study of how power has been used and misused within the church.

In the light of all that was said in Chapter Two, we must approach the question of power and structures within the church by seeing what the bible, the world around and within us, and what has been handed on to us have to say, and we must balance each of these against the other two, using all the powers of discernment and collective wisdom available to us.

THE BIBLE
AMBIVALENCE

In the First Book of Samuel there are two stories of the appointment of Saul as the first king of Israel, with one viewing the appointment in a favourable manner[1] and the other in an unfavourable manner.[2] This is the bible's way of saying that there was ambivalence in the appointment. On the one hand, the nation of Israel faced all the practical problems that any nation faces and needed a government. On the other hand, it was a basic belief that the nation was ruled by God, while kings, with their own personal vanities and ambitions, could become a barrier between the people and God. Kings were appointed, but their presence remained ambivalent.

In the bible's need to tell two stories of the one event there is a permanent truth, valid for all religious bodies. It is always to be hoped that a religious body will in all major aspects be ruled by God, and yet it is an identifiable and large community of people that faces a thousand and one practical problems, and so needs a form of government. This government will place human beings in positions of authority, and it is inevitable that the human beings will all too often get in the way of God, distort God's message or replace the divine with the human. In any religious body there always has been and always will be a tension between the need for divine rule and the need for human rule. The perfect religious organization, with the divine and the human in total harmony, never has existed and never will exist.

THE COMMUNITY OF JESUS

Once Jesus himself had returned to his Father and once the community of the followers of Jesus had grown to a certain size, it was inevitable that the community would begin to acquire a structure. There are indications that Jesus understood and accepted this fact.

From the large crowds who had gathered to hear him, Jesus freely chose a group of twelve people. It is only in the third gospel, that of Luke, that they are called 'the apostles'. The gospels of Mark and Matthew move easily between the two terms, 'the twelve' and 'the disciples', so that it is not always easy to know whether the writer is referring to all those who had accepted Jesus or only to the inner circle of twelve who had been chosen out of this much larger group.

The twelve were clearly destined to be in some manner a basis of the future community but, from the scanty evidence in the gospels, it is not possible to build too large an edifice concerning their later role in the Christian community. What is surely clear is that Jesus wanted his work to continue after he had gone and saw the need to have a special group of twelve people who were with him at all times, saw every single thing he did and heard every single word he said.[3] Their later leadership would be primarily a leadership in bearing witness to all that Jesus had said and done.

THE ROLE OF SIMON, CALLED PETER

The role of the first disciple to be called needs special treatment. Unquestionably the Second Testament presents Peter in a role of leadership of the group of twelve chosen as the constant companions of Jesus and says that this role was either given to him by Jesus himself or arose naturally from the group and was accepted and confirmed by Jesus. There is a consistency in the presentation of this role in all four gospels, in the letters of Paul and in the Acts of the Apostles.

Simon is the first disciple to be called, he is named first in the list of the twelve and is given the name of Peter or "rock". It is he who makes the fundamental profession of faith in the name of all, 'You are the Christ of God'.[4]

The first twelve chapters of the Acts of the Apostles also clearly portray Peter as both leader and spokesman. He took the lead in replacing Judas (1:15), spoke on behalf of the group at Pentecost (2:14-36) and defended the group before the authorities (4:8-12). He acted as judge (5:1-11) and took the revolutionary step of beginning the mission to the Gentiles (10:1-48).

At the same time, Peter was not outside or above the community. It was the twelve as a group that decided to appoint deacons and, with the approval of the community, did so (6:1-7). When Peter began his mission to the Gentiles, the church in Jerusalem demanded an explanation from him and he gave it (11:1-18). At the Council of Jerusalem, Peter was present and spoke (15:6-11), but it was James who took the role of leadership (15:19).

PETER IN THE GOSPEL OF MATTHEW

The gospel of Matthew deserves particular attention, for it is on the basis of this gospel that the major claims of the Catholic Church have been based.[5]

In the gospel of Matthew we find the scene in which Simon is formally renamed Peter and Jesus says,

'Blessed are you, Simon, son of Jonah! For flesh and blood has
not revealed this to you, but my Father in heaven. And I tell you,
you are Peter and on this rock I will build my church, and the
gates of Hades will not prevail against it. I will give you the keys
of the kingdom of heaven, and whatever you bind on earth will be
bound in heaven, and whatever you loose on earth will be loosed in
heaven.'[6]

These are certainly solemn words about Peter, they come from the gospels and we must pay full attention to them. The words clearly speak
of Jesus delegating something of his own authority over the community to Peter. There are, however, three points that must be noted as
a balance to these words.

Firstly, it must occasion some surprise that the name Jesus gave
to Simon was that of Peter, meaning 'the rock', for a rock does not
do anything, it simply is. It is solid and firm and makes an excellent
foundation, but its role is passive. Needless to say, it is only an image
and we must never push images too far. Jesus immediately went on to
speak of binding and loosing and this is a more active role. Nevertheless, Jesus, who could have chosen from a multitude of images, freely
chose the powerful and yet passive image of a rock as the image that
gave Peter his name, the image that before all others gave him his
identity. The statement that Peter was a rock was more basic than the
statement that he was the keeper of the keys, for it was the first statement, not the second, that gave him his name.

Secondly, this thought is strengthened by the fact that just two
chapters later almost identical words about binding and loosing are
spoken by Jesus again, but this time to 'the disciples'.

'Truly I tell you, whatever you bind on earth will be bound in
heaven, and whatever you loose on earth will be loosed in heaven.'[7]

I have already noted that in Matthew the term 'the disciples' can refer
either to the twelve or to all the followers of Jesus, and the effect in this
passage is that both groups share in this authority to bind and loose.[8]
Is not the logical conclusion that Peter alone is the rock, but Peter, the
twelve and the whole church all have a share in the authority to bind
and loose? If we are to be faithful to the gospels, can we ever exclude
the rest of the church from the authority to bind and loose?

That a ruler, a single person, had the power to bind and loose was a commonplace in the ancient world. But that a group and even the whole community had a share in the power to bind and loose was a most surprising idea, and is typical of the quite radical manner in which Jesus looked at traditional ways of acting. May we not conclude that the followers of Jesus were free to think in new ways and were meant to think in new ways?

Thirdly, the words of blessing of Peter occur in 16:17-19. A mere two verses later, in v.21, Jesus

'began to show his disciples that he must go to Jerusalem and undergo great suffering.'

In v.22 Peter did not speak in the name of the whole group, but solely in his own name, for

'Peter took him aside and began to rebuke him, saying, 'God forbid it, Lord! This must never happen to you.''

Jesus answered with the strongest words he ever spoke to any human being,

'Get behind me, Satan! You are a stumbling block to me; for you are not intent on the things of God, but on the things of human beings.'

These verses seem to go out of their way to reverse the message of the earlier verses. In the earlier scene Peter had been placed in the position of blessing, in front of the eleven and speaking in their name. Now he is placed in the position of rejection, behind Jesus, away from the eleven and speaking only in his own name. Earlier he had been called the rock of the church; now he is called a rock that would trip Jesus on his path, a stumbling block. Then he had been told that it was not flesh and blood that had revealed truth to him, but God in heaven. Now he is told that his thoughts do not come from God, but are the unholy thoughts that arise when God is ignored. In fact, Jesus actually told him that he was speaking on behalf of Satan rather than God.

In the First Book of Samuel we were given two stories of the appointment of Saul as king, and together they stressed the ambivalence of kings in Israel. Here something remarkably similar happens, for we are given two stories about Peter side by side, one favourable, the other unfavourable. May we conclude that the message is the same as that concerning kings in the First Testament, that is, that the church will need leaders but, because those leaders will be human, they will be a mixed blessing and will frequently get in the way of God?

The words concerning the renaming of Peter and his being given an authority to bind and loose are powerful, but can they ever be properly understood unless they are balanced with the scene of Peter's failure that takes place immediately afterwards and with the scene in which Jesus, in virtually identical words, gave also to 'the disciples' an authority to bind and loose?

SUCCESSORS

Did Jesus intend that Peter and the apostles should have successors, that is, that their roles should continue forever in the church? As the first part of an answer, we must say that Jesus called the twelve so that they could be the eyewitnesses to every single action and word of his life, death and resurrection. When another was chosen to take the place of Judas, he was to be chosen from

> 'one of those men who have accompanied us during all the time that the Lord Jesus went in and out among us, beginning from the baptism of John until the day when he was taken up from us'.[9]

This was their primary and unique role and it died with them. Needless to say, there would still need to be witnesses after the death of the apostles, and in this sense their role would continue, but the witnesses would no longer be direct eyewitnesses.

Just as the role of witnessing would continue, could there be successors to other parts of the role of Peter and the twelve, e.g. binding and loosing? While still limiting myself to the bible rather than including history and the wisdom of the world around us, several statements can be made leading towards an answer to this question.

Obviously there could be successors, for there was nothing to stop the church from freely choosing to continue the roles of Peter and the twelve into the future.

There is no evidence of an explicit *order* by Jesus that there must be successors forever to Peter and the twelve. If we keep always in mind that it is not proven that Jesus acted with perfect knowledge and we cannot assume the divine origin of any particular structure of the church, this lack of a clear order becomes important.

On the other hand, the early church appeared to *assume* that there would in fact be successors to Peter and the twelve. The best information we have would say that Peter died under the Emperor Nero (64-67), and at least three of the gospels and the Acts of the Apostles were not completed until well after this date. Why would Matthew stress that Peter and the twelve had a role of binding and loosing if Peter and the twelve were already long dead and their role had no further relevance at the time he wrote, if it were of no more than historical interest? Why did all four gospels insist that Peter's very name came from his being the rock of the church if his role as rock had already come to an end and had no relevance for the future?[10]

This argument is strengthened by the fact that there are several instances of the leaders appointing others to take over parts of their ministry and complete the work they had begun.[11]

The Second Testament does not present Peter as an absolute ruler over the twelve or over the whole church. There were occasions when he was made answerable to the church[12] and there were occasions when others took the role of leadership of the assembly and announced the decision of the group[13].

Before we try to take these questions further, we must look at what has been handed on to us and the world around us.

What Has Been Handed On to Us

In speaking of what has been handed on to us, it cannot be enough to look only at the *words* of popes and councils. Surely we must look also at their *actions*, at what actually happened in the life of the church.

Within the limits of this chapter, it would be quite impossible to give a detailed account of the complex story of the last two thousand years. I shall try to trace a few lines through a number of crucial incidents.[14] I stress that I shall be looking solely at the question of governance, and this is not always where the greatest beauty in the church is to be found.

PETER

There was a period in the early church in which structures were 'fluid'[15]. The two great apostles Peter and Paul, however, had both died as martyrs in Rome, and the crucial importance of these two apostles is shown by the fact that the ministry of Peter occupies the first half of the Acts of the Apostles, while the ministry of Paul occupies the second half. It was because of the martyrdom in the one city of both of these apostles that Rome came to be seen by the whole of the early church as the supreme place of the apostles' witness to the person and life of Jesus Christ. This inspired the whole church to give to the local church of Rome a unique and eminent place, so that union with the see of Rome became the sign and guarantee of union with the witness of the apostles themselves. It was not at this time a primacy of jurisdiction of one bishop over other bishops, but a primacy of honour of one local church, that of Rome, over all other local churches.

Because other apostles had given witness in other cities and because of the unavoidable practical importance of the structures of the Roman Empire, the cities of Constantinople, Antioch, Alexandria and Jerusalem also became patriarchal sees. Below these there were other levels of authority, and bishops met in local councils with relative frequency to exercise their joint responsibility.

LEO THE GREAT (440-461)

Leo I was the most influential person in the movement from the primacy of honour of the *diocese* of Rome based on the deaths of the two great apostles to the primacy of jurisdiction of the *bishop* of Rome based on the promises made to Peter in Matthew 16. He began to use a more legal language than popes before him, and he intruded himself into the affairs of other churches when he believed it to be necessary. However, he also knew when to hold back and let churches solve their own problems. He always saw his task as being that of supporting the churches in their profession of the faith of the apostles. He did not insist on Roman customs and allowed great plurality between different churches and even within his own diocese.

> 'His authority seemed indeed more like a power of resort, attentively answering appeals, than a force imposing everywhere his views and the customs of his local church.'[16]

The conflicts of the Arian controversy had by his time weakened respect for local councils of bishops, for there had been too many examples of rival councils producing incompatible documents. This scepticism was stronger in the West than in the East, so the West accepted Leo's ideas with some enthusiasm. In the East and in Africa, on the other hand, there were strong reservations about placing the one Western patriarchate (Rome) above the four Eastern ones (Constantinople, Antioch, Alexandria and Jerusalem), and in placing one bishop above all other bishops.

LEO III (795-816)

One of the causes of contention between West and East was the so-called *filioque* clause (literally 'and from the son') introduced in various places in the West into the Creed developed by the councils of Nicea and Constantinople, concerning whether the Spirit proceeded only from the Father or also from the Son.

> 'Trouble broke out at Jerusalem on Christmas Eve 808. The Latins appealed to Rome. Pope Leo declared the doctrine of the *filioque* to be convincing but gave judgement that he was unable to allow a change of any sort in the letter of what had been issued from an ecumenical council. Let the Latins teach the filioque for it belongs to their tradition. But let them not make it a part of the common faith by inserting it into the creed of the Fathers. He then had the Creed of the One Hundred and Fifty Fathers (the Niceno-Constantinopolitan Creed) engraved on silver plaques, without the *filioque* clause, in Greek and Latin, one for the Confessio of St. Peter, the other for the memorial of the apostles in St. Paul-outside-the-walls.'[17]

This was seen by many as an ideal action by a pope, always serving the unity of the church, not imposing his own views but allowing diversity and insisting on nothing that was not an essential part of the faith of the apostles and of the great councils that gave expression to it.

GREGORY VII (1073-1085)

With the conversion of the Frankish king Pepin to Christianity (753), the vacuum created by the fall of the Roman Empire was filled by the creation of 'Christendom', the attempt to build a state on the basis of Christian principles and a Christian way of life. This eventually led to the coronation by Leo III of Charlemagne as Holy Roman Emperor on Christmas day 800. In this Christian empire, however, problems soon arose. The clergy were by and large the only educated people, so kings and emperors relied largely on clerics to staff their civil service. Appointment as a bishop inevitably became an important civil as well as ecclesiastical appointment. Thus church and state became inextricably mixed, and no one knew how to separate them and assign a proper role to each. There was, therefore, continuing conflict between pope and emperor concerning who was supreme. At various times popes insisted on crowning and even choosing the emperor, and at other times emperors insisted on authority over the church, on the right to actually appoint and depose popes, and especially on the right to name and control bishops.

The matter reached its climax in the confrontation between Pope Gregory VII and Emperor Henry IV. The emperor had an absolute power, so an absolute pope was opposed to him, for in this epic confrontation there was no room for a pope whose power was in any way restricted by that of the bishops. It was in this atmosphere of a struggle for control over both church and state that powerful statements were made concerning papal supremacy over the whole church and they have influenced the church ever since.[18]

At around the same time, relations between the Eastern and Western parts of the church were coming to a head for, not long before the time of Gregory VII, the *filioque* clause was finally inserted into the Creed in Rome itself. Discussions between East and West could have resolved the question, for it would have been possible to find a formula of words that satisfied both sides. The question of the *filioque* clause, however, raised again in an acute form the serious reservations that the East had always had about the papal claims made by Leo I. The objection made by the Eastern bishops was that two councils of the entire church (Nicea and Constantinople I) had determined the Creed without the *filioque* clause and, in their view, only an equal council of the entire church could change the decision and add such a phrase – not a council of the Western part of the church alone, and certainly not a pope acting alone. The final break between East and West occurred only after 1203 when the armies of the Fourth Crusade sacked the city of Constantinople, but the claims concerning papal authority were the background against which this final act was played out.

INNOCENT III (1198-1216)

The theory of papal supremacy developed by Gregory VII soon required an elaborate machinery to sustain it. The popes ruled through councils, legates, tribunals and an ever increasing stream of papal letters concerning every aspect of life, spiritual and temporal. The most brilliant of the popes of this era was Innocent III, who created a voluminous correspondence and contributed greatly to the building up of a system of law.

> 'Innocent III is the pope in whose time the papal monarchy, that is to say, the effective sovereignty of the pope over the whole public life of Christendom, is usually considered to have reached its zenith. The Church was now, at last, a world State, not so much international as supra-national, organised as a State with its judiciary and its law, its centralised bureaucracy, its financial system and its armies, prepared to coerce by force of arms, by the threat and the reality of a holy war, any rebellion against the standard doctrines of belief and conduct or against the papal policies.'[19]

There was both bad and good in this situation. On the negative side, Innocent again claimed authority over the state as well as the church, and he was prepared to use force on the basis that heresy was a danger to the social order. The Inquisition found its origin here. On the positive side, the strength of the papacy prevented the anarchy that was always close to the surface in those centuries and enabled a more ordered and peaceful society. The system of laws developed by these lawyer popes was basically humane and represented a significant step forward for the civilised world. Many modern legal systems owe a large debt to it. It must also be remembered that, because the pope was by far the strongest and most reliable authority of the age, he did not have to go out and seek business, for it flowed in to him. The decisions of his tribunals would stand in a way that the decisions of other tribunals would not, so the business of the papal tribunals grew. The papacy became the victim of its own strength, for it was now heavily involved in secular as well as spiritual affairs.

A striking example of this is to be found in the events following Innocent III's deposing of the emperor Otto and selecting of Frederick, the king of Sicily as his successor. Frederick proved a very ungrateful client and there was long and bloody conflict between him and the papal forces until his death in 1250. The popes again had a large part in the choice of his successor and determined to keep Sicily apart from the empire. They secured the appointment of a Frenchman, Charles of Anjou, as king of Sicily. The unpopularity of this foreign king and his foreign soldiers led in 1282 to an uprising (the 'Sicilian Vespers'). For many years the papacy then found itself in the situation of using military force to put down a popular uprising. Less than one hundred years after its zenith, papal authority was being seriously eroded.

Boniface VIII (1294-1303)

Once it had begun, the loss of moral authority by the popes seemed to continue in an inexorable manner. The end of the century saw an intransigent pope with an exalted sense of papal authority opposed to a French king, Philip the Fair, dedicated to the new theory that the largest autonomous unit of society should be the territorial or national state, so that Christendom would be replaced by a series of nation states. Because of the near anarchy that had prevailed for centuries, this idea was popular, so Philip mobilised public opinion and opposed the pope's fulminations with an effective smear campaign and an attempt to abduct the pope. He did not succeed in the abduction, but the act caused the pope to die shortly afterwards. A French pope was elected and he transferred the papacy to Avignon in France in 1305.

Urban VI (1378-1389)

The popes returned from Avignon to Rome only in 1376 and a new election took place in 1378. It was one of the most extraordinary elections ever held, with the Roman crowd taking a belligerent part, demanding the election of a 'Roman or at least an Italian' and eventually breaking into the palace where the election was being held in order to enforce their will. When Urban VI was finally elected, he turned out to be the most irascible and impossible pope of all times. He was so bad that the cardinals soon decided that his election had been invalid because it had been coerced by the Roman crowd. So they elected another pope, and the Great Schism had begun. The Christian world was divided, with saints and scholars on both sides. Many attempts were made to resolve the dilemma, but the rival popes solemnly excommunicated each other and refused to resign so that a new and universally accepted pope could be elected. They even raised armies to crush each other and increased taxation to pay for the armies, making the papacy even more unpopular. In desperation many decided that in such a crisis a council was superior to a pope, so a council was called at Pisa, but the only effect it had was the incredible one of creating a third pope. The solution finally came from an unexpected quarter, the intervention of the surviving Holy Roman Emperor and a new council, this time at Constance in 1415. The problem was resolved, but not before the council had decreed that:

> 'First of all it declares that, having assembled legitimately in the Holy Spirit, and being a general Council and representing the Catholic Church militant, it has its power immediately from Christ, which every state and dignity, even if it be the papal dignity, must obey in what concerns faith, the eradication of the mentioned schism and the reformation of the said Church in head and members.'[20]

The Council also passed the decree *Frequens*, obliging the pope to call councils at regular and frequent intervals.

Eugene IV (1431-47)

In accordance with the decree *Frequens*, Pope Eugene IV called a council at Basel in 1431. In the aftermath of the Great Schism, this council quickly began to be concerned with questions of its own superiority in relation to the pope, so the pope issued a decree closing it down. The majority of those in Basel refused to accept this decree, but then, instead of tackling the matters in the church that were in dire need of reform, they concentrated on seeking to deprive the pope of all money and make him a penniless figurehead dependent on the council. At one stage some five hundred members were present, but only twenty were bishops. The council degenerated into a farce, with both sides reading out their decrees at the top of their voice at the same time, with the side that finished first breaking into a *Te Deum* to drown out the other. The pope transferred the council to Ferrara and then Florence, where he enjoyed great (but not lasting) success on the matter of reunion with the East. The result was that papal supremacy was restored, but at the cost of not carrying out the necessary reforms in the church and creating an atmosphere where no pope wanted to call another council.

LEO X (1513-1521)

The Great Schism had seriously harmed the church at every level and there was a crying need for reform. Unfortunately, a number of the popes of the fifteenth century were more interested in their secular rather than their spiritual role, in pomp rather than humility, in pleasure rather than reform. There were many attempts at reform at lower levels in the church, but without support from the top, these attempts could not coalesce into a serious movement. When Martin Luther posted his theses in 1517, there was much to complain about, vast sections of the church were profoundly disillusioned, and Pope Leo X was quite lacking in the ability to appreciate what was happening or to react to it in an adequate manner.

PIUS V (1566-1572)

It took twenty-eight years from 1517 before the Catholic Church was able to react to the Reformation by calling a council and then it took another eighteen years for this council to complete its work.[21] By that time the horse had well and truly bolted. In its theology the Council of Trent was conservative, responding to the Reformation by restating Catholic positions and restoring a basically medieval concept of church with a thoroughly centralised structure. The council appeared to be constitutionally incapable of admitting that the reformers had got anything at all right. During and after the council, however, a serious revival did take place, and it came to be known as the 'Counter-Reformation'. The greatest leader of reform was Pius V, a pope who set the highest standards of personal conduct. He threw himself heart and soul into reform and tackled head on all of the most difficult questions. Much was achieved, but it was far too late to repair the divisions that had occurred.

INNOCENT XI (1676-1689)

The seventeenth and eighteenth centuries were not a good time for the church, for a divided and warring Christianity had lost power, prestige and credibility. The battle between church and state continued, but with the church now in a weakened position. In both Catholic and Protestant states, the tendency was to reduce the church to a department of the state. The more powerful states also interfered in papal elections, vetoing candidates who appeared too strong; so many elections were the result of compromise, and a number of mediocre leaders were elected. One strong leader to emerge was Innocent XI, who found himself pitted against the strongest king of the time, Louis XIV of France. Louis was determined to dominate the church, and he and Innocent fought over the issue for years, with neither coming out a complete winner. Because of the loss of credibility by the church, a number of brilliant minds, in a movement called the Enlightenment, began looking for a new explanation of the world and everything in it. By and large, the church defensively condemned rather than actively engaged with this movement.

Pius VII (1800-1823)

While the church was often dominated by the state, it still retained a privileged position within the state. It was for this reason that, among its many targets, the French Revolution of 1789 came to attack the very union between church and state that had lasted since the time of Charlemagne, or even since the time of Constantine. There was conflict between Napoleon and one of the most innately good, decent and kind persons ever to hold the office of pope, Pius VII. Napoleon imprisoned Pius for several years and fought hard to use the church for his own ends. In the end, however, it was Napoleon who fell, while Pius won back much prestige for the church by his character and manner of acting. The Revolution killed many priests and nuns, took away privileges and robbed possessions, and yet, in doing so, it liberated the church from its subservience to the kings of Europe. As a result, stronger popes were elected and Rome once again became a centre of interest and attention for the church.

Gregory XVI (1831-1847)

Out of the Revolution came a movement called liberalism. It came at first with both the scepticism of the Enlightenment and the excesses of the Revolution, but then took so many forms that by different routes it led, on the one hand, to representative government and many of the freedoms we enjoy today, and on the other hand, to both communism and capitalism. There was a serious attempt by a number of

Catholic thinkers to engage with this movement, taking from it what was good and setting aside what was harmful, but unfortunately for the church the popes took a more negative stand. In 1832 Pope Gregory XVI published a sweeping condemnation in his encyclical *Mirari vos*.[22] This put the church on the side of the old regimes that were fast disappearing and meant that the church was against the major trends of the age, and so having little influence on them.[23]

Pius IX (1846-1878)

The times were confusing for the church and, to meet this confusion and to give the pope a spiritual authority to replace the temporal authority over the Papal States in central Italy that was being taken away from him, Pius IX strongly favoured a policy of papal authority and condemnation of errors rather than engagement and dialogue, and he worked hard to bring people to his way of thinking. In 1864 he issued his Syllabus of Errors, listing eighty errors to be condemned, including the idea that the pope should reconcile himself to 'progress, liberalism and modern civilization'. He then called a council at which the major issue was papal authority in the forms of infallibility and the universal jurisdiction of the pope over every part of the church.

Leo XIII (1878-1903)

The next pope is best remembered for his work in beginning a social teaching that sought to address the real concerns of a newly industrialised and urbanised society. All the forces within the church that wished to engage with modern culture supported this development, and over the following century it absorbed much energy that might otherwise have turned against the papacy.

Pius X (1903-1914)

While the social teaching was important, it left many other questions concerning the response of the church to all the movements of the preceding century, and they would not go away. A number of scholars from many disciplines sought to confront these questions, but those who were against this direction branded them all as 'Modernists' and Pius X supported them. There were faults on both sides, but 'Modernism' was always a vague term and the condemnation of many scholars looked suspiciously like a witch-hunt. While the following pope, Benedict XV, ended the open condemnations, 'Modernism' continued to be used as a term of condemnation for many years afterwards. As a young priest in the 1960s I was still required on frequent occasions to take an 'Anti-Modernist Oath'. And the questions still would not go away.

John XXIII (1958-1963)

In 1959, to the surprise of everyone, Pope John XXIII called a general council of the church, the Second Vatican Council, which met in four sessions from 1962 to 1965. He spoke of opening windows, bringing the church up to date and of seeing much that was good in the world around him. In this council the church finally did take an open look at the world and culture in which it lived and sought to engage with it. It finally looked at many of the questions the church had failed to look at over nearly two hundred years. In sixteen documents it ranged over most aspects of the life of the church and opened up many possibilities.

LESSONS TO BE LEARNED

There are lessons to be learned even from a history as brief as this. Several can be mentioned here.

Surely it is obvious that what I have recounted is the *story of a journey*, similar in many ways to the story of a journey found in the bible, with the same mixture of human and divine, and with the same steps backwards as well as forwards.

The world has changed constantly over the last two thousand years and the structures of the church must be flexible enough to meet the many different circumstances that can arise. They should not become so fixed that they cannot adapt.

There should always be a proper balance between the two legitimate needs of the proclamation of necessary certainties and the search after elusive truth. In the Second Millennium the proclamation of certainties has followed the rise of papal power. While the bible spoke constantly of uncertainty and struggle, this story has had a tendency to accent certainty and obedience.

The same rise of papal power in the Second Millennium has meant that, the higher the papacy ascended into the realms of being perfect, the greater had to be the covering over and denial of anything that did not fit this image. And what was said of the pope in the universal church tended to flow down to the bishop in his diocese and to the priest in his parish.

For more than a thousand years the church committed much of its efforts to the creation of 'Christendom', a Christian society in which there would be a secular ruler who would be under the ultimate authority of the pope; in which heresy could be suppressed because it was seen as an offence against the social order; and in which serious pressure could be brought to bear on individuals to conform their actions to those of the society. This attempt lasted for so long that it cannot be a cause of surprise if the church is still coming to terms with the forced abandonment of this goal. In the terms I used in an earlier chapter, it is the massive paradigm shift from seeking the external kingdom of a Christian society to seeking to be a humble agent of God's eternal plan of life in all its fullness, through the reign of God within the hearts and minds of individuals.

The Present Situation
The Effects of the First Vatican Council (1869-70)

The euphoria that followed the proclamation at the First Vatican Council of papal infallibility and universal jurisdiction was so great that it swept away the somewhat more sober wording of the documents of that council. Exaggerated phrases were used and their effects are still with us. The euphoria created a pope who lived in solitude, set apart, transcendent, rather than as part of the body of bishops. Rather than the pope serving this body, the bishops were to serve the pope. The original idea of a pope as the principle of unity had become the idea of a pope as the principle of direction. To quote one of the phrases used at the time, the entire universal church became 'the pope's diocese'. Instead of a circle with the bishop of Rome as its human centre holding it together, the church became a pyramid with the pope at the top.

The original idea of the diocese of Rome possessing a primacy because it was the place of witness of the greatest of the apostles vanished almost entirely in favour of the idea of a pope possessing a personal primacy because of the words of Jesus in the gospel of Matthew. May we ask whether this introduced a distinct imbalance into the Catholic understanding of the Church?

PAPAL POWER AND TECHNOLOGY

Papal infallibility was declared in 1870, not long after the technology introduced by the Industrial Revolution had begun to make its presence felt. The official upgrading of papal authority through the declaration of infallibility and a practical increase in papal power through technology occurred together.

In the middle of the nineteenth century the Australian bishops sought advice from Rome on a problem confronting them. They wrote their letter and then waited some months for the next sailing ship to depart. The ship travelled around the long southern coast of Australia, across the Indian Ocean to South Africa and up the length of the Atlantic Ocean until it eventually reached England about eight months later. The letter then travelled by coach from London to Rome. The Roman authorities deliberated, then sent their response by the same route. In all, it took over two years for the response to be received.

In 1999 an Australian bishop made a decision of which some did not approve, and within two days his action had been reported to Rome and a facsimile reply from a Roman cardinal lay on his desk ordering him to stop.

From two years to two days! While this development is a result of technology rather than of any changes in theology, it has brought with it a quite massive practical increase in the power of the pope. It has enabled a detailed control of every aspect of the church in every part of the world in a manner that popes of earlier centuries, even one as recent as Pius IX, could not have dreamed of.

The technology used to gain greater papal *control* over the church could have equally been used to *listen* to the views of the whole church, but it must be said that this has not happened.

The Effects of the Second Vatican Council (1962-65)

The Second Vatican Council was an immense achievement, one of the greatest in the entire history of the church. It was, however, the beginning of a journey rather than its end, for in four brief sessions it attempted to engage with all the complexities of the modern world in a manner that had not happened for a very long time.

On a number of issues there was fierce debate between opposing views. If the council refused to endorse many older positions, it did not always find a clear expression of a new position, and there are many compromises in the documents, with something being given to each side. Indeed, its usual method of resolving disagreement was to place statements reflecting both views side by side. Despite this, the bishops voted overwhelmingly in favour of the final texts, thereby acknowledging the conflict of views and their own inability to reconcile them.

It has always been possible, therefore, to quote the council selectively, and over the last forty years a vast amount of this has been done by both sides. Some people on one side have gone beyond anything the council said in the name of a sometimes vague 'spirit' of the council, while some people on the other side have argued that, if the council did not specifically replace an older formulation of some truth with a new formulation, then the older formulation remained fully in possession. Each side has accused the other side of 'abuses' of the council, and there has been a significant measure of truth in the accusations on both sides.

In closing the council, Pope Paul VI referred to unfinished business,

> 'Since the council had not intended to resolve all the problems raised, some were reserved for future study by the church, some were presented in restricted and general terms, and therefore they remain open to further and deeper understanding and a variety of applications.'[25]

In seeking to deal with this unfinished business, it is not possible to find a way forward by doing no more than embracing either one of the conflicting views placed side by side in the council documents. In placing these views side by side, the bishops of the council were saying, clearly if implicitly, that the earlier formulations could no longer be considered, in and of themselves alone, as full expressions of the church's faith, and yet the alternative view was also inadequate. On each particular question something new is needed, involving a synthesis that incorporates the strengths of both sides, and much of this work still remains to be done.[26]

The bishops of the council also established a principle that one writer, Ormond Rush, has called 'discontinuity for the sake of a greater continuity', that is, in attempting to reconcile opposing views, the bishops often reached back behind a particular formulation of truth to an earlier and greater truth.[27] For example, the council:

> i) went behind the neo-Scholastic categories that had dominated for a long time to the riches of the early Fathers of the church;
>
> ii) went behind the same more static neo-Scholastic categories of the church as a 'perfect society' to a more dynamic concept of a pilgrim church on a journey and involved in history;
>
> iii) went behind the second millennium's emphasis on hierarchy to the first millennium's greater balance between hierarchy and communion;
>
> iv) went behind a thousand years of exclusively clerical decision-making on all matters of faith to revive the ancient idea of the *sensus fidei*, the 'sense of faith' of the whole people of God;
>
> v) went behind a thousand year's of teaching that a bishop's power of governance came from the pope to the idea that all of a bishop's power comes from ordination;
>
> vi) went behind some fifteen hundred years of teaching that only truth has rights to the idea that it is people who have rights, even when they are in error;
>
> vii) went behind much of both the first and second millennium to a rejection of the idea of 'Christendom';
>
> viii) went behind Gregory VII's virtual rejection of the bishops in his confrontation with the emperor to a teaching concerning the college of bishops as an equal holder of supreme power within the church;
>
> ix) went behind the Council of Trent and the whole Counter-Reformation to an appreciation of the independent reception

of the Great Tradition by the separated churches and to open
dialogue with them;

x) went behind the same Council of Trent and Counter-
Reformation to a better balance between scripture and
tradition in the life of the church;

xi) went behind the attitudes and style of Gregory XVI, Pius
IX and Pius X in their condemnations of 'modernity' to the
sentiments expressed in the first sentence of Gaudium et Spes.[28]

In all of these cases there was discontinuity with a more recent tradition in the name of a fuller continuity with the Great Tradition, the
handing on of the person and story of Jesus Christ. In seeking to hand
on the Great Tradition, a particular age makes a decision that it sees as
opportune, but a later age sees that this decision was too circumscribed
by its own time and that there is need to set it aside in order to be
faithful to the Great Tradition.

THE RECENT EXERCISE OF PAPAL POWER

In recent decades, in addition to the increase in power coming from
technology, there have been three developments in the exercise of papal power that must be queried.

WILL AND INTELLECT

When speaking, not of infallible statements, but of less solemn statements of the pope, the Second Vatican Council spoke of a submission
of the will first and then the intellect to the teaching authority of the
pope,[29] but more recent documents have reversed the order (speaking
of a submission of intellect and will) and changed the object (what
is taught rather than the teaching authority).[30] By putting the will
first and speaking of the teaching authority, the council stressed the
willingness, the wanting to accept the teaching authority of the pope.
In practice it meant that, when I picked up a new papal document,
I willed it to be right, and this willingness had its effect on the way
I read the document. It did not mean that I surrendered the powers of
my intellect; it did not take away my right to disagree. It simply meant
that I was willing to read the document in a favourable spirit, seeking
to understand the force of the arguments presented rather than seek-

ing only to find things I might disagree with. I had no problems with this teaching. By reversing the order of will and intellect, however, and by speaking of what is taught rather than of the teaching authority, the more recent documents stress, not willingness to accept the person teaching, but intellectual assent to what is taught.[31] It is the difference between willingness to accept the pope as a teacher and acceptance of every word the pope teaches.

'CREEPING INFALLIBILITY'

Papal infallibility was solemnly proclaimed in 1870 and some people thought that it would lead to many infallible statements. In fact it did not and there has been only one infallible statement since that time (in 1950). What happened instead was that there was an increase in the level of authority and certainty of every statement of a pope. There has been a process that a number of people have called 'creeping infallibility'. Terms have been used that reflect this trend, e.g. teaching that is not infallible, but irreformable or definitive.

'In necessary matters there must be unity, in doubtful matters there must be freedom, in all matters there must be love.' I had always understood this ancient saying to mean that the necessary matters on which unity was essential should be kept to a minimum and that as much freedom as possible should be allowed. But I believe that 'creeping infallibility' has involved a tendency to move many matters from the realm of the doubtful or not strictly necessary, where freedom reigned, to the realm of the necessary, where unity was demanded. I find that this trend imposes unnecessary demands on people, and goes against the 'freedom to grow' that is at the heart of this book.

A symptom of this is 'The Catechism of the Catholic Church', published by Pope John Paul II in 1992. If it were nothing more than a guide to the teachings of the church, it could be a useful document, though it would always have to be used with caution, for it runs the serious risk of reducing faith to intellectual assent to a series of propositions rather than seeing it as a response of love from one person to another. However, it contains infallible statements, definitive but not infallible statements and statements that one presumes are not definitive, with little guidance as to which category any particular statement belongs to. This is not a good situation and it seems to be part of the same tendency to upgrade the solemnity and certainty of every state-ment. Certainly there are people who are using this catechism as the yardstick of all orthodoxy.

Gradual Infallibility

Some recent quasi-official opinions have told us that when popes constantly repeat the same teaching, there is a point at which this re-peated teaching becomes infallible. I have four major problems with this idea.

Firstly, through its many discontinuities for the sake of a greater continuity with the Great Tradition, the Second Vatican Council set aside many things that had been consistently taught for more than a thousand years and would, by this criterion, have been infallible.

Secondly, it contradicts another statement of the same council, 'No doctrine is understood to be infallibly defined unless this is mani-festly demonstrated.'[32] This statement appears to be common sense. The Catholic people of the world are entitled to know with crystal clarity which statements are infallible and must be believed and which are fallible and may be disagreed with. And yet if an opinion can gradually become infallible simply by being repeated, this clarity is destroyed. If one adopts this criterion, people cannot have certainty on the status of many teachings put forward by the teaching authority.

Thirdly, the argument that constantly repeated opinions become infallible is exactly the argument that has been applied to the two most controversial papal statements of the last forty years – those on contra-ception and on the ordination of women. It is a claim used to add fur-ther authority to two papal teachings that, as a simple matter of fact, have failed to convince by the force of the arguments used in them. These two issues have today become the touchstone of orthodoxy. I find it strange that, if I were to tell a cardinal in the Vatican that I was struggling with doubts about the existence of God, I would re-ceive sympathy and support. But if I were to tell the same cardinal that I had doubts about papal teaching on contraception and the ordina-tion of women, I would receive a stern lecture on loyalty to the pope.

Fourthly and most fundamentally, this argument comes too close to turning the *tool* of discernment into a third *source* of our religious knowl-edge, and it is never legitimate to do this. I shall return to this idea.

The Desire for Certainties

In many people there is a psychological need for a religion of certainties. The euphoric celebration of papal infallibility in 1870, the three developments in papal power I have just spoken of, and the immense practical rise in papal power that came from the use of technology, all reflect this desire for a religion of certainties. From the beginning of time this has been a powerful human desire and it has affected every religion that has ever existed. Indeed, it affects even quite secular modes of thinking, as can be seen from the success of populist politicians in a number of countries. People want simple certainties, they demand simple certainties, and leaders frequently feel constrained to give them simple certainties, even when they are not really certain themselves.

In his encyclical Evangelium Vitae[33], Pope John Paul II says that at a consistory on 4-7th April 1991 the Cardinals unanimously asked him 'to reaffirm with the authority of the successor of Peter the value of human life and its inviolability, in the light of present circumstances and the attacks threatening it today.'[34] This placed obvious pressure on the pope to produce an answer. The most crucial question was whether, not just 'human life', but an actual 'human person' is present from the first moment of conception or not, and if not, at what moment a human person first exists. No one can deny the importance or the urgency of the question and no one can deny how immensely convenient it would be to have a clear and simple answer. But is it really possible to have this clear and simple answer? If one gives such an answer, do the arguments given in support add up to the certainty one desires? Or is authority being used to go further than the arguments can go? If so, has authority, a tool of discernment, at this point been turned into a source of religious knowledge? And yet, within the Catholic Church as it is structured today, it would be extremely difficult for a pope to say, 'The question is both important and practical, but I cannot answer this question with certainty.'[35]

In relation to the bible I have argued that God quite deliberately did not give people a whole book full of certainties. One of the most powerful messages of the bible is that human life is a search and a struggle through a world of uncertainty. May we not ask the question: Would God now give through the pope a world of certain answers to every question that God refused to give through the bible? Would God who, through the bible, wanted us to grow by struggling in the midst of uncertainty and taking responsibility for our actions, now wish to return us to a world where all we were supposed to do was listen and obey? Would God wish to reduce the responsibility appropriate to adults to the obedience appropriate to small children? We grow, not by obeying certainties imposed on us, but by searching and struggling for the truth and by taking responsibility for all we believe and do in this struggle.

The Danger of Five Vicious Circles

Is there evidence that through these recent developments the papacy could run the risk of five vicious circles?

i) The more a pope insists on authority rather than on the persuasive force of arguments, the less people will listen. The less people listen, the more a pope can feel the need to insist on authority.

ii) The more a pope insists on intellectual assent to what is taught, the less people will be willing to accept that pope as teacher. The less people are willing to accept a pope as teacher, the more that pope can feel the need to insist on intellectual assent to what is taught.

iii) The more insistence there is on authority, the more faith will be presented as intellectual assent to propositions rather than as a response of love to a person. The more faith is presented as intellectual assent to propositions, the more people will turn away from the propositions towards a religion of love and relationship.

iv) The more people of today emphasise the individual and stress their right to their own opinion, the more a pope will feel the need to stress the community nature of religion. The more a pope stresses community, the more people will demand a more participatory community in which their opinions are listened to and taken into account.

v) The more people clamour for a voice in the affairs of the church, the more a pope can tend to turn towards a small group of 'loyal' advisors rather than seek 'the faith of the church'. The more a pope does this, the louder will become the popular clamour.

THE COLLEGE OF BISHOPS

In the circumstances I have outlined, the college of bishops does not play the role in the church today that it should.

In the twenty years I worked as an active bishop I can remember very few occasions when the pope consulted the body of bishops and none when the pope asked the bishops to vote on an issue. We were not asked to vote before the publication of the document on the ordination of women, not even when the Cardinal Prefect of the Congregation for the Doctrine of the Faith spoke of this teaching as 'infallible', with the pope doing nothing to contradict him. If bishops are not asked their opinion even when the word 'infallible' is in the air, the college of bishops would seem to have no practical importance in the church, and the statement of the Second Vatican Council that this college is a co-holder of supreme power would seem to have little meaning. No explanation was given as to why the bishops were not consulted, but one may surely ask whether the reason was that some people close to the pope were afraid that the bishops would not give this teaching the near-unanimous endorsement that alone would have given credence to the use of the word 'infallible' in speaking of it.[36]

I do not know what the result would have been if the bishops of the Catholic Church had been asked to express an opinion on whether women could be ordained to the priesthood. But I am certain that a majority would have been opposed to the idea of attaching the word 'infallible' to any teaching on the subject.

The Synod of Bishops meets every three years and many people perceive this as a powerful body, but in fact it, too, is very carefully and thoroughly controlled. It is the pope alone who determines what a synod finally says, so the bishops can do no more than offer advice, and even the advice is carefully filtered. On at least two occasions the bishops have been told that they may not even discuss a certain matter.[37]

At the Synod for Oceania in 1998 I was told by the Cardinal Secretary of the Synod that the meeting worked by consensus, not majorities, and that only a vote of 90% constituted a consensus. And yet the Vatican officials appointed to that synod made up more than 10% of the whole synod and so could block even a near unanimous vote of all the other bishops present.

So why don't the bishops rebel and speak out? I have yet to meet the bishop who has no criticisms of any kind of the way things are done in the Vatican, and there is widespread dissatisfaction with what happens at a synod, so why don't the bishops use their collective power? This is not an easy question to answer. I can only say that it is a combination of loyalty, love and fear.

Before his ordination every bishop is required to take an oath of fidelity to the pope, so rebellion is breaking an oath made to God. Bishops take this oath seriously, and they are quickly reminded of it if they step out of line on even a trivial matter, as I know well from personal experience.

The 'rock' of Peter is immensely powerful in holding the Catholic Church together, and a bishop who criticised would feel, and would be made to feel, that he was performing the unthinkable act of abandoning the rock.

International meetings of bishops do not occur unless they are controlled by Vatican officials,[38] so there is little opportunity for bishops to formulate common proposals or to act as one. No bishop would wish to create an atmosphere of the bishops on one side against the pope on the other side.

Loyalty to the rock has been translated into personal loyalty to each individual pope. Consequently, if no bishop is totally happy with the way things are done in the Vatican, the unhappiness is directed towards this or that cardinal or other official, never towards the pope. The dissatisfaction frequently becomes a criticism of individuals rather than of the system these individuals are collectively bound to uphold.

All bishops had a genuine admiration for the great strengths of the pope of the last quarter of the twentieth century – his early courageous story under Nazi occupation and his later courage against Communist domination, his great intellect, his obvious holiness. No bishop has wanted to present himself as in any way better than this pope. In these circumstances, the identification between the rock and the particular pope has blunted all criticism.

A disagreement between a group of bishops and a Vatican cardinal is an unequal contest, for the cardinal can gain the support of the pope for his ideas, knowing that the bishops will not oppose the pope.

There are many degrees of unhappiness with 'the Vatican' or 'Rome', and there are many different causes and objects, so that a bishop who criticised could be left high and dry by his fellow bishops.

Bishops love the church and gave their lives for it, and they are aware that a stand-up, knock-down fight between a group of bishops and the Vatican would bring great harm to the church.

Please believe me when I say that all of the above and more have been in my mind as I have written this book.

THE ROMAN CURIA

I have had only limited personal dealings with the members of the Roman Curia, those senior church officials who work in the various offices of the Vatican. In those dealings I have found many to be likeable and charming. Each has a personal life-story that eventually led to his present position. Many came from quite humble origins and I do not believe that they are all driven by ambition or a lust for power.

I accept that they are a necessary public service in the church and that the pope could not function without them. The Catholic Church exists in almost every country in the world, and I accept that the Curia has an essential and difficult task in preserving the unity of the church in the midst of incredible diversity. I am sure that, if the members of the Curia were to speak openly, they could tell many stories of great stupidity by various bishops and of serious threats to unity.

Furthermore, if the college of bishops and the faith of the whole church provide few restrictions on the exercise of the power of the pope, the Roman Curia does provide significant restrictions. Many talks given by the pope would be first drafted by the Curia, or at least revised, amended and given the Curia's seal of approval.[39] The pope also depends on the Curia in every aspect of his work and could no more do his job without them than a government could survive without its civil service. As a result, there are many ways in which the members of the Curia would be able to influence the words and actions of a pope.

The Roman Curia is a restriction on the exercise of the power of the pope and this restriction is more real and effective than that which comes from the college of bishops or the faith of the whole church. In the absence of other restrictions it is good that this one exists, for it largely prevents any pope from being wilful and arbitrary or from indulging in the excesses of past centuries.

On the other hand, it ensures that the past dominates the present and prevents the church from breaking away from problematic aspects of its past. It is beyond doubt that the Curia has been a major force in using technology to control but not consult, in promoting the three developments in papal power that I have spoken of and in keeping under strict control both the college of bishops and the faith of the whole church. The members of the Curia protect papal power, and they make no secret of the fact that this is the task above all others that they are specifically employed to do.

The signature of a pope cannot make a wrong document right, so there is also the danger of thinking that the mantle of always being right must cover not only the pope who signs so many documents, but also the members of the Curia who draft most of these documents for signature. The experience of the bishops of the church would be that the Curia has not always avoided this danger.

It is not surprising, therefore, that there is resentment of the Curia by many bishops and other people who have had dealings with the Vatican. The most usual complaints concern an insistence on control of all affairs of the church, high-handedness and a pervasive atmosphere of secrecy.

The words of the great theologian Yves Congar are powerful. He speaks of being 'crushed, destroyed, excommunicated by a pitiless system which can neither emend itself nor even recognise its errors, but which is run by men who are disarming in their goodness and piety.'[40]

The fundamental problem does not lie in the individual persons who make up the Curia, but in the system that they are bound to uphold. Papal power has gone too far and there are quite inadequate limits on its exercise. The authority of the college of bishops has been marginalised and the faith of the whole church has been rendered powerless.

The Roman Curia has been heavily involved in this process and it is committed to supporting unrestricted papal power. No changes of personnel within the Curia will resolve the problem, for that is not where the problem ultimately lies. Only serious changes to the papal system the Curia is bound to uphold can bring about a true resolution.

Learning From the World Around Us

There is much that a church can learn from the science that has developed in recent years concerning the ways in which communities function, but this is not the place for a lengthy treatment of this topic. I must limit myself here to a bare minimum.

RESTRICTIONS ON THE USE OF POWER

There are many different forms of power. There is physical, psychological, spiritual, political, military and economic power. There is parental power and there is delegated parental power, e.g. the power exercised by teachers and babysitters. All of these different forms of power can be abused.

It is for this reason that there is a hard-won lesson of history that all societies need to place restrictions on the exercise of power, and will most probably encounter serious problems if they do not. It was Lord Acton who gave this truth the form most often quoted, 'All power tends to corrupt, and absolute power corrupts absolutely.'

Thus a prime minister must answer to a parliament. In the parliament a strong opposition should balance the power of the party in government. The judiciary acts as a check on the executive power of government. The military must be subject to the parliament. Wise laws must curb the exercise of great economic power. The chief executive of a business firm should answer to a board. The power of both a father and a mother in a family should be limited by the power of the other partner and, within strict limits, by the power of the State. The greater the power a person exercises, the greater should be the restrictions on the exercise of that power.

The world around us is one of the two sources of religious knowledge we should look to. The wisdom of restrictions on the use of power is a truth that we can learn from that world and it is a truth that we ignore at our peril. The scandal of sexual abuse has carried the powerful message that spiritual power can be abused just as easily as any other power, so the need for restrictions on power within a church must be assumed, and the contrary would require serious proof.

TENSIONS

There are always a number of tensions within any society. As just a few examples, there is a tension between the needs of the individual and the needs of the community, between the need for unity and the need for diversity, between the need for stability and the need for flexibility.

These tensions cannot be resolved by seeking to crush either side. We must not crush either the individual or the community. We must not seek to abolish either unity or diversity, either stability or flexibility. In all circumstances we must seek to hold the two sides in creative balance.

Within a church, as I have noted, the first tension is between rule by God and rule by human beings. There have been churches that had too much human authority (e.g. the Catholic Church) and they have encountered serious problems. There have also been churches (e.g. some Protestant churches) that had too little human authority and they have run the constant risk of being unable to resolve the tensions that have inevitably arisen and of splitting into separate groups.

In every modern nation there is a tension between the power of the people, the power of the parliament and the power of the president or prime minister. There are certain matters affecting the very constitution of the society that only the whole people can decide. It is impossible, however, to hold a referendum on every matter that arises, so it is necessary to have a parliament and for that parliament to possess considerable power. The parliament needs a leader and, in practice, the president or prime minister will also possess a real power. There are many different forms of balance between these three powers in different countries and there is no perfect answer. All countries must live with the inevitable tensions that arise.

In a church the same three levels of governance as in any other society would have to be assumed– the whole people, some form of synod or parliament and a leader. If any of the three were to be omitted by a particular church, it would seem that the onus would be on that church to show how it could survive and prosper without that level of governance. There would need to be appropriate means to deal with the tensions that would necessarily arise.

LEADERSHIP

Within any society, and certainly within a church, the concept of authority must be complemented by that of leadership. Leadership is the acquired gift of helping both the members of a community and the community as a whole to grow into all they are capable of becoming. Growth is always what God desires for human beings, and authority without leadership will not achieve this. There is an extensive literature today on the qualities required for leadership and the art of leadership, and these topics must be given greater attention.

THE POWER TO SERVE

All power is power to serve, so all power brings with it responsibilities. Both history and the world around us tell us that it is extremely difficult to *serve* a community by exercising *absolute* power over it. When considered as a *system* involving many people at many levels of governance over many centuries, it is naïve to think that such a system could work. As a system it will fail on countless occasions and in countless ways.

The world around us (and this includes the history of the church itself) would tell us quite strongly that true *service* of the community by its leader or leaders demands restrictions on the use of power, the sharing of power by the leader(s) and participation in its exercise by the community, accountability of the leaders to the community, and the promotion of a true sense of responsibility among all members of the community.

Meditation

For two thousand years Christian people have attempted, in myriad different ways, to learn from the bible and the world around them, and use their reason, feelings and spiritual insight to apply these sources to their lives. Their attempts have created another story of another journey, with the good and the bad once again side by side, with steps forwards, backwards and sideways, with bitter divisions and attempts at reconciliation. We can learn much from the best of this story, but we must also learn the lessons of its many mistakes.

Muddy human fingers have always stained the beauty of the divine, so that there is no perfect church, and there never will be. Any Christian church is daily and permanently in need of reform. It must never forget the lessons of its own history.

While paying lip service to the idea of the constant need for reform, it is all too easy for a church to come to believe that in all important matters it has things in their proper place. Such thinking is always dangerous.

There will always be the need for a constant and untiring effort to reclaim the spirit of Jesus.

Footnotes

[1] 1 Samuel 9:1-10:16

[2] 1 Samuel 8:1-22; 10:17-24; 12:1-24.

[3] Mark has the call of four disciples as the very first act of the public ministry of Jesus (1:16-20), to emphasise that their witness would be complete.

[4] Lk.9:20. See Mk 8:29 and see the same phenomenon in a different context in John 6:67-69.

[5] See First Vatican Council (1869-1870), Fourth Session, Dogmatic Constitution *Pastor Aeternus*, chapter 1, *The Establishment of Apostolic Primacy in Peter*.

[6] 16:17-19

[7] 18:18

[8] The passage begins at 18:1, '*At that time the disciples came to Jesus and asked, 'Who is the greatest in the kingdom of heaven?' He called a child, whom he put among them, and said......*' 8:18 is part of the following discourse and it is clear that the discourse is directed to all disciples of Jesus. For example, the first words of the discourse are, 'Truly I tell you, unless you change and become like children, you will never enter the kingdom of heaven' and it cannot be said that these words are directed only to the twelve and not to the rest of the disciples.

[9] Acts 1:21

[10] Article 20 of *Lumen Gentium* says that the bishops 'have by divine institution taken the place of the apostles as pastors of the Church'. However, the limits of what the Council said on this subject must be kept in mind. For example, in commenting on this article, Karl Rahner says, 'This transmission (of the apostolic office) is proved (or merely asserted?) very briefly by appealing to the eschatological definitiveness of the gospel. How far this proof is valid, when taken alone is, of course, not decided, and hence it remains a question to be freely debated by both sides in ecumenical discussion...... From the purely historical point of view, it can hardly be denied that in the age of primitive Palestinian and Pauline communities the constitution of the Church still seems to have been somewhat `fluid'. Thus the question arises as to the exact theological interpretation of the element of divine right in the structure of the Church, a question not further discussed in the text..... (The text) merely says that the Council `teaches' (*docet*), which is a less forcible expression than those used in earlier drafts.' *Commentary on the Documents of Vatican II*, ed. Herbert Vorgrimler, Burns and Oates, London, 1967, Vol.1, pp.190-191. At the risk of being repetitious, it must be added that the Fathers of the Vatican Council assumed the perfect knowledge of Jesus and what they said must be revisited in the light of the fact that this perfect knowledge can no longer be assumed.

[11] *Lumen Gentium* no. 20, footnote 5, quotes 'Acts 20:25-27; 2 Tim.4:6ff; in

conjunction with 1 Tim. 5:22; 2 Tim.2:2; Tit. 1:5.'

[12] Acts 11:1-18.

[13] Acts 15:6-21

[14] Since it is a brief overview that I am concerned with here, my main sources for this section are books giving a history of the whole two thousand years of the church. In particular, see Thomas Bokenkotter, *A Concise History of the Catholic Church*, Image Books, 1979; Philip Hughes, *A Short History of the Catholic Church*, Burns and Oates, London, 1974; John Jay Hughes, *Pontiffs, Popes who have Changed History*, Our Sunday Visitor Publishing Division, Huntingdon, Indiana, 1994. For a deeper analysis of particular events, I owe a debt to the six-volume work, *The Pelican History of the Church*, editor Owen Chadwick, Penguin Books, 1964. For a perspective on different eras I have made use of *Christianity, Two Thousand Years*, edited by Richard Harris and Henry Mayr-Harting, Oxford University Press, 2001.

[15] See the comments of Karl Rahner in an earlier footnote.

[16] J.M.R. Tillard O.P., *The Bishop of Rome*, Michael Glazier, Wilmington, Delaware, 1983, p.184

[17] J.M.R. Tillard, *op.cit.*, p.163.

[18] Gregory's Dictatus Papae makes for strong reading.

[19] Phillip Hughes, *op.cit.*, p.109.

[20] Quoted from *The Christian Faith in the Doctrinal Documents of the Catholic Church*, eds. J. Neuner and J Dupuis, pp.219-220.

[21] 'The Council of Trent is important, in the first place, because it failed to meet until 1545.' Owen Chadwick, *The Reformation, The Penguin History of the Church*, Penguin Books, 1964, vol.3, p.273.

[22] 15 August 1832, *Acta Gregorii XVI* 1:169-174.

[23] Among other things, Gregory condemned the recent invention of trains, making a play on words in French by saying that the *chemins de fer* (ways of steel or railways) were *chemins d'enfer* (ways of hell).

[24] *Op.cit.*, pp.42-43.

[25] Quoted by Ormond Rush, *Still Interpreting Vatican II, Some Hermeneutical Principles*, Paulist Press, New York, 2004. p.29.

[26] cf. O. Rush, *op.cit.*, p.29.

[27] cf. O. Rush, *op.cit.* References to this phenomenon occur throughout Rush's work.

[28] 'The joy and hope, the grief and anguish of the people of our time, especially of those who are poor or afflicted in any way, are the joy and hope, the grief and anguish of the followers of Christ as well. Nothing that is genuinely human fails to find an echo in their hearts.' Second Vatican Council, *Pastoral Constitution on the Church in the Modern World*, no.1.

[29] *Lumen Gentium*, no.25. 'This loyal submission of the will and intellect must

be given, in a special way, to the authentic teaching authority of the Roman Pontiff....'

[30] See e.g. The Code of Canon Law (1983), can.752. 'While the assent of faith is not required, a religious submission of intellect and will is to be given to any doctrine which either the Supreme Pontiff or the College of Bishops, exercising their authentic magisterium, declares upon a matter of faith and morals....'

[31] See Francis A Sullivan SJ, The Response Due to the Non-Definitive Exercise of Magisterium, *Studia Canonica*, 23 (1989), pp.267-283; Ugo Betti, L'ossequio al magistero pontificio 'non ex cathedra' nel n.25 della 'Lumen Gentium, *Antonianum*, 62 (1987), pp.432 ff.

[32] *Lumen Gentium* 25; cf. canon 749 #3.

[33] Encyclical Letter 'on the value and inviolability of human life', 25th March 1995, Libreria Editrice Vaticana, Vatican City.

[34] *Op. cit.,* no.5, p.9.

[35] The pope's answer is to quote two statements from the Congregation of the Doctrine of the Faith which go within a whisker of saying that from the first moment of conception a foetus is a new person, and then add that the matter is so important that, even if it is not so, we must act as though it is, so that 'the human being is to be respected and treated as a person from the moment of conception.' *Op.cit.*, no.60, pp.107-108.

[36] In fact, a kind of consultation did take place, but it only serves to strengthen the points I have made. The presidents of the Bishops' Conferences of the world were called to Rome. There they were presented with a completed document banning the ordination of women and were asked to endorse it in the name of all the bishops. The presidents replied that they could not speak in the name of all their members without first consulting them. They also asked for two changes in the document: the omission of the words 'having heard the views of the bishops' and of the word 'irreformable'.

[37] At the synod on the laity they were told that they may not discuss the question of the ordination of women, and at the synod on the priesthood they were told that they may not discuss celibacy.

[38] See canon 459 #2.

[39] My suspicion is that the famous Regensburg address of Pope Benedict XVI in 2006, which caused such a strong reaction in the Muslim world, did not go through this process of revision.

[40] From *Journal of a Theologian*, edited by Etienne Fouilloux, quoted by Alain Woodrow in *Congar's Hard-Won Victory*, The Tablet, 28th April 2001, p.605.

CHAPTER SEVEN

The Authority of 'the Church'

The Second Vatican Council made at least a partial move in the direction of change when it spoke of the pope and the college of bishops as being co-holders of supreme power in the church.[1] (N.B. The college of bishops is not the bishops over against the pope, for the pope is the head of the college of bishops and the college does not exist without the pope).

As indicated in the previous chapter, there were many compromises at the Second Vatican Council, and placing the power of the pope and the power of the college of bishops side by side as being equally supreme is one more of these compromises. It is difficult to maintain the idea of two bodies holding the same supreme power within a community, for it is inevitable that one or the other will in practice dominate, that one will in fact be supreme and the other will not. In the time since the council, it has been evident that, in fact and in practice, the pope has possessed supreme power, while the college of bishops has not.

A solution to this dilemma would be to maintain that the college of bishops, with the pope at its head, is the holder of supreme power, with this power then being *exercised* collectively by the whole college or individually by the head of the college, the pope.   On this basis it would be possible to draw up a set of wise rules governing the exercise of supreme power, such that both the college and the pope would exercise their proper role and neither would be dominated by the other.

Instead of doing this, however, can we go further and ask whether all authority in the church belongs first and foremost to 'the church'?

Here a word about the meaning of the word 'church' is essential. Within the Catholic Church, the word is often taken to mean either the institution or the pope and the bishops, e.g. 'church teaching', 'the response of the church to sexual abuse' etc . The church, however, is not primarily an institution, but the People of God[2]. It is not simply the lay members of the church, even though they make up 99%; it is all members of the church. It is this community that laity, pope, bishops, priests and religious all serve. The power of none of them is absolute, for all serve the community of the church, so that the church may serve the reign of God within the hearts and minds of all people in the world. All individuals in the church, including the pope, are subject to the church, for all are subject to the reign of God.

This is the sense in which I am using the word 'church' here, though the common misconception that the word refers to an institution or to pope and bishops explains why I have felt constrained to place the word between inverted commas in the title of this chapter.

Would it be in accord with the two texts of Matthew 16:19 (the power to bind and loose given to Peter) and Matthew 18:18 (the power to bind and loose given to the 'disciples') taken together, to say that authority belongs to the *church*, the entire community, with this authority then being *exercised* universally by the whole church, collectively by the twelve and their successors and individually by Peter and his successors?[3] If this were accepted, each level would possess all the power it required to serve the community of the church and wise laws could be enacted to ensure that the three levels worked in harmony. I can do no more here than say a few words about each of the three levels.

A PETER-FIGURE

Building on what is said and assumed in the Second Testament and looking at both history and the world around us, there are two strong arguments in favour of a Peter-figure. Both come from the role as rock, the image that gave the Peter-figure a name.

The first argument is best illustrated by a recent story. At the time of the Second Vatican Council (1962-65), a French archbishop, Marcel Lefebvre, became the leader of the resistance to many of the changes brought about by the Council. The issue that gained most media attention was that of the language of the Mass (Latin or the language of the people), but this was only a minor issue in his broad rejection of the whole council. Eventually he left the Catholic Church and founded his own new church. There were many millions of people within the church who were in sympathy with him. By and large they did not like the changes made by the council and they preferred the church the way it had been before the council. If asked to choose between the views of Archbishop Lefebvre and Pope Paul VI at that time, many would have chosen the views of the archbishop. And yet only a very small number of these people followed Archbishop Lefebvre out of the church. The major reason why the many others did not follow him, despite their sympathy for his position, was that to do this would mean abandoning the rock, and this they would never do. Protestant Churches have frequently split into smaller groups over differences of understanding,[4] but the Catholic Church has had an extraordinary ability to hold together a very large and disparate group of people. Outsiders often have a monolithic idea of the Catholic Church, and do not appreciate just how disparate its members are and how hard it is to hold them together. And the rock of Peter has been crucial to this holding together.

Indeed, the opposite situation also proves the point. In this book I have criticised the pope's lack of an adequate response to sexual abuse. And yet, if the pope had responded immediately and forcefully, speaking directly to victims and demanding a humble, honest and compassionate response from all members of the church, the power of the rock is so great that the response of the Catholic Church could have been a model.

The second argument is that there is great power in the idea of rare and momentous occasions when, after full consultation with the whole church and speaking solely in the name of the whole church, the very rock itself would actually open its mouth and proclaim the faith of the church. In ecumenical dialogue, a group of Lutheran scholars has said,

> 'Our Catholic partners have stimulated us to consider how vital it is for the Churches to speak, when occasion demands, with one voice in the world, and a universal teaching office such as that of the pope could exercise a ministry of unity which is liberating and empowering rather than restrictive or repressive.'[5]

WHAT KIND OF PETER-FIGURE?

In speaking of a Peter-figure, should we have in mind the pope of the Catholic Church with some adjustments? Or, rather than start with the papacy as it now is and suggest changes, would it be possible for the entire Christian world to go back to the bible, all aspects of what has been handed down and the wisdom of the world of today, and create a new synthesis? The essence of the idea would be a Peter-figure who was the calm rock of unity and who, after consultation with the church and speaking in the name of the church, proclaimed the faith of the church.

To put this in another way, I do not believe in the church of Pacelli or Roncalli or Montini or Luciani or Wojtyla or Ratzinger (the family names of the last six popes), but in the church of Jesus Christ. The views of the particular individual who carries out the role of Peter should not have the importance they have had in the past. When a vacancy occurs, there should not be the intense speculation we have recently witnessed concerning who the next pope will be, for it should not make a difference to anything truly important. It should be quite impossible to be loyal and orthodox under one pope and then somehow less loyal and less orthodox because another human being has taken his place. Indeed, the first task of any pope should be to make loyalty easier by giving to the rock a human face of both holiness and warmth.

THE DIOCESE OF ROME

In doing this, could we look again at the original idea of the primacy of the diocese of Rome because it was the place of witness of the two great apostles — of Peter, who had said, 'You are the Christ, the son of the living God'[6] and Paul, who had written, 'I live now, not I, but Christ lives in me'[7]? Could this concept be combined with the idea of a successor to Peter continuing to fulfil the role of rock of the church? The two ideas of the diocese of Rome having a primacy and the bishop of Rome as the rock of the church go together very well. It is only the third element of the power of binding and loosing that has caused problems, and even then only when this power has been separated from the power of the bishops and of the People of God. Could we not solve many of the most profound and bitter difficulties experienced within the church by one more 'discontinuity for the sake of a greater continuity'? For little that is being proposed here is actually new; in the main, it is a return to and elaboration of something that has already existed and in its own time was endorsed by popes, councils and the People of God.

THE POPE AS BISHOP

The Second Vatican Council made the significant change of saying that a bishop's power comes from ordination rather than from a delegation of power by the pope. The change has profound consequences, and among them are consequences for our understanding of the papacy. As we all know, becoming pope involves no new ordination. The only ordination a pope has received is that as bishop, and there is not the slightest difference between this ordination and that of any other bishop, so the pope is essentially a bishop. What is different is not the ordination, but the diocese to which the pope is elected, for since the time of the deaths of both Peter and Paul in Rome that diocese has been pre-eminent among all the churches. The power the pope exercises is that of a bishop but, because of the pre-eminence of the diocese of Rome, the bishop of that diocese has a special task that no other bishop has. That task is to be the rock of unity. A very satisfying theology could be built on this foundation.[8]

Peter and Paul

One further fact needs to be mentioned. Not one, but two apostles gave witness of martyrdom in Rome. So the bishop of Rome is to do everything possible to make present in the church the witness of both Peter and Paul, and is never to be a witness to Peter alone. On one famous occasion Peter and Paul clashed,[9] and at all times they stood for different, if complementary, values. Among other things, Paul stood for the priority of the hierarchy of holiness over the hierarchy of power, for the Spirit over the letter and the Word over all human endeavours. This must be part of the witness of the bishop of Rome.[10]

SOME ESSENTIAL ELEMENTS OF THE ROLE

The gospel of Matthew tells us specifically that Peter was also given a power to bind and loose, and it would surely be wrong to go from one extreme of unfettered papal power to an opposite extreme where the Peter-figure had no power at all and was a mere rubber stamp for what others had decided. The events of the council of Basel would underline this need. The basic statement is surely that the Peter-figure must have the powers necessary to fulfil the role of rock of the church and a proper share in the power to bind and loose.

After all the necessary work had been done to determine the faith of the church, the Peter-figure alone would have the authority to speak in the name of the whole church and proclaim this faith.

While the choice of persons would be made by different people at different levels, the actual appointment to all major offices in the church could be signed by the Peter-figure, with the candidate then making a public commitment to remain anchored to the rock.

In accordance with laws that would have to be established, the Peter-figure should have the coercive power to make warring bishops sit down together, and authoritatively urge them to find a peaceful and equitable solution to their disagreements.

The Peter-figure would have a role as sentinel for the faith of the apostles, along the lines followed in their actions by Leo I and Leo III.

The Peter-figure must have a role of leadership. Peter spoke in the name of all the apostles in affirming faith in Jesus,[11] took the lead in replacing Judas,[12] spoke on behalf of the group at Pentecost [13]and defended the group before the authorities.[14] The Peter-figure must answer to the church, just as Peter did, but the position can not be so circumscribed that a role of leadership is not possible.

It is generally agreed that the fall of Communism in Eastern Europe began in Poland with the Solidarity Movement, and that this movement gained courage and inspiration from the presence of a strong Polish pope in Rome. John Paul responded to the cry of his people in Poland, just as Leo I had responded to the cry of the people of Italy when Attila invaded. Surely a Peter-figure of the future should be free to use influence in a similar way, though safeguards and limitations would have to be included.

SOME ESSENTIAL LIMITS ON THE ROLE

Should another schism occur (and who can say it cannot happen?), there must be a means of resolving this problem. Should the Peter-figure suffer a severe and irreparable cerebral haemorrhage, there must be a means of responding to this situation. Should a Peter-figure be prevented by an external force from carrying out necessary duties, provisions must be made. It has long been said that a Peter-figure can be deposed for heresy, but it has never happened and there is no mechanism for putting it into effect if it did happen. And who can say that we will never have another leader like Urban VI, who was so impossible and was causing such damage that the cardinals felt an overwhelming need to rectify their own mistake in electing him? To say that the church can do nothing when faced with any one of these five situations is to say that the Peter-figure is not merely above the bishops and the laity, but above the church itself, and not even the First Vatican Council said that.

I am not advocating Conciliarism or Gallicanism or Febronianism or Modernism or any other 'ism' of church history. I am simply saying that the Peter-figure serves the church, as the church serves the reign of God within the hearts of all people. This appears to be fully in accord with what is said in the Acts of the Apostles concerning the relationship between Peter and 'the church'. It must mean that circumstances can arise when the Peter-figure must answer to 'the church' or when 'the church' must act to preserve its integrity and its relationship to the reign of God. There must be laws of 'the church' safeguarding these values that even the pope is subject to and cannot change.

It is not good enough that each successive Peter-figure should freely decide whether to consult anyone else. It is not good that one should decide to consult and the next decide the opposite. On this subject also there must be laws of 'the church' that even a Peter-figure is subject to and cannot change. I shall return to this question in a later chapter.

It is clear that there would be many matters to discuss, but it seems that a united Christian church of the future must give the most serious consideration to the idea of continuing the role of Peter.

The Middle Level

The one church of Christ possesses two essential dimensions, the universal and the local (e.g. the church of Manila or Budapest or Nairobi). They are both basic and neither can be reduced to the other.

On the one hand, the church is not a federation of pre-existing local churches, which are free to decide whether or not to federate. A local church is not a local church at all unless it makes present the universal church that Jesus founded. On the other hand, local churches are not mere administrative divisions of this universal church, for the universal church exists only in and out of the local churches. The church is one, not despite the local churches, but in the variety of the local churches. The phrase of the Second Vatican Council which best captures this idea is 'The variety of local churches harmonising (*conspirans*) into one'.[15]

Much thought needs to be given to the relationship between the universal church and the local churches and the ways in which the leaders of local churches should share in the governance of the universal church.

The Second Vatican Council speaks of 'the holding of councils in order to settle conjointly, in a decision rendered balanced and equitable by the advice of many, all questions of major importance.'[16] In addition to councils, there are also synods and other kinds of joint meetings. The manner of giving effect to this principle of decisions 'rendered balanced and equitable by the advice of many' is important but has its difficulties. Several points can be made.

In the Catholic Church alone there are more than three thousand dioceses or local churches, and there are more than four thousand bishops. A parliament of several thousand is unworkable.

Any particular structure set up to give expression to the college of bishops would be a contingent structure, but it would be wrong to deny, either in theory or simply in practice, the authority of the college solely because any expression of it must be contingent. It would be better to say that the structure is a contingent expression of a basic principle of church life that does have a serious foundation, and is to be judged, not by its contingency, but by its effectiveness in giving expression to the basic principle of the authority of the college. In its simplest terms, if effective structures are not in place, the basic principle is being denied.

The physical presence of all bishops is not essential to a council or synod or parliament, as long as there is some means of having the bishops of the world confirm or reject the decisions taken by the representative group.

Modern means of communication enable forms of consultation, including even a council, that do not need to bring large numbers of people together into the one place for lengthy periods of time.

There is no reason why other people besides bishops could not also be members of the council, synod or parliament.

There could be different rules for e.g. an occasional council, a regular synod and an ongoing parliament.

Clearly there are many matters here to be studied. I shall return to some of these questions in a later chapter, for the history of the Catholic Church makes it clear that any statement of the importance of this middle level of government is meaningless unless contingent structures that make it a reality are firmly in place.

THE FAITH OF THE WHOLE CHURCH

The word 'pope' or 'papa' means 'father', and I have no objection to popes being seen in a parental role, as long as they remember at all times that they are parents of *adult* children. They should always be listened to with respect because they are parents, but they cannot order their adult children to do everything the way they want it done and they cannot order them to think the way they think. They cannot take away their sense of responsibility for their own lives. They must never reduce the responsibility appropriate to adults to the obedience appropriate to small children.

In Christian history there is a Latin term, *sensus fidei*, that is not easy to translate. Its meaning can be expressed in a longer phrase as 'the instinctive sensitivity and power of discernment that the members of the church collectively possess in matters of faith and morals.'[17] It is a good term because, while it most certainly includes rational thinking, it is in itself a sensing, an instinct, an intuition, a head-and-heart discernment of truth.

While each member of the church can possess this 'instinctive sensitivity and power of discernment', in both individuals and groups it can be suffocated or led astray by other concerns. It certainly does not mean that every individual is always right. Since humility is always desirable in the search for truth, it is probably true that, the more an individual claims to have this 'instinctive sensitivity and power of discernment', the less one is inclined to believe that he or she does.

We are surer of its presence when there is a genuine consensus of opinion on a particular topic, but even this is not always enough. For long periods of history there was a consensus among Christian people that slavery was a normal part of life, that torture was an ordinary means of interrogating persons suspected of a crime, and even that every flash of lightning was an expression of God's anger. We are never excused from the serious work of discernment.[18]

Despite these limitations, Christian tradition has always recognised that a consensus of belief among all the members of the church is something that must be listened to and given its full weight. In the words of St. Augustine, 'The whole world judges securely.' John Henry Newman took this idea further by saying that, 'while the multitude may falter in its judgment', we have certainty when the whole church 'in due course rests and acquiesces in a deliberate judgement.'

The Second Vatican Council took up this idea. The draft document first presented to the council had followed a traditional pattern by speaking first of the pope and then working down through the various levels of the church until it reached the laity. The council changed this, so that its final document speaks first of the mystery of the church, then of the people of God, and only then of the hierarchy of the church. This means that the church is first a work of God and a means of God's presence, then it is a community of people, and then, and only then, it is a community with a structure and a hierarchy within it in order to carry out its task. It was within this context that the council made the statement that 'the whole body of the faithful.... cannot err in matters of belief.'[19]

Because this was the Second Vatican Council, however, conflicting ideas were once again placed side by side, so that the whole message given by the council was that the body of the faithful cannot err in matters of belief, but in coming to these beliefs it must follow the teaching authority of the pope and bishops.[20]

Despite these ambiguities and conflicts, we must affirm that the council, in the name of continuity with the Great Tradition, once again created a discontinuity with more recent history by returning to the ancient idea of the *sensus fidei* of the whole church. The council clearly reintroduced this concept into church thinking, and it cannot be made to go away.

We would also have to say that the solution cannot lie in embracing either extreme. On the one hand, it cannot lie in seeing the *sensus fidei* of the whole church as above or independent from the pope and bishops. On the other hand, it cannot lie in so subjecting the sensus fidei to the pope and bishops that it is meaningless. It is a new synthesis that is required.

The essence of this synthesis must surely lie in the idea of dialogue. Just as, before the church proclaims a truth, it should ensure that this truth is not contrary to the bible, *or* the world around and within us *or* what has been handed on, so it should ensure that the truth is not contrary to the faith of the pope, *or* the faith of the bishops *or* the faith or *sensus fidei* of the whole church. This can only be achieved through dialogue.

The need for this dialogue is fundamental. If the whole body of the church is to have the freedom to grow, it must have a say in the foundational beliefs of the church.

In speaking of the bishops, I said that 'any statement of the importance of this middle level of government is meaningless unless contingent structures that make it a reality are firmly in place', and I indicated that the current structures concerning bishops are too controlled to function properly. How much more true it is, then, that there must be structures in place to listen to the *sensus fidei* of the whole church, for virtually no structures are in place at the universal level and quite inadequate ones at the more local level. Rather than discuss theory, therefore, I shall try to make a reality of the *sensus fidei* by suggesting particular structures in a later chapter of this book.

In the last few years of the Second Millennium the church has been devastated by one of the worst scandals in its history, that of sexual abuse. It has not been good that the response of the whole church has depended to a large extent on the understanding and limitations of one person, the pope, however admirable that person may have been in many other fields. It would have been far healthier if the strong views of the entire People of God had been part of the response. If the church is to move forwards, this painful lesson must be learned.

Meditation

All individuals in the church serve the community of the church, so that the church may serve the reign of God within the minds and hearts of all people in the world. No one is above the church, for no one can be above the reign of God.

Responsibility is the single most crucial element in human growth. And people will feel truly responsible only for that which they have in some manner helped to create, whether it be a local project or a universal church.

Ideas concerning such matters as participatory government and subsidiarity, which the church constantly preaches to nations, must be applied to the church itself.

Just as, before the church proclaims a truth, it should ensure that this truth is not contrary to the bible, or the world around and within us or what has been handed on, so it should ensure that the truth is not contrary to the faith of the pope, or the faith of the bishops or the faith or *sensus fidei* of the whole church.

This can only be achieved by dialogue, "in order to settle conjointly, in a decision rendered balanced and equitable by the advice of many, all questions of major importance."

Footnotes

[1] 'Together with their head, the Supreme Pontiff, and never apart from him, they (the bishops) have supreme and full authority over the universal Church.' *Lumen Gentium*, no.22.

[2] For the constitution *Lumen Gentium* of the Second Vatican Council the church is first a mystery (chapter one), then a community of people, the People of God (chapter two), then a community with its own structures and hierarchy (chapter three).

[3] Yves Congar speaks of a power given universally to the church, personally to the twelve and singularly to Peter. (*The apostolic college, primacy and Episcopal conferences*, Theological Digest 34:3, 1987, p.211). Father David Coffey, formerly of the Catholic Institute of Sydney, suggests that it is better to say 'collectively' to the twelve, and I have followed this.

[4] It is only a joke told to me by a Protestant bishop that a church once split over the question of whether, in the phrase 'eternal punishment', the word 'eternal' expressed a sufficiently lengthy period of time. This may be a joke, but it is not always easy for a Catholic to understand why there are so many Protestant churches and sects.

[5] '*Teaching Authority and Infallibility in the Church*', Lutherans and Catholic in Dialogue, Minneapolis, VI (1980), Lutheran Reflections 18, quoted by J.M.R. Tillard, *op.cit.*, p.11.

[6] Mt.16:16

[7] Gal.2:20.

[8] J.M.R. Tillard develops this theme well, *op.cit.*, especially at pp.40-41.

[9] Gal.2:11-14.

[10] Once again see J.M.R. Tillard, *op.cit.*, pp.92ff.

[11] Mk.8:29

[12] Acts 1:15

[13] Acts 2:14-36

[14] Acts4:8-12

[15] Lumen Gentium, n.22.

[16] *Lumen Gentium*, no.22.

[17] I have adapted this phrase from the book *Vatican Council II, the Conciliar and Post-Conciliar Documents*, editor Austin Flannery OP, where the translator of no.12 of *Lumen Gentium* says that the *sensus fidei* refers to 'the instinctive sensitivity and discrimination which the members of the Church possess in matters of faith'. (p.363)

[18] For a discussion of some of the limits of the *sensus fidelium*, see J.M.R. Tillard O.P., *A Propos du 'sensus fidelium'*, Proche-Orient Cretien, Vol.XXV (1975), pp.113-134.

[19] *Lumen Gentium,* no.12.

[20] See the whole text of both no.12 and no.25 of *Lumen Gentium* taken together.

CHAPTER EIGHT

Free
and
Responsible

The field in which the power of the church has been most controversial is surely that of morality, for it concerns the practical actions of people. As we shall see in the next chapters, the use of power in this field impinges on matters closely connected with abuse. In the next chapters I shall, therefore, discuss the role of the church in relation to teaching on questions of morality (what we should do) before writing of questions of belief (what we should believe).

THE BIBLE

Concerning the question of how we should relate to other people, we find in the bible the same development of ideas and a similar story of a journey as we have already seen in other areas. We find a gradual rise from a more primitive to a higher morality, though with constant steps backwards as well as forwards. I believe that we can distinguish six levels of morality that gradually evolved.

Six Levels of Morality

Level Six

The first two chapters of the Book of Genesis contain the two stories of creation, chapter three deals with the fall, and chapter four, vv.1-16 with the story of Cain and Abel. Immediately following this is a passage that deserves to be better known (4:17-24). It tells us that, right from the time when human beings first inhabited this earth, their natural genius began to assert itself and they quickly learned to live together in community and to develop agriculture, industry and culture.

> 'Cain knew his wife, and she conceived and bore Enoch; and he built a city, and named it Enoch after his son Enoch....... Lamech took two wives; the name of the one was Adah, and the name of the other Zillah. Adah bore Jabal; he was the ancestor of those who live in tents and have livestock. His brother's name was Jubal; he was the ancestor of those who play the lyre and pipe. Zillah bore Tubalcain, who made all kinds of bronze and iron tools.'

But, having done this, the passage immediately draws a strong contrast between this technical and cultural progress and the moral ability of people to relate to each other in a manner that would help them to grow as human beings.

> 'Lamech said to his wives:
>
> 'Adah and Zillah, hear my voice.
>
> You wives of Lamech, listen to what I say:
>
> I have killed a man for wounding me,
>
> a young man for striking me.
>
> If Cain is avenged sevenfold,
>
> truly Lamech seventy-sevenfold.'[1]

This is surely the most primitive level of relationships between people, the very starting point of a long journey. If a whole society were to adopt this criterion of seventy-sevenfold vengeance for any wrong done, it would be condemned to an endless cycle of violence and chaos, and all its technical and cultural progress would be wasted. It may be called the level of *superiority and vengeance*. One does not have to look hard to see that even today there are individuals, groups and whole nations that can at times fall to this level of morality. It is important to realise that no one is immune from falling back to this level at any moment. Indeed, whenever a serious wrong is done to us, it is often our first spontaneous reaction: 'If you hit me, I'll hit you twice as hard.'

Level Five
The next level is that of the well-known biblical saying, 'An eye for an eye, a tooth for a tooth.'[2] This saying is not an order from God concerning the manner in which we should act, but part of the long *story* of the human race in rising above the moral level of Lamech. Far from being as primitive as it is often thought to be, this law was a conscious attempt to rise above the earlier level, for its force was 'Not seventy-seven teeth for one tooth; not even two teeth for one tooth; no more than one tooth for one tooth.' Far from requiring vengeance, it sought to restrict it, for it meant that, if A knocked out a tooth of B, B would knock out a tooth of A and the violence would stop there. It may be called the level of *justice without mercy*. In practice, it was still too close to the level of Lamech, and Mahatma Gandhi's comment on it was, 'An eye for an eye leaves the whole world blind.' It is the morality of 'getting even', and one is reminded of the chilling phrase attributed to Joseph Kennedy, 'Don't get mad; get even.' If humanity were to make serious progress, this rule had to give way to higher levels of morality.

Level Four
Throughout human history people have related to other people on one of two bases: either the usefulness of others to themselves or the essential dignity of others. Sadly, in all cultures and at all times (including our own) the first has tended to dominate, with people esteeming those who were useful to themselves while despising those who were seen as useless. This is the moral level of *self-interest based on the usefulness of others to oneself*. Needless to say, most of our relationships are reciprocal, that is, we both give and receive, and this is a good thing.

But it leaves the question of how we should relate to both individuals and whole categories of people who seem to have nothing to offer us.[3] This level is reflected in many incidents in the bible and in statements such as the one I have already quoted,

> 'When you sit down to eat with a ruler,
> observe carefully what is before you,
> and put a knife to your throat if you have a big appetite.'[4]

Level Three

The third level is that of the Ten Commandments[5], the level that best reflects the influence of the great Covenant between God and the people of Israel. The Ten Commandments are a serious attempt to base human relationships on the essential dignity of all persons rather than their mere usefulness. They may be called the level of *respect for dignity*. Five consecutive commandments call for respect for one's neighbour's dignity as a human being. In the first four they do this by demanding respect for:

> i) life and physical integrity (you shall not kill),
> ii) the relationships that make life worth living and give it meaning (you shall not commit adultery),[6]
> iii) material goods (you shall not steal),
> iv) a person's good name (you shall not bear false witness).

When these four are taken together, they are a powerful affirmation of one's neighbour's dignity.

In the fifth of the series the commandments forbid even *desiring* to harm one's neighbour ('You shall not covet your neighbour's house; you shall not covet your neighbour's wife, or male or female slave, or ox, or donkey, or anything that belongs to your neighbour').

The Ten Commandments were a gigantic step upwards from the previous levels. They are also the essential level on which any higher level must be built, for it is impossible to truly love another person unless one first has a genuine respect for the dignity of that person.

Level Two

The third level was based on negative commandments, 'You shall not', that is, 'Because you respect your neighbour's dignity, do no harm.'

The second highest level requires that we not merely do no harm, but also do positive good to our neighbour. If I respect you as my equal, I will at least do you no harm and I will wish to see you given all that belongs to you by right. If to respect I add love, I will wish for more, for I will wish for all that is good for you and that is within my power to give you. It is the level of *love built on respect* and of the Golden Rule: 'Love your neighbour as you love yourself'[7] or 'In all things treat others as you would like them to treat you.'[8] The Beatitudes of Jesus start here but then continue into the highest level of morality.

LEVEL ONE

The highest level is also based on love, but this time on *God's love for us*. It is the level of the actions of Jesus, 'I give you a new commandment: love one another...as I have loved you.'[9] Some might think that this level is a mere ideal that human beings could never live up to and that they can ignore in practice. Just occasionally, however, a story appears on our television screens, e.g. of a stranger running into a burning house to rescue children. To do something like that involves far more than loving as one loves oneself; it is a genuine rising up to love as God loves. None of us will ever know whether we are capable of this level of heroism until we are faced with the test, and then we might surprise ourselves. Surely an overwhelming majority of parents rise to this level at many critical moments in their child's life, for there are many moments when they must love their child, not as they love themselves, but far more than they love themselves.

There is no one who cannot fall back to the sixth or lowest level at any moment, but there is also no one who is not capable of rising to the highest level.

Frequent examples of all six of these levels of morality are found in the bible. There were, of course, steps backwards as well as forwards, but in these six levels of morality there is the story of the communal journey of the people of Israel, and it can become the story of a personal journey for each one of us. The moral teaching of the church must seek to assist people on this journey.

Religious Liberty

Many scholars believe that the most radical changes introduced by the Second Vatican Council concerned religious liberty. For some fifteen hundred years the Catholic Church had held that truth alone had rights, while error had no rights, that the Catholic Church alone contained the complete truth, so it alone had rights that other groups did not have.

Against this, the council said that it is people who have rights, not truth or error, and that people retain their rights even when they are in error. On this basis it defended the right of all people to religious liberty, that is, the right to choose their own religion and to practise it in their life without hindrance from others. This included the right to choose and practise no religion.

The French bishop, Marcel Lefebvre, left the Catholic Church after the council and took a number of people with him, and the council's teaching on religious liberty was one of his main reasons for leaving.

Conscience

If there was clarity on the issue of religious liberty at the Second Vatican Council, there was not the same clarity on the closely related issue of conscience. On this topic the documents of the council contain many ambiguities and even contradictions, mainly concerning the question, 'What should I do when the teaching authority of the church says one thing and my conscience tells me the opposite?'

This controversy goes back to the beginning of the Christian era. It is perhaps most clear in the differences between Augustine and Thomas Aquinas on the subject.

Augustine and Thomas Aquinas

On the authority of conscience the dominant view for centuries was that of Augustine (354-430). Using an example of his time, he argued that, just as a lower official cannot pass a law that contradicts the law of the Roman Emperor, so conscience cannot tell us to do something that contradicts God's law, and it is the church which is the appointed interpreter of divine law.[1][6] He concluded that, if our conscience and church teaching are in conflict, we must obey church teaching. Against this Thomas Aquinas (1225-1274) was truly radical in saying that conscience must always be followed, even when it is mistaken, provided only that the mistake is an honest one.[2][7] He argued that we must always be seeking God's truth and goodness, and must certainly listen to the church in doing this, but that we must then constantly make decisions based on our present imperfect understanding of that truth and goodness. The relationship between divine law and conscience is always a dialogue. He concluded that, if our conscience and church teaching are in conflict, we must obey our conscience.

THE SECOND VATICAN COUNCIL

This fundamental difference between Augustine and Aquinas was expressed in many ways in Christian history and the Second Vatican Council did not resolve it. Compare two quotations from the same document, *Gaudium et Spes*. The first speaks of the nature of conscience and reflects the views of Aquinas.

'Deep within our conscience we discover a law which we have not laid upon ourselves, but which we must obey. Its voice, ever calling us to love, and to do what is right and avoid what is wrong, tells us inwardly at the right moment: do this, shun that. For we have within our hearts a law inscribed by God. Our dignity lies in observing this law, and by it we will be judged. Conscience is our most secret core and sanctuary. There each of us is alone with God, whose voice echoes in our depths.'[12]

The second quotation applies conscience to the question of birth control and reflects the views of Augustine.

'In the end, it is the married couple themselves who make this judgement before God. In their way of acting, however, Christian couples should be aware that they cannot proceed solely according to their own ideas, but must always be ruled by a conscience that seeks to follow the divine law, and they must be docile to the teaching authority of the Church, which authentically interprets the divine law in the light of the Gospel.'[13]

It is important to realise that this ambiguity on the subject of conscience exists within the Second Vatican Council itself. It would be wrong to quote either side as being the authentic and consistent teaching of that council. It must be admitted that the council was reflecting a very long history of division on this point and that it was unable to resolve the tension.[14]

Since the council this ambivalence continues to exist and has, indeed, been sharpened. On the one hand, the encyclical Veritatis Splendor says,

'The Church puts herself always and only at the *service of conscience*'.[15]

On the other hand, there has been a constant insistence that people must conform their thinking to the teaching of the church. The issues of the time since the council that aroused the most controversy have been contraception and the ordination of women. Separately or together they have frequently been seen as today's litmus test of orthodoxy and loyalty.

THE MEANING OF MORALITY

Is there a way to resolve this tension by creating a new synthesis? Yes, I believe there is, for the conflict exists only when we limit our understanding of morality to doing right things. But is morality solely about doing right things or is there more to it?

I believe that the point at which we must agree with Aquinas and part company with Augustine is in the latter's comparison between God and the Roman emperor. For the emperor, his own power and glory and the obedience of his subjects came high on his list of priorities. The personal growth of all subjects came a long way down his list, so obedience to his commands was strictly and harshly enforced. For God, on the other hand, the first consideration is always that people, both individuals and communities, should grow to become all they are capable of being. To adapt a sentence from an earlier chapter, we must move from a God-emperor whose glory is to be found in our obedience to a loving God whose glory is to be found in our growth.

Thus the ultimate difference between Augustine and Aquinas is that, at least on this one point, Augustine was serving a sterner god who demands obedience, while Aquinas was serving a god of love and challenge who desires growth. For the God of Aquinas what is important is that people should grow towards all they are capable of being, and obedience is not sufficient, of itself alone, to achieve this goal. If we are to grow towards the higher levels of morality contained in the bible, two things are equally essential: we must do right things and we must take responsibility for them.

DOING RIGHT THINGS RESPONSIBLY

Augustine was right in saying that performing right actions and avoiding wrong ones is an essential part of moral growth, e.g., in the midst of a powerful history of communal or tribal hatreds, a certain person makes a genuine conscience decision before God alone that he should take part in the massacre of his perceived enemies, an act of 'ethnic cleansing', and does so. In the words of the Second Vatican Council, I would be compelled to say that his very dignity lies in following his conscience, even when he is wrong. Despite this, I would have to add that his decision has hurt him. He has become a murderer, and for the rest of his life, whenever he looks in a mirror, that is what he will see. To make serious progress as a human being, he would need to recognise that his decision in conscience had been wrong, and he would need to do all he could to repair the damage he had caused.

Deliberate actions that hurt other people hurt ourselves as well. We cannot grow by deliberately doing things that hurt others, no matter how right we might think we are at the time. To grow we must do right things.

Aquinas was also right, however, in saying that for growth as moral persons more is required than simply performing right actions. It is also required that we take personal responsibility for our choice of actions, e.g., as children grow, it is important that they learn right habits, but it is also important that they gradually learn to take responsibility for their own actions. If they do not learn to take responsibility, obedience to parents will eventually become an obstacle rather than a help to their true growth as persons. If a fifty-year-old man is still obeying his mother in all things and never thinking for himself, we know that there is a serious problem present. If this is true in all aspects of life, it is true also of moral life.

Years ago much marriage counselling was directive, that is, a couple presented their problem and the counsellor responded by indicating the best way to resolve the problem. All too often, however, the couple went away not fully convinced the solution would work, or even not wanting it to work, tried the solution in only a half-hearted way and, when it consequently did not work, blamed the counsellor. So all counselling became non-directive, that is, the counsellor undertook the harder task of helping the couple to find their own solution to the problem, a solution they were both convinced of and committed to. Even if the solution the couple decided on was not the one the counsellor thought ideal, it was the best solution in the circumstances because the couple took *responsibility* for it.

There are persons who, because of fear or laziness, do not want to take personal responsibility for moral choices. They want either the bible or church authority or a charismatic leader or popular opinion or a peer group to take the responsibility for them, so that all that will be left to them is to follow this authority. This cannot be called 'the very dignity' of these persons, for they have not taken personal responsibility for their decisions and will not grow as they should. Mere obedience, to either religious authority or popular opinion, is not 'the very dignity' of a person.

The importance of taking personal responsibility for our actions is fully in accord with church teaching.

> 'Human dignity therefore requires us to act out of conscious and free choice, as moved and drawn in a personal way from within, and not by blind impulses in ourselves or by mere external constraint. We gain such dignity when ... we press forward towards our goal by freely choosing what is good....'[16]

> 'By free will one shapes one's own life. Human freedom is a force for growth and maturity in truth and goodness.'[17]

> 'The right to the exercise of freedom, especially in moral and religious matters, is an inalienable requirement of the dignity of the human person.'[18]

Thus it is important that we take personal responsibility for our decisions and it is also important that we get them right. We will not grow unless we take personal responsibility. But, even if we do take personal responsibility, we will still not grow if our decisions are wrong ones, that is, if they harm other people or our own true good. For growth both of these elements are essential.

A SOUND AND SERIOUS CONSCIENCE

I earlier quoted Aquinas as seeing the relationship between divine law and our imperfect understanding as a dialogue. The place where this dialogue takes place is called conscience.

When we must face a serious moral decision, it is important that we leave behind all the noise of the world around us and enter more deeply within ourselves. There we need to listen, to study and to think. We will listen most carefully to those sources for which we have the greatest respect. The first source might be sacred writings or a religious leader or a religious community to which we belong. Other sources might be a person whose life of service to others we greatly admire. It might be someone who has lived through the very problem we are now facing and seems to have grown in the process. It might be a friend we trust. How much value we give to each of these sources will depend on ourselves.

The amount of time and energy we spend on a question will depend on several factors: the greater or lesser importance of the question, the time available before action is required, the availability of persons to consult or material to study, the extent to which the decision will involve personal action, and the effect the action will have on others.

All of this is a time of serious study and thinking, but it is not yet the moment of conscience. To find that moment we must leave even this area behind and enter into a room deep within ourselves where we are completely alone with God. It is a spacious room but we may bring nothing and no one into it other than what is in our head and our heart. To be a true moment of conscience we must be entirely alone with God, staring into God's eyes, who sees the very depths of our being.

What happens next will depend on the kind of God we believe we are alone with. If we believe in an angry God, we will probably not think for ourselves; we will probably wish only to obey and get out of the room as quickly as we can. This will not lead to a decision that produces true moral growth, for we will not be taking personal responsibility for our decision. If our belief is in the opposite extreme, a God who is over-indulgent with soft love, we will probably seek the easiest way out, the softest option, the answer that asks least effort and sacrifice on our part. This, too, will not help our growth. If we have worked to find the middle way between these two extremes, we will be alone with a God who loves us unconditionally but also wants to see us grow and so is not afraid to challenge us to see where true growth lies.

Alone with God, we will try to enter into a dialogue concerning the moral choice we must make. We shall first seek self-knowledge, for we will know that it is all too easy to convince ourselves of the rightness of whatever it is that we want to do. We shall then think about the decision we must make as carefully and intelligently as we can. We shall always seek humility, for we can be dealing with subtle and profound matters.

When we believe that, within the limits of the concrete circumstances in which we must act, we have done all that God would ask of us, we will calmly make a decision because we know that God wants us to make decisions and to take responsibility for them. We may be a long way short of certainty in our choice, but we know that we have to make a choice. We may be mistaken in the choice we make and we may later have to change our thinking and even make amends for harm we have caused. However, provided we have made our decision as conscientiously as we can in all the circumstances of our lives, it is a true decision of conscience.

The Second Vatican Council tells us that our very dignity lies in following such decisions of our conscience. Our very dignity lies there, for it is only through such decisions that we can grow to become all we are capable of being.

This is a serious idea of conscience, but the moral life is serious, for my moral identity, who I am, is serious.

Assisting Conscience

If we apply these ideas, it must follow that the task of church authority in the moral field is that of assisting consciences. To quote again the words of Pope John Paul II,

'The Church puts herself always and only at the *service of conscience*'.[19]

There is a twin danger in this idea. For individual persons the danger is that of speaking of conscience when they have not done the work necessary to justify the use of this word, when they do no more than go along with the crowd or decide what they would like to do and call that 'conscience'. This is a constant danger for every single person and much that is called 'conscience' does not deserve that name. The idea of responsibility must be taken seriously: as well as the right to choose, it also means that I am answerable to God, to other people and to my own deeper self for the choices that I make.

The danger for church authority, on the other hand, is to think, 'We have a responsibility and an authority to teach in the name of Jesus Christ. Therefore, if people had formed their consciences correctly, they would agree with us. If they don't agree with us, they can't have formed their consciences properly and must be in bad faith.'

For two thousand years there has been a constant tug-of-war between these two forces. The solution is surely to be found in Aquinas' idea of a constant dialogue between conscience and God, for this should mean a constant dialogue between two parties who both want the greatest possible moral growth for the individual and will accept no counterfeit.

SOME ELEMENTS OF THE DIALOGUE

INDIVIDUAL AND COMMUNITY

As need arises, I am in dialogue with a mechanic concerning my car, a doctor concerning my health, a dentist concerning my teeth, and so on. In line with this, it does not make sense to call myself a member of a church community and not be in dialogue with that community on moral matters.

It is not possible for individuals to form their consciences on all matters entirely on their own. People can form their consciences only by humbly joining with many others in the search for truth.[20] If I have no respect for the collective wisdom of the community I belong to, I can hardly call myself a member of that community. One of the very first requirements of a true conscience is humility.

HUMANAE VITAE

In July 1968 Pope Paul VI published an encyclical entitled *Humanae Vitae* in which he said that all artificial forms of birth regulation are morally wrong. This document marked a watershed in the teaching of the papacy for, leaving aside all questions of right and wrong, it is simple fact that over a period of time very large numbers of Catholic people made conscience decisions to reject the teaching of that encyclical. For most of these people their decisions fulfilled all the requirements of conscience that I have spoken about. The rejection eventually became a flood involving many moderate and even some rather conservative Catholics. Many of these people then began to say to themselves, 'If the pope is wrong on this question, how can I be sure that he is right on other questions?' The change has been profound and it is unlikely that the church will ever fully return to the situation that existed before this document was published.

For individual Catholics, there has been a loss of trust in the authority of the church in moral matters and this has left many people without real guidance in their moral lives. What happened was nothing less than the breakdown of the dialogue between the teaching authority and many Catholics, and it is important that this situation be redressed.

On a wider scale, in the Western world today we need serious moral debate on the many important issues that arise, e.g. the many profound and far-reaching bioethical issues that arise daily. It is not good that many people in our society believe that there is no serious spiritual authority to sustain one side of the debate. It is important for our whole society, not just for Christians, that there should be such an authority.

THE FORCE OF ARGUMENTS

All people have an instinctive awareness that, in order to grow, they must take responsibility for their decisions. In fact and in practice, therefore, the effectiveness of any document setting out moral teaching will always depend first and foremost on the power of the arguments contained in the document. The authority of the writer will never be able to make up for a lack of power in the arguments. A document containing powerful and persuasive arguments written by a person with little authority will always be more convincing than a document lacking persuasive arguments written by a person with great authority. If the arguments in a document fail to convince even people of good will, no amount of authority will make up for this.

A system of documents based on authority rather than arguments could be justified only if the sole issue were that of doing right things. But if it is also essential that people take responsibility for their decisions, such a system has no legitimate basis. If people are convinced by the arguments put forward, they will make a decision based on personal conviction and will be ready to take responsibility for the decision. If they are quite unconvinced by the arguments presented and do something only because of the authority of the person who wrote the document, they will not take the same degree of responsibility for the decision and will not grow in the same way.

The Importance of Authority

Despite what has just been said, authority does matter. If I am sick, I want the opinion of a qualified doctor rather than the opinion of someone ignorant of medicine. Sometimes I might want a second medical opinion or a referral to a specialist, but it is undeniable that in most matters authority does count.

I must, of course, decide whether I will accept the word of the doctor. There will be many factors involved in this decision, and one of them will usually be whether the doctor has taken the time to explain to me exactly what is wrong and what needs to be done. In other words, I will have most faith in those authorities who do not rely on authority alone, but who attempt to lead me as far as possible along the road of making my own informed decision.

The Power of Collective Wisdom

In assessing a moral authority, one of the criteria will usually be whether the opinion expressed represents the collective wisdom of the whole community or only the private wisdom of an individual or group, no matter who that individual or group may be.

Infallible Advice?

It is surely a contradiction in terms to speak of infallible advice to conscience. If a statement is presented as infallibly true, it is no longer advice.

Over the centuries popes have sometimes made infallible statements on dogmatic matters, that is, on what people should or should not *believe*, but no pope of the past ever attempted to make an infallible statement on a moral matter, that is, on what people should or should not *do*.

There are several reasons for this, but the reason that concerns us here is that an infallible moral statement would subvert the role of conscience. Moral statements can be more or less certain and they can be made with more or less authority. But if they are to respect the essential role of conscience in moral growth, they must stop short of infallibility.

A POSITIVE ROLE FOR CHURCH AUTHORITY

The world of today often seems to present to people, on the one hand, a dogmatic and authoritarian church with an absolute answer to every question and, on the other hand, the total freedom of the individual, and then ask: Which of these two do you prefer? To this I must reply: Why should we choose either of these extremes? Can not a greater truth be found in the middle? I see four roles for the church.

EDUCATING TO THE USE OF CONSCIENCE

The first task is to assist people to educate themselves in the fields of conscience and moral principles.

In relation to *conscience*, the church should help people to understand what is and what is not conscience, how it works, how one forms a conscience properly, and the dangers to be aware of in the difficult and subtle world of moral decision making. It should do everything possible to help people to have a truly serious understanding of conscience, because that is the only way in which they will grow to become all they are capable of being.

In relation to *moral principles*, the church must not present a long series of statements beginning with 'Thou shalt not.....', for a negative morality cannot be an adequate basis for a person's life. It must be a positive morality, consisting of positive principles, e.g. 'How can I best witness to truth and justice in this situation?', 'How can I best help to bring peace and understanding between these persons in conflict?', 'What can I do in this situation that will best help both others and myself to grow towards perfect love?'

Since such principles require a profound sense of realism and honesty, the church should then seek to give to people the best spiritual-moral insights it can from the scriptures, the whole of Christian history and the world around and within us. The better people are educated in the field of moral principles, the better they will be able to make moral decisions and the more they will grow.

GUIDANCE IN MORAL MATTERS

The second role I see for the Christian church is to present the facts and the arguments on many issues that commonly arise in the lives of people.   In doing so, the church must not rely simply on the moral authority of its leaders. Rather, it should always present the arguments in favour of its position as fully and as fairly as it can, that is, it should rely above all on the force of its arguments.

Indeed, I believe that in all such statements the church should first present as fully and as fairly as it can the case against its own position. If it does this, it will truly be assisting people to make mature decisions in conscience before God alone. There is one obvious condition.

> 'Your exposition of your opponent's beliefs should be so accurate, so true to his beliefs, that he will gladly sign his name at the bottom of your exposition as a witness to its accuracy.'[21]

If the church acquired a reputation for putting the arguments against its own views as powerfully, clearly and honestly as they can be put, its credibility would soar dramatically.   If people were able to say, 'You will never see the arguments in favour of this action put more clearly than they are in the document of the church', they might really start listening to the moral arguments the church gives against that action.

PROTECTING THE COMMUNITY

The third role is a more negative one, but necessarily so. A community must protect its members against the decisions of individuals that harm other people, even when these decisions are made in conscience. The state will imprison people who murder or steal, and a church community must, for example, dismiss from a teaching post a person who repeatedly displays racial bias against some students. Because harm is being caused to people, neither the state nor the church will accept conscience as a defence. There are serious difficulties and dangers in this field, but it cannot be ignored.

Encouraging People

The fourth role I see for the church is the important one of giving constant encouragement to people to believe in God's love and God's assistance, to have the courage to face the challenges that confront them, and to make all the conscience decisions they need to make. The church should encourage people not to seek an easy way out, but to grow through challenges towards all they are capable of being. It can encourage them to have faith that they can grow to heights they have not dreamed of.

FREEDOM AND RESPONSIBILITY

Freedom (the right to choose) and responsibility (being answerable to God, other people and my own deeper self for the choices I make) must go together. The aim of morality is that people should grow to become all they are capable of being. Freedom without responsibility is the surest way to prevent growth, while responsibility cannot be exercised without freedom.

Placing freedom and responsibility together is a middle ground between the two extremes of freedom without responsibility (I decide to do something and that makes it morally right for me) and responsibility without freedom (don't think, just obey). The terms of the debate in our modern society are all too often either total obedience or unlimited freedom, but both are dead ends that allow no growth and no escape. The only road that opens us to true growth is that of freedom and responsibility taken together.

I, and I alone, am finally responsible for who I become. It would be a pity if, at the end of life, a Christian person had to say to God, 'Lord, I must confess that I largely ignored the death of your son on the cross and I consistently followed the easier way. What I wanted was freedom without responsibility'. What God wants is growth and that must involve a truly responsible use of freedom.

As children grow up, their parents must gradually stand back and allow them to make their own mistakes and learn from these mistakes. If the children abuse their freedom, the parents can only hope that the day will come when they see that their actions are not contributing to their growth, health or happiness, and will want to change. Through all of this process, however long it takes, the most important thing for the parents is to keep their relationship with their children and continually show them that they love them, so that the children will want to turn to them when they experience the need. A church should act in the same way.

Meditation

We grow in moral and spiritual stature when we do two things together:
- seek to act according to God's truth and goodness, despite the cost to ourselves,
- and take personal responsibility for our actions.

It is possible to move beyond a subjective understanding of goodness to a more objective understanding of what God's goodness asks of us, but it involves a serious and never-ending search, both for individuals and for the whole human race.

We should spend our whole life in this search, while also constantly making decisions and acting on the basis of our present and inadequate understanding of that goodness.

The relationship between our conscience and God's goodness should be a constant, humble and loving dialogue.

We should constantly remind ourselves of six levels of moral living:

6) Superiority and Vengeance
The pointless and endless cycle of revenge

5) Justice without Mercy
An eye for an eye, a tooth for a tooth

4) The Usefulness of Others to Ourselves

3) Respect for Human Dignity
　　Respect for Life and Physical Integrity
　　Respect for the Relationships that Give Life
　　　Meaning
　　Respect for Material Possessions
　　Respect for Good Name

2) Love as You Love Yourself

1) Love as God Loves Us

There is no one on this earth who cannot fall back to the lowest level at any moment, but there is also no one who is not capable of rising to the highest level.

Footnotes

[1] Gen.4:23-24.

[2] Ex.21:25, Deut.19:21

[3] For the Christian view on this, see Luke 14:12-14.

[4] Prov.23:1-2

[5] Ex.20:1-17; Deut.5:6-21

[6] I shall comment on this commandment later in the chapter on sexuality.

[7] Lev. 19:18

[8] Mt.7:12

[9] John 13:34.

[10] *Sermo sexta De Verbis Domini, cap.8*, quoted in *Confronting the Truth*, Linda Hogan, Dartman, Longman and Todd, London, 2001, p.81.

[11] *Commentary on the Sentences*, in Hogan, *op.cit*, p.81

[12] Second Vatican Council, *Gaudium et Spes*, Pastoral Constitution on the Church in the Modern World, no.16. I have changed the English to an inclusive form.

[13] *Gaudium et Spes*, no.50.

[14] The first quotation is a good example of a beautiful and inspiring pastoral statement, but without the clear theological foundation that is necessary. In the Vorgrimler commentary, Joseph Ratzinger says of Article 16 of *Gaudium et Spes*, '....It affirms the transcendent character of conscience: it is the 'law written in the heart by God', the holy place in which man is alone with God and hears God's voice in his innermost centre. This, of course, simplifies the problem..... How conscience can err if God's call is directly to be heard in it, is unexplained..... (There is an) inadequate use made of the insights of modern philosophy and allied disciplines, which here makes it particularly difficult to avoid an impression of pre-critical thought.' Commentary on the Documents of Vatican II, edited by Herbert Vorgrimler, Burns and Oates/ Herder and Herder, 1968, vol.5, pp.134-135.

[15] no.64, emphasis from the text itself.

[16] *Gaudium et Spes*, no.17.

[17] *Catechism of the Catholic Church*, no.1731.

[18] ibid. no.1738

[19] no.64, emphasis from the text itself.

[20] 'Through loyalty to conscience Christians are joined to other people in the search for truth and for the right solution to so many moral problems which arise in the lives of individuals and from social relationships.' *Gaudium et Spes*, no.16.

[21] Donald Nicholl, 'Wrestling with Truth', *The Tablet*, October 9, 1993, p.1292.

CHAPTER NINE

A Turbulence
and a
Whirlpool

If the Catholic Church is to regain some credibility after the many scandals of sexual abuse, it must first learn to speak with humility, intelligence, realism and compassion about all aspects of human sexuality.

Sexuality is the field above all others in which the Catholic Church has been in the greatest danger of denying the goodness of God's creation and the completeness of Christ's redemption. God created everything good, including sex, and Jesus Christ redeemed all aspects of human life, including sex. This must be our starting point. And yet sexuality was often relegated to the field of the material, the bodily and the worldly, and had no part in the spiritual life, not even of a married couple.

I have moved a long way on this topic over the forty-five years I have been a priest. The changes began when I was a young priest hearing confessions in the local parish church. I knew many of the people confessing to what they called 'bad thoughts' as good and sincere people, people I admired. I asked myself whether God would really condemn these people to an eternity of punishment in the fires of hell for one 'bad thought'. I had the same reaction to the confessions of masturbation by good young people growing up in the parish and discovering their own sexuality. The same seemed to be true of good young engaged couples thinking about sex and experimenting with its feelings as they approached their wedding.

I now realise that what changed for me in those early years was not so much my understanding of sex as my understanding of God. I was in those years gradually abandoning an angry God and coming to accept a loving God. I began to feel that there was a total lack of proportion between the offence of a 'bad thought' and the punishment of eternal damnation, and that it was quite unthinkable that a loving God would act in this way. I began to ask whether any system that said such a thing must be seriously deficient. In other words, I was gradually coming to realise that the 'tradition' behind teaching on and attitudes towards sexuality must be questioned.

My first objection was to the idea that sexual sins are always and in all circumstances mortal (*ex toto genere suo*), so that there cannot be venial sins in the field of sexuality. Rape and a single 'bad thought' (deliberately thinking about something sexual) were equally mortal sins and led to the same eternal punishment. I began to ask whether this was not a quite unhealthy idea, leading to a concentration on the sexual sin in itself and leaving out the important question of the effects the act might have on another person. In many good people the idea that every 'bad thought' was mortal led to the conviction that it was impossible to avoid mortal sin, so many became discouraged in the moral life. For many people it led to the idea that, if a thought and a complete sexual act were morally equal, both being mortal, then one might as well commit the complete act. Within this environment it was difficult for the church to avoid the accusation that it considered sex itself as in some manner 'bad'.

When the sexual revolution struck, however, I instinctively knew that I had no desire to go to the opposite extreme where 'anything goes'. I was a priest and this had brought me into contact with many people who had been badly hurt because of the sexual desires both of others and of themselves. I knew that sex needed to be treated much more seriously than the 'anything goes' mentality allowed. I became convinced that what was happening was a classic case of a reaction against one extreme taking people quickly to the opposite extreme without stopping to see if the truth lay in the middle.

I thus found myself in an uncomfortable position, no longer agreeing with the church of which I was a public representative but quite unwilling to follow those who would lead me to the opposite extreme. There were times when good young Catholic people were talking about sexual morality and I would have loved to join them, but as one like them seeking answers, not as one giving out instant official answers to all questions. I felt that I was prevented from doing this because I was a priest.

I realise that, once a breach is made in the church's teaching, it is hard to find another point at which to say 'stop'. This is, perhaps, one of the major reasons why most Christian churches have been slow to move. The matter is often presented to young people in these extreme terms: you either follow the Christian ethic where 'nothing goes' outside marriage, or you follow the modern ethic where 'anything goes'. I believe that it is essential that we find a middle ground.

I do not know of any individual, any culture or any religion that has ever had all the answers in this delicate and complex field. I am acutely conscious of the fact that I emphatically do not, that, indeed, I am very ignorant on this subject. Despite this, I believe it is vitally important that an intelligent conversation should begin. So what I shall attempt here is limited. I shall look at some aspects of the bible, what has been handed on to us and the world around and within us, and then ask some questions.

The Bible

Most statements in the bible that touch on the broad subject of sex are moral statements. The major difficulty in dealing with this material is that the bible contains several different ethics of sex, that is, several different criteria for making moral judgements, several different viewpoints for looking at the subject, several different questions that are asked. For example, a justice ethic will ask, 'Is this action just?', while a love ethic will say, 'It may be just, but is it a loving thing to do?' Thus these two ethics can come to opposing conclusions, with one approving and the other disapproving of the same action.

ETHICS OF LOVE, JUSTICE AND GOODNESS

In relation to sex there is certainly a love ethic in the bible, the best example being the Song of Songs. In fact, for centuries many people were so afraid of this poem's uninhibited glorification of sexual love that they believed it had to be an allegory of something else, but scholars today say that it is quite simply what it appears to be – a lyric rhapsody concerning the love of a man and a woman, with sexual desire as an obvious and natural expression of that love. It has been noted that the couple do not live in the same house[1] and so are not married, and yet their love is clearly sexual.[2] Despite the fact that God is never mentioned, both Jews and Christians have always included this book in the bible. So it, too, contains things that God 'wanted written', 'truths for the sake of our salvation'.

Among other statements reflecting a love ethic, we may include the following:

'When a man is newly married, he shall not go out with the army or be charged with any public duty. He shall be free at home one year, to be happy with the wife he has married.'[3]

'Rejoice in the wife of your youth,
a lovely deer, a graceful doe.
May her breasts satisfy you at all times;
May you be intoxicated always by her love.'[4]

'I will take you for my wife forever; I will take you for my wife in righteousness and in justice, in steadfast love and in mercy. I will take you for my wife in faithfulness....'[5]

'I remember the devotion of your youth,
the love of your bridal day.'[6]

In the prophet Malachi we find what may be called an ethic of both justice and love taken together:

'You cover the Lord's altar with tears, with weeping and groaning because he no longer regards your offering or accepts it with favour at your hand. You ask, `Why does he not?' Because the Lord was a witness between you and the wife of your youth, to whom you have been faithless, though she is your companion and your wife by covenant.... For I hate divorce, says the Lord, the God of Israel.'[7]

And, of course, on the very first page of the bible we find what may be called a 'goodness ethic':

'So God created humankind in his image,
In the image of God he created them;
Male and female he created them.
God blessed them, and God said to them, 'Be fruitful and multiply, and fill the earth and subdue it'.... And God saw everything that he had made, and indeed, it was very good.'[8]

These sayings are an integral and important part of the biblical tradition. And yet, in a book that tells the story of a journey and reflects every part and every level of that journey, the obverse side of the love ethic could not fail to be present. Thus the author of the Book of Ecclesiastes, who finds little that is good in any human being, says,

'One man among a thousand I found,
 but a woman among all these I have not found.'[9]

The bible was written by men and inevitably contains many male prejudices against women.

'Like a gold ring in a pig's snout
 is a beautiful woman without good sense.'[10]

The same book of Proverbs paints a very masculine picture of the perfect wife, a woman who is constantly working from before dawn to well after dusk, while her husband seems to spend most of his time sitting with the elders at the city gates.[11]

The most damaging remark comes from the book of Ben Sira (Ecclesiasticus) in a classic misinterpretation of the *story* of creation,

'From a woman sin had its beginning,
 and because of her we all die.'[12]

Both the good and bad comments that come out of ethics of love, justice and goodness are rare when compared to the far more frequent sayings that come out of two other ethical viewpoints: the purity ethic and the property ethic. These we must now consider.

In dealing with these two ethics of purity and property I am largely reliant on one book, *Dirt, Greed and Sex, Sexual Ethics in the New Testament and their Implications for Today*, by L. William Countryman.[13] I shall draw extensively on this book.

THE PURITY ETHIC IN THE FIRST TESTAMENT

The purity ethic asks the question, 'Is this thing or action ritually clean or unclean?'

To be a Jew did not mean only to profess a certain faith, but also to belong to a particular people. So the Torah was not only religious law, but the basic law of Israel in all areas of life. Since Israel placed a very high value on being distinct from other peoples, the laws that made them different had a value greater than their intrinsic worth. High among these were the prohibition of images, the disapproval of marriage with Gentiles, circumcision, Sabbath observance and the purity laws.[14] They became an important part of the national identity during times when there was immense pressure to abandon this identity and merge with other peoples.[15] [16]

The rationale of the purity laws appears to be that God's holiness calls for the completeness and purity of all of creation. Only that which is complete and only that which is pure, that is, not a mixture of kinds, may be offered to God or stand in God's presence.[17] The particular rules were a spelling out of these two principles of completeness and purity, and it seems that they were meant to be practical, everyday things that raised the mind to a meditation on God's completeness and purity.

In relation to completeness, for example, only an unblemished animal could be offered to God and only an animal that had a divided hoof and chewed the cud was considered complete, and hence clean. Since blood was considered the life force of a human being, a menstruating woman was considered incomplete and therefore unclean. On the part of the man, an emission of seed was considered a diminution of the life principle, so he too became unclean.

In relation to the second principle, that of purity, it was forbidden to sow two different crops in the same field or to use two different types of thread (e.g. cotton and wool) in the same cloth. Homosexuality was forbidden because the man playing the female part was both male and female at the same time, and so a mixture of kinds.[18]

Some of these laws could be justified on rational grounds (e.g. the laws concerning adultery, incest, and leprosy), but others reflected particular cultural ideas of what made something 'complete' (e.g. that only an animal that had a divided hoof and chewed the cud was complete), or they reflected the instinctual ideas that every nation has and that are not subject to rational analysis (e.g. some peoples eat snails, dog-meat or certain insects, while others recoil from them).

If I may intrude some of my own thoughts on those of Countryman, it seems to me that the purity code of the First Testament places three separate ideas in close proximity: sinful, unclean and dirty. They are separate, for 'sinful' refers to a moral offence, 'unclean' refers to ritual uncleanness such that a person could not, for example, enter the temple while unclean, and 'dirty' refers to the instinctual reaction that different cultures have to different things.

In the purity codes these three ideas were put so closely together that it must have been hard not to cross from one to the other. If a couple had intercourse, they had to 'bathe in water'[19] in order to become 'clean' again, so it was easy to think that something dirty had happened. If menstruation was unclean, it was easy to think of it as dirty, and since the woman carried the contagion to any chair she sat on or person or object she touched, it was all too easy to conclude that she herself was dirty, at least at that time of her periods. After all, the menstruating woman, without the slightest fault on her part, was considered to be lacking in 'holiness', that is, she was in 'a state of being incompatible with the holiness of the Lord and hence prohibitive of any contact with him.'[20]

Indeed, it was easy to think of females as more unclean than males at the best of times, e.g. after giving birth to a male child a woman was unclean for seven days, but after giving birth to a female child she was unclean for fourteen days.[21]

It was also easy to start thinking that there had to be some moral stain on the menstruating woman if she carried the contagion of uncleanness everywhere she went and passed it to every object she touched. After all, the forms of sexual activity that were forbidden under the purity laws were adultery, incest, homosexuality, bestiality and intercourse with a menstruating woman. It is obvious that this listing could suggest some moral parity between the adulterous, incestuous, homosexual and menstruating woman. I am not competent to comment on how the Jewish people have handled these issues, but I am concerned about the effect they later had on Christian people.

Homosexuality is called an abomination, but the word 'abomination' is used 138 times in the bible, and if homosexuality is an abomination, so is eating lobster or prawns,[22] so we should not put more weight on the word than it deserves.

THE PURITY ETHIC IN THE SECOND TESTAMENT

To return to the ideas of Countryman, the gospel of Mark states, 'Thus he declared all foods clean'.[23] It is unlikely that Jesus made a crystal clear statement abolishing the purity laws, for then it would be difficult to explain the controversies that occurred later, but this was the firm and clear conclusion the writers of the Second Testament reached from their observation of all that Jesus had said and done. For him they were too external a measure, and it was possible to be externally clean while internally most unclean. What mattered for him was purity of the heart.[24]

Jesus abolished the purity laws across the board. He did not abolish only those concerning foods, while retaining those that spoke of leprosy, witchcraft or sex.[25] If any of these things were still to be considered wrong, it would have to be on some grounds other than the purity ethic.[26]

Despite this, Jesus himself on occasions followed the purity laws, at least when there was a valid external reason for doing so, e.g. in sending the leper to the priests to be declared free of leprosy before rejoining the community.[27] This tendency became stronger in the followers of Jesus, and Paul may serve as an example. Paul was a Jew and had been brought up from earliest childhood according to a strict observance. Inevitably, he had acquired a level of instinctual reaction against those things that were forbidden because they made a person unclean. He thus found himself in the difficult position of defending mightily the freedom of his Gentile converts from the requirements of the purity laws while observing most of them himself.[28] He developed his teaching on the strong and the weak,[29] and this teaching was reflected in the Council of Jerusalem in the year 50 CE.[30] The answer given by this council was a compromise and a postponement. It was a compromise because it asked Gentile converts to observe a modified purity code, and it was a postponement because the provisions made were less than completely clear and could be interpreted in different ways by different groups.[31] It became a step in the longer process of transition to freedom from the purity laws, but it also served to reinforce the idea that purity laws had not entirely disappeared.[32]

The major practical day-to-day problem that faced the new Christian community was whether Gentiles and Jews could share a meal together, so the statements about food laws are more frequent and more explicit in the Second Testament. No replacement argument was ever given for abstaining from these foods.[33] This left a certain ambivalence in relation to those parts of the purity code, especially sexual matters, where some other argument could be given against certain actions.

Once again intruding my own ideas, if a whole community has been told for centuries that certain sexual actions are wrong, and is now told that those same actions are still wrong, but not for the reason they were formerly thought to be wrong, the argument will be too subtle for many people to grasp. The fact that these actions are still constantly proclaimed as wrong will, in the minds of many, serve to perpetuate the idea that aspects of the purity code remain in force. This feeling will be all the stronger if the reasons now given for why the actions are wrong are not convincing. Following the teaching of Jesus, the early Christians had to abandon the purity ethic, but it must be said that they did not find a clear sexual ethic to replace it, so various aspects of the purity ethic retained their force.

PHILO OF ALEXANDRIA

Countryman suggests that, in order to understand how these ideas affected Christian history, we must go outside the bible for a moment. Philo of Alexandria, a contemporary of Jesus (13 BCE – 45-50 CE) was a Jewish philosopher, familiar with Greek philosophy, and living in a Gentile world. Some of these Gentiles were attracted to the Jewish religion, but found its purity laws an insurmountable barrier. So

Philo tried to explain the purity laws in terms that Gentiles could accept. He found that this was near impossible in relation to the food laws, but that he could find common ground when speaking of the purity laws concerning sex. From Plato he took the duality of body and soul and the necessity for human beings to free themselves from the sensual element, while in accordance with the Stoics he regarded indulgence and pleasure as hedonistic and animalistic and exalted self-control and orderliness.[34] The Stoics often described what is morally right as 'according to nature', so Philo appealed to 'nature' as something that would justify his religion's antagonism towards certain sexual acts. He therefore argued that the natural purpose of sex was to beget children, so to sow seed in a menstruating woman was like 'sowing seed in a swamp', while homosexual sex was like 'sowing seed in a desert'.[35]

This work of Philo had two unintended effects. Firstly, for the Jews who listened to him, it changed the nature of the purity laws, for the sexual laws were no longer simply purity laws, but also 'natural laws'. Secondly, because his whole purpose in writing was to explain the reasonableness of the purity laws, the Gentiles who accepted his arguments would find it difficult not to take on certain aspects of a purity law. Philo was read with respect by a number of Christian thinkers, e.g. Clement of Alexandria, Origen, Gregory of Nyssa and Ambrose, and his ideas passed into Christian thinking. An ethic of what is 'according to nature' began to replace the purity ethic.[36]

Furthermore, Philo was far from being the only person to be influenced by Plato and the Stoics. At the time when the Second Testament was written, scholars tell us that there was a widespread and even now poorly understood revulsion which a number of people in late antiquity felt towards the human body. So the extreme attitudes which Paul combated in I Cor.7:1-2[37] and which the Book of Revelation may have accepted in the vision of the 144,000 male virgins (14:1-5) had their origin in the spirit of the age rather than in the bible. This widespread revulsion towards the body affected Christians as well as others. From the late second century onwards, there were Christian sects which held that salvation was contingent on sexual continence (the Encratites) or that the material world was wholly evil and sex was to be rejected on that account (Marcionites and some Gnostics). By the fourth century, there were also orthodox writers, such as Jerome, who were greatly concerned with physical purity. In the light of all of these facts, it may be argued that aspects of a purity code continued in the Christian world, especially when Christianity became the official religion of the Roman Empire and felt the need to be concerned with public morality.[38]

THE PROPERTY ETHIC IN THE FIRST TESTAMENT

I now turn to the second ethic affecting sex that is found throughout the First Testament, the property ethic. The property ethic is a form of justice ethic that begins by asking the question, 'Whose property is it?'

> '(In the bible) marriage is assumed to be the calling of every human being. Virginity is a tragedy; infertility a curse. God's blessings are given through the process of procreation.'[39]

The family, not the individual, was the basic unit of society in the whole of the ancient world, not just in Israel. It consisted of a male head who possessed one or more women as wives or concubines, and children who would either carry on the family (sons) or be used to make alliances with other families (daughters). There were no 'individuals' in the modern sense, unless eunuchs and bastards might fit that category. Those persons, such as widows and orphans, who had no connection with a patriarch, were necessarily marginal to the society.[40]

The male head ruled the family, but this does not mean that he was a completely free agent, for he, too, was the servant of the family, with the serious task of maintaining and increasing the family's wealth and public standing in the community.[41] An irresponsible or lazy or violent man could be taken to task by the community.

The other members of the family were the property of the male head, and the wives and concubines were his sexual property. In chapter 31 of the Book of Job, Job defends himself with a series of arguments saying, 'If I have taken another's property, let another take my property.' In applying this principle to various matters, he then says,

> If my heart has been enticed by a woman,
> and I have lain wait at my neighbour's door,
> then let my wife grind for another,
> and let other men kneel over her.' (vv.9-10).

From our modern point of view we might say, 'This is unjust. If he has offended, let him be punished, not her.' But Job was not speaking out of a love ethic or an ethic of individualism; he was speaking out of a property ethic. In a similar way, the book implies that the children born after Job's trials were over replaced the children he had lost at the beginning of the trials.[42] If one is speaking out of a love ethic, later children cannot replace lost ones; they can if one speaks out of a property ethic.[43]

Intruding my own thoughts again, the example of Job surely makes it clear how difficult it is for a love ethic and a property ethic to co-exist. Even a man who began his marriage on the basis of a love ethic could easily find that he later moved to a property ethic. Do we not see this property ethic alive in our own day in many ways, e.g. in those men who kill their wife and children rather than see them become the 'property' of someone else?

Returning to Countryman, there is little evidence of significant development in this ethic between the writing of the Torah and the time of Jesus. Apart from the waning of polygamy and an occasional protest against the abuse of divorce, the Torah's definition of sexual property was the one which Jesus and Paul found current in their own time.[44]

THE PROPERTY ETHIC IN THE GOSPELS

Under the property ethic, a man could divorce his wife, for she was his property, but a woman could not divorce her husband, for property cannot disown its owner. Under the same ethic, adultery was the violation of the property rights of a man. If a married woman had intercourse with a man other than her husband, it was always adultery, for she was violating her husband's property rights. But if a married man had intercourse with an unmarried woman, it was not adultery, for he was not violating the property rights of any man.[45]

In his debate with the Pharisees on the question of divorce, on the other hand, Jesus called back to the story of creation, saying that the will of God as originally intended in the act of creation could not subsequently be annulled by any rule communicated through (or created by) Moses during the exodus from Egypt.[46] In doing this, he redefined adultery, for he said, 'Whoever divorces his wife and marries another commits adultery *against her*'[47], an unheard of and quite revolutionary idea. It meant that, if we must use the language of property, we must at least say that he was as much her sexual property as she was his. If this were so, she was no longer simply his property and he had lost his ultimate authority to maintain his patriarchal position. In this one saying Jesus completely undermined the patriarchal family that had existed in every culture for thousands of years, and a completely new basis for the family had to be found.[48]

Not the father, but the most powerless person in the family structure, the child, became the model for entry into the kingdom.[49]

Jesus actually went even further, for, instead of setting out some new basis for the family to replace the structure he had abolished, he subjected family to the reign of God and constantly put discipleship before family ties.[50] Some of his statements appear quite outrageous, e.g. 'Follow me, and let the dead bury their own dead',[51] or 'I have come to set a man against his father, and a daughter against her mother'.[52] Family was no longer the central and unquestioned value it had been for thousands of years, for one must be prepared to sacrifice even family for the sake of the reign of God.[53]

Because of this approach, Jesus gave no detailed idea of family structures to replace the patriarchal structures he had rejected. His followers, therefore, had the extremely difficult task of picking up the pieces left by his radical approach, and this is where they would fail.

THE PROPERTY ETHIC IN THE REST OF THE SECOND TESTAMENT

In a number of his letters Paul was quite convinced that the Second Coming of Jesus was an imminent event. In these letters he saw little value in seeking to change ancient, deep-seated family structures, for what was the point if the world was about to end?

His advice to people was, therefore, to stay as they were. If they were married, they should stay married. If they were single, they should stay single. If they were about to get married, the choice was theirs. They did nothing wrong if they got married, but they were probably better off if they did not, for his overriding concern was that people should be able to wait on the imminent coming of the Lord without distraction. There was simply no time for Christians to be making sweeping changes in the life of the world, and any attempt to do so would itself be a distraction.[54]

He was, therefore, quite conservative in his attitudes towards many family matters and the role of women in society and in the church. It is possible that this was his natural disposition but, since he believed that the end of the world was about to occur, it is hard to judge him severely.[55] He at least admitted in theory that Jesus had demanded radical changes in the structure of families.

The First Letter of Peter, on the other hand, did not make this admission, for the overriding concern of the writer was the public hostility to Christians that threatened to break out into serious persecution[56]. For this reason, the writer did not wish to see Christians seeking to overturn societal and family structures. Respectability[57] and conservative family life[58] were essential in order to avoid persecution. Unlike Paul, however, this writer made a permanent principle out of a temporary need, converting Paul's provisional acceptance of traditional family structures into a principled insistence on them.[59] The impetus of the radicalism of Jesus concerning family life has here very nearly spent its force.[60]

There may have been powerful external and internal reasons persuading the early church not to embark on the arduous task of a radical reform of the family and of male-female relationships, but the Second Testament outside the gospels has had the effect of largely nullifying the radical reforms on these subjects that are found on the lips of Jesus. For most of the last two thousand years every word of the bible has been treated as directly inspired by God. In this atmosphere, it has been inevitable that First Peter, Timothy, Titus and Ephesians in particular have had a powerful influence on Christian thought on the subjects of sex, marriage and women.

FORNICATION AND MASTURBATION

Neither fornication nor masturbation is mentioned in the purity laws. Under the heading of the property ethic, intercourse with an unmarried woman and the visiting of prostitutes were frowned on because they could harm the good of the family, which was always the man's prime duty, but it cannot be said that they were absolutely condemned. The presence of prostitutes was taken for granted and at least those who were not slaves or cult prostitutes were considered 'sinful women', but it does not necessarily follow that the men who visited them were considered 'sinful men'. The fact that fornication received no specific mention in the purity laws meant that it did not receive the same attention or condemnation as those things that are contained there. The word 'masturbation' does not occur anywhere in the bible[61], and the practice is not condemned under any heading, though some of the rabbis later called it 'adultery of the hand'.

HOMOSEXUALITY

The Second Testament constantly condemns sexual immorality. It contains twenty-two lists of vices and the most common word to be found in those lists is *porneia* (in twelve of the twenty-two lists). There are, however, two problems. Firstly, on a number of occasions the meaning of the words used is not clear, and *porneia* is itself a classic example of this.[62] Secondly, in following Jesus, the writers of the Second Testament had to abandon the purity laws as the basis for sexual prohibitions, but the replacement arguments they give are not always clear or convincing, so we can be left with assertions backed by authority rather than rational arguments.[63]

There is not the time here to go into a detailed discussion of all the particular sayings that have had a significant influence on the Christian world in relation to sexual matters. One thinks, for example, of Romans 1:26-27 and 1 Corinthians 6:9-10 in relation to the morality of homosexuality. A few points can be made.

The meaning of key words in these passages is not clear and translations often contain interpretations.[64] It is essential to go back to the Greek texts and to spend much time studying the exact meaning of words. Loaded words such as 'lusts' should not be used where the Greek has a more neutral word such as 'desires'. Definite meanings should not be given to words where this is not possible.[65] We must be particularly careful when the words are placed in the mouth of Jesus himself.[66]

In the letter to the Romans it is not easy to determine whether Paul is using the language of sin or of uncleanness, and hence whether he is saying that homosexuality is sinful or unclean.[67]

In the same letter he appears to say that homosexuality is a penalty imposed by God on pagans because of false worship, and one must have profound questions about the idea of God this concept presents.

The context of the sayings is important. While the other letters of Paul are responses to particular events and issues in communities he has already visited, the letter to the Romans is an attempt to present a more complete picture of himself to a community he had not visited. He deliberately speaks first to the Jews and later to the Gentiles and seeks to win the approval of both groups. His comments about the Gentiles in chapter 1 must be seen in this context, just as his negative comments about Jews in chapter 11 must be seen in the same context.[68]

We have already seen that Paul and the other writers of the Second Testament outside the gospels failed to maintain the radicalism of Jesus on both purity laws and property laws. If their sayings on those subjects are not divinely inspired truth, we must have serious reservations as to whether their other sayings on sexual matters can be taken, in and of themselves alone, as final proofs, and hence whether assertions without convincing arguments are sufficient. Are we once again dealing with the story of a journey that ended only in the person of Jesus and not in anyone else who came before or after him? For example, did Paul share the almost universal opinion of his time that all people are in fact heterosexual, so to engage in homosexual relations is a free (and perverted) choice by a heterosexual person?

There is much here that still needs to be studied and resolved.

At this point my reliance on Countryman comes to an end and I shall move on to other matters.

THE TEN COMMANDMENTS

The sixth commandment says, 'You shall not commit adultery' and, within the Catholic Church, an entire world of sexual teaching has been built on this foundation. In the older books of moral theology, the entire teaching on sex was called *de Sexto*, 'concerning the sixth commandment'. I believe that this understanding of the commandment is in need of radical reassessment.

Even in the First Testament the commandment against adultery must be seen as going beyond property law.[69]   If it referred solely to property law, its content would already be covered by the commandment 'you shall not steal', so we must assume that this commandment adds important elements to the one against stealing. The people of Israel knew all about romantic love and they knew about other friendships that gave meaning to life (e.g. the story of Jonathan and David in 1Sam.), and I suggest that this commandment includes at least something of this element. Malachi's condemnation of divorce speaks directly to the tension between a love ethic and a property ethic.

Furthermore, while most commandments are expressed in a negative form ('You shall not...'), they each have a positive content.

> 'The (eight commandments formulated negatively) implicitly
> commend their positive side..... e.g. not bearing false witness
> invites speaking well of one's neighbour, not killing suggests efforts
> to preserve life.'[70]

If we see adultery solely in terms of the property rights of the male, it is hard to see that there could be a positive side (building up his property rights even further?). If we include at least something of an ethic of justice and love, there is a large and important positive side.

In the gospels it is certain that the commandment goes far beyond property rights. Jesus told the man who asked about goodness to keep the commandments. In all three synoptic gospels he cites the commandments concerning murder, adultery, theft and false witness.[71] In citing the commandment against adultery, it is quite certain that he was going beyond all ideas of the woman as the man's sexual property, for we have seen that he did not think in these terms. Surely it is true that Jesus saw adultery as an offence against both justice and love. In other words, in rejecting the ethics of purity and property, he went back to the ethics of justice, love and goodness that we have seen were already present in the bible and were far closer to his own heart. In Matthew's gospel alone Jesus adds to the list, 'and you shall love your neighbour as yourself'.[72] In doing this, I suggest that he is saying that this statement of love of neighbour sums up the commandments that go before it, for those commandments taken together are a powerful expression of love of neighbour.

Indeed, in the previous chapter I noted that four consecutive commandments call for respect for one's neighbour's dignity as a human being, and I believe that they should be seen as a unity, for they demand respect for four complementary aspects of human life, namely:

i) life and physical integrity (you shall not kill),

ii) the relationships that make life worth living and give it meaning (you shall not commit adultery),

iii) material goods (you shall not steal),

iv) a person's good name (you shall not bear false witness).

I believe that, just as 'do not kill' includes 'do not wound', so 'do not commit adultery' includes 'do not harm any relationship that gives love, meaning and happiness to a person's life, e.g. those with parents or children or siblings or friends'. I suggest that the sixth commandment refers to all human relationships, but makes its point by concentrating on the central relationship of marriage.

Are human relationships so important that they fully deserve their place in the ten commandments alongside life and health (you shall not kill), material goods (you shall not steal) and a person's good name (you shall not bear false witness)? When the four are taken together, do they become a powerful expression of what respect for my neighbour's dignity means? Can we leave relationships out of this list without fatally weakening it? If I respect life, material goods and good name, but destroy a person's most important relationships, where is the respect for dignity?

I would, therefore, see the sixth commandment referring to a world of sexual teaching only in so far as wrong sexual actions can harm relationships, and any discussion of sexual morality must be placed within that context.

CONCLUSIONS FROM THIS STUDY OF SEX IN THE BIBLE

While there are statements concerning sex in the First Testament that come out of an ethic of love or justice or goodness, they are overwhelmed by the far more frequent statements that come out of the ethics of purity and property. In the gospels Jesus radically rejected both the purity ethic and the property ethic. The rest of the Second Testament rejected the purity ethic concerning foods, but in relation to sexual matters it neither entirely abolished the idea of purity laws nor replaced them with any other consistent ethic. It seriously compromised Jesus' radical rejection of the property ethic. As a result, neither the purity ethic nor the property ethic has been abolished from Christian thought. Philo of Alexandria's ideas concerning the 'natural' purpose of marriage continue to be influential in Catholic thinking.

There is a need, therefore, for a new and serious study of the bible in relation to all matters sexual, with a view to regaining and renewing the radicalism of Jesus himself on these questions.

It is extraordinary how little Jesus said about sex when compared with virtually every other founder of a new religion in history. There is much to think about in this absence of any detailed instructions on the subject. There is no reason to think that Jesus was so unworldly that he was not aware of the importance of sex and how it can both build human relationships and complicate and disrupt them. Since he was fully human, we must assume that he experienced sexual desire like any other human being. It is safer to conclude that in his overall teaching on the Christian life he believed that he had said everything he wished and needed to say about sex, and saw no need to single out the topic for particular comment. In this the Christian world has not followed his example.

Should we conclude that, if people followed the ideas of Jesus in all aspects of their lives and approached other people with the same frame of mind as he did, they would find the answers to all their questions concerning sex? Should the basic rule for all sexual relations be the same as the basic rule for all Christian living: 'This is my commandment: love one another as I have loved you'?[73]

The placing of the sixth commandment in the context of the three that surround it would be a good first step towards the building up of a new sexual ethic, one that combines justice and love and that looks at the morality of sex both in terms of respect for the relationships that give meaning, purpose and direction to human life and in terms of loving one another as Christ has loved us?

What Has Been Handed on to Us

Is there not proof of extensive and deep-seated bias against women in the traditions on this subject of sex? Can we read some of the sayings of the great Fathers of the church on the subject of women without a sense of shame and embarrassment at what they said? Has the Christian view of the world been overwhelmingly a masculine one? Are there still strong traces of both the purity ethic and the property ethic in Christian life? Did the distrust of the body that was so marked in certain groups at the time of Jesus have permanent effects on Christian understanding? From early times was sexuality caught in the duality of spirit and matter, sacred and profane that has plagued Christian thought? If it would be wrong to sweep away the whole tradition, is it just as dangerous to assume that, because certain views have been held for two thousand years, they are automatically correct? If even the documents of the Second Testament outside the four gospels failed to live up to the radicalism of Jesus, how could we claim that the last two thousand years of church history have been fully faithful to him? Is there not a need for a new, serious, honest and unbiased study of what the traditions might have to offer us in relation to sexuality?

At the same time, we must be impressed by the fact that every society throughout history has seen the need to have some controls over sexual conduct. This is true, not just of societies influenced by Jewish or Christian thought, but also of societies without the slightest trace of such influence. The controls have varied greatly and have taken many forms, but they have existed in every society. The sexual drive is a powerful force, a source of immense energy within human beings, and all societies have seen that a totally uncontrolled force of this magnitude and power would pose serious dangers to the society. Many controls were rules made up by men that were grossly unfair to women, many involved turning relative values into absolutes, many were needlessly draconian, but in all societies there were controls. Unless we would arrogantly dismiss the past, must we not pay serious attention to this 'handing on', this wisdom of the past, of the whole world?

Meditation

In so far as a sexual act between two persons is based on love, it is a means of giving expression to the very deepest longing of the human heart. It can neither fully express nor totally satisfy that longing, but it is one of the most profound and rewarding expressions of love there is in human life. It helps to reinforce the truth that *agape* (self-giving love) must constantly be renewed by *eros* (desire) and *philia* (affection).

Because the deepest longing of the human heart is as serious a topic as there can be on this earth, one of its most profound and rewarding expressions is also serious. Indeed, for those who see the deepest longing of the human heart as the foundation of all that is spiritual and the source of all meaning in life, its sexual expression is something we should treat with the greatest care, and even reverence.

Sex can, of course, be pleasurable and desirable in itself, irrespective of whether it is an expression of love or not, so sex and love are easily divided, and there are many dangers when this division occurs.

At the same time, persons who find a lifelong relationship in which sex and love are at all times and in every way in perfect harmony most probably don't exist, and it is obvious that one cannot speak of failure for all who fall short of this near-impossible standard.

Sexual union is also the means by which new human life is created, and the relationship between the expression of love and the creation of new life is both complex and delicate. The complexity must never be oversimplified or underestimated.

Sexuality is a mixture of body, mind and feelings and it seems to touch the mystery of life itself, for it is a place where blind instinct, rational thinking and strong emotions meet like three separate streams forming a turbulence and a whirlpool. It is always ambiguous and paradoxical. There is nothing quite like it in human life to mock our rationality and give the lie to our claims of calm control.

When we begin to speak of morality in this field, we must tread lightly and carefully.

Footnotes

[1] See 3:1-4, 5:2-8.

[2] See again 3:1-4 and, indeed, the whole poem.

[3] Dt.24:5

[4] Prov.5:18-19

[5] Hos. 2:19-20

[6] Jer. 2:2

[7] 2:13-16

[8] Gen.1:17-28,31

[9] Ecclesiastes 7:28.

[10] Proverbs 11:22.

[11] Proverbs 31:10-31.

[12] Ben Sira (Ecclesiasticus) 25:24.

[13] Fortress Press, Philadelphia, 1988.

[14] Though individual purity laws are scattered throughout the five books of the *Torah*, the two most substantial collections are found in Leviticus 11-16 and 17-27.

[15] The most famous stories are those of Eleazar (6:18-31) and the mother and her seven sons (7:1-42) in the Second Book of Maccabees.

[16] Countryman, *op.cit.*, pp.20-21.

[17] Countryman says that this insight comes from the anthropologist Mary Douglas, whose study of purity codes in many cultures led her to see the unity of those in the bible. See her book *Purity and Danger: An Analysis of Concepts of Pollution and Taboo*, London, Rutledge and Keegan Paul, 1966.

[18] 'If a man lies with a male as with a woman, both of them have committed an abomination.' (Lev.20:13)

[19] 'If a man lies with a woman and has an emission of semen, both of them shall bathe in water, and be unclean until the evening.' (Lev.15:18)

[20] *The New Jerome Biblical Commentary*, Geoffrey Chapman, London, 1989, p.68.

[21] Lev.12:2-5

[22] 'Everything in the waters that has not fins and scales is an abomination to you.' (Lev.11:12)

[23] Mk.7:19

[24] Countryman, *op.cit.*, p.85.

[25] He touched the leper (Mk.1:41) and allowed the woman with a flow of blood to touch him (Mk.5:25-34), in both cases without appearing to be concerned by issues of clean and unclean.

[26] Countryman, *op.cit.*, p.96.

[27] Mk.1:43-44

[28] Countryman, *op.cit.*, pp.99-101.

[29] Countryman, *op.cit.*, pp.101-104.

[30] See Acts 15:28-29. 'For it has seemed good to the Holy Spirit and to us to impose on you no further burden than these essentials: that you abstain from what has been sacrificed to idols and from blood and from what is strangled and from fornication.'

[31] Countryman, *op.cit.*, p71. There were some difficulties with the phrase 'what has been sacrificed to idols', but the major difficulties were with the requirement to refrain from *porneia*. In the NRSV this word is variously translated as 'unchastity', 'fornication' and 'immorality'. It derives from the verb *pernemi*, ' to sell', and so indicates 'bought sex' or 'harlotry'. Elsewhere it is used in the figurative sense of idolatry. No one can really explain with certainty what the word is doing in a list of things that were permissible in themselves but were to be avoided because of the sensitivities of the Jewish converts, or what the word means in this context.

[32] Countryman, *op.cit.*, pp.70-77.

[33] Countryman, *op.cit.*, p.101.

[34] Following the Septuagint, Philo places adultery in first place, before murder. 'Such being the disasters wrought by illicit intercourse, naturally the abominable and God-detested sin of adultery was placed first in the list of wrongdoing.' William Loader says, 'Philo considers the blame as lying in most of these cases not with the soul but with the balance of elements of fire and moisture in the body, when `the moisture is sluiced in a stream through the genital organs, and creates in them irritations, itchings and titillations without ceasing". William Loader, *The Septuagint, Sexuality and the New Testament*, William Eerdmans, Grand Rapids, Michigan, 2004, p.13.

[35] Countryman, *op.cit.*, p.59-61.

[36] Countryman, *op.cit.*, pp.59-64.

[37] 'Now concerning the matters about which you wrote: 'It is well for a man not to touch a woman."

[38] Countryman, *op.cit.*, pp.142-143

[39] Luke T. Johnson, *The Biblical Foundations of Matrimony*, The Bible Today, March/April 2003, p.114.

[40] Countryman, *op.cit.*, pp.166-167.

[41] Countryman, *op.cit.*, p.150.

[42] 42:10. 13-15.

[43] Countryman, *op.cit. pp.*148-150.

[44] Countryman, *op.cit.*, p.156.

[45] Countryman, *op.cit.*, pp.157-159.

[46] Countryman, *op.cit.*, p.174.

[47] Mark 10:11.

[48] Countryman, *op.cit.*, pp.168-189.

[49] See my book, *A Change of Mind and Heart, the Gospel according to Mark*, Parish Ministry Publications, Sydney, 1994, pp.347 ff.

[50] Mt.10:37-38

[51] Mt.8:22

[52] Mt.10:35

[53] Countryman, *op.cit.*, pp.169-173.

[54] See I Cor.7:25-31.

[55] Countryman, *op.cit.*, pp.190-220.

[56] 4:12-19

[57] 2:12-17

[58] 3:1-7.

[59] Countryman, *op.cit.*, pp.224-225.

[60] Countryman, *op.cit.*, p.234

[61] *NRSV Exhaustive Concordance*, ed. Bruce M Metzger, Thomas Nelson Publishers, Nashville, 1991.

[62] In the NRSV this word is variously translated as 'unchastity', 'fornication' and 'immorality'. It derives from the verb *pernemi*, ' to sell', and so directly indicates 'bought sex' or 'harlotry'. Elsewhere it is used in the figurative sense of idolatry. In translation it seems best to avoid the over-specific word 'fornication' and keep to vaguer words such as 'sexual immorality'.

[63] The arguments given by Paul in 1 Cor.11:2-16 concerning why a woman should wear a head covering as a sign of submission are a good example of this, leading to his final recourse to authority: 'But if anyone is disposed to be contentious – we have no such custom, nor do the churches of God.'

[64] Compare the NRSV translation of Rom.1:24, 'Therefore God gave them up in the lusts of their hearts to impurity, to the degrading of their bodies among themselves' with Countryman's more neutral translation of the same text, 'For this reason (idolatry), God surrendered them in the desires of their hearts to uncleanness so that they would dishonour their bodies among themselves.'

[65] In 1Cor.6:9, the Greek words *malakoi* and especially *arsenokoitai* do not allow of certain translation. NRSV ('male prostitutes and sodomites') is interpretation more than translation, and so is the Jerusalem Bible ('self-indulgent, sodomites'). Raymond F. Collins comments, 'Paul does not use these terms in any other place of the extant correspondence. This lack of usage makes it difficult for the modern reader to understand what Paul meant... It is usage that allows one to understand the meaning of a word.' *Sexual Ethics of the New Testament – Behavior and Belief*, Crossroad Publishing

Company, New York, 2000. p.87.' For his fuller discussion of the difficulty of understanding these two terms, see pp.87-90.

[66] A passage frequently quoted in this regard is Mark 7:14-22 (cf. Matthew 15:10-20). Here Jesus gives a list of six sets of wrong acts and six wrong frames of mind that defile a person. In the context of the passage he is saying that it is not forbidden foods coming from outside the body that defile, but wrong acts and frames of mind coming from within. Listed first among the wrong acts is 'fornication'. However, 'fornication' is a less than accurate translation of the plural word *porneai*, better understood as a generic word meaning 'sexual offences'. In context, Jesus is saying no more than that there are wrong sexual acts, and there is no one who would disagree, e.g. paedophilia and rape. He is not specifying particular acts, so no vast edifice can be built on this phrase alone. Among the wrong frames of mind is listed 'licentiousness', but this is not limited to sexual offences, for it refers to a wanton person, a person without shame who sins openly and without qualm in any field.

[67] See Countryman, *op.cit.*, p.114.

[68] See Countryman's comments on this matter, *op.cit.*, pp.121-123.

[69] 'For ample reason the commandment has been much more broadly understood in Jewish and Christian communities.' *The New Interpreter's Bible*, Abingdon Press, 1994, vo.1, p.848.

[70] Terence E. Fretheim, *Exodus*, Interpretation Series, John Knox Press, 1991, p.221.

[71] Mk.10:17-22, Mt.19:16-22, Lk.18:18-23. Jesus also cited the commandment about honouring father and mother, but that commandment is specific to those two people, while the other four apply to all people, so I leave it out of further consideration here.

[72] 19:19

[73] John 15:12.

CHAPTER TEN

The Return to an Original Sexual Ethic

The constantly repeated argument of the Catholic Church is that God created human sex for two reasons: as a means of expressing and fostering love between a couple (the unitive aspect) and as the means by which new human life is brought into being (the procreative aspect).[1] The argument then says that the use of sex is 'according to nature' only when it serves both of these God-given purposes, and that both are truly present only within marriage, and even then only when intercourse is open to new life, so that all other use of the sexual faculties is morally wrong.[2]

ORIGINS OF CURRENT CATHOLIC TEACHING

This argument is drawn from the world around and within us rather than from the bible, and it relies heavily on the fact that it has been often repeated (tradition). In the balance between the bible, the world around us and tradition, the accent is first on tradition, and then on the world around us (what is considered 'natural'), with the bible coming a poor third.

It must occasion great surprise that the teaching of the Catholic Church on something as important as sexuality draws so little on the bible. Why would a Christian church put the bible aside and assume that a new and elaborate sexual ethic needs to be developed that is not contained in the gospels or even based on anything that is said there?

Furthermore, this teaching of the church would say that the essence of sexual sin is that it is a direct offence against God because, irrespective of whether harm is caused to any human being, it is a violation of the divine and natural order that God established. Following the ideas of Philo of Alexandria, sexual sin is said to be against 'nature' as established by God. This raises two serious questions, one concerning nature and the other concerning God.

In relation to nature, should not the church's argument give a number of examples of other fields where God has given a divine purpose to some created thing, such that it would be a sin against God to use that thing in any other way? Why do church documents not attempt to do this? I remember reading years ago the mocking argument that the natural God-given purpose of eyes is to look forwards, so rear vision mirrors in cars are against nature and hence immoral. Granted that this is a mocking argument, does it not raise questions about what we mean by 'nature' and how difficult it is to draw moral consequences from a claim to a divinely established nature?

In relation to God, the argument was used in the past that striking a king was far more serious than striking a commoner, and, for the same reason, an offence against God was far more serious than an offence against a human being. In this view, the most serious sins were those directly against God. In practice, this applied above all to sins of blasphemy and sexual sins. This attitude seems to make the same mistake as Augustine in implying that God reacts to human events in a manner similar to the Roman Emperor. When a person takes great offence at even a trivial remark, we tend to speak of that person as a 'little' person, while a person who can shrug off most negative comments is a 'big' person. If I may return to the bible for a moment, my reading of it leads me to believe in a very big God indeed who, quite unlike the Roman Emperor, is not easily offended by direct offences. I believe, for instance, that God shrugs off much of what is called 'blasphemy' as an understandable human reaction to the felt injustice of evil and suffering in this world. I do not believe that God is in the least offended when parents who have just lost a child rage in anger against God.

In this vein, I must ask whether God will be offended by any sexual thought or action *in and of itself alone*, considered only as a direct offence against God before any question of its effect on other persons, oneself or the community is taken into account. After all, the God who determined that sexuality can be both unitive and procreative also created the turbulence and whirlpool within which these purposes were to be lived out.

The parable of the prodigal son may help us here[3]. The younger son had received the entire share of the property that would come to him and he had wasted it. He had no right to one further square centimetre of the property, for the entire remaining property would now go by strict right to the elder son ('You are with me always and all I have is yours' v.31). The father respected his elder son's rights and would take nothing from him. When, however, it came to the hurt the prodigal son had caused by abandoning his parents and wasting the property they had worked so hard for, the father brushed this aside out of love for his son and insisted that he be welcomed and treated as a son rather than a servant. The message is surely that God cares about the rights of human beings and what they do to one another, but is big enough, loving enough and forgiving enough not to get angry at direct offences against God. May we ask whether the God portrayed in this parable would condemn a person to eternal punishment for sometimes getting unitive and procreative purposes out of a perceived ideal harmony in the midst of the turbulence and whirlpool of sexuality?

Does it not follow that there are serious dangers in basing the church's moral teaching concerning sex on the concept of direct offences against God?

It must be added that, in the response to revelations of sexual abuse, this became a most serious problem, for far too many church authorities saw the offence primarily in terms of a sexual offence against God, to be treated according to the criteria governing such

offences — repentance, confession, absolution and restoration to the
status quo. There was never going to be an adequate response to abuse
as long as many people thought primarily in terms of sexual offences
against God rather than harm caused to the victims.

No one disputes the fact that sexuality can help couples to express
and strengthen their love and that it is the means of creating new
life, but the crucial question is whether the procreative aspect must
be present, not only in marriage as an institution of the whole human
race, but also in each individual marriage, no matter what the circumstances, and, indeed, in every single act of sexual intercourse.

There are always problems when human beings claim that they
know the mind of God. So is the statement that it is God's will, and
indeed order, that both the unitive and procreative aspects must necessarily be present in each act of sexual intercourse a proven fact or
a simple assertion? If it is a proven fact, what are the proofs? Why
do church documents not present such proofs?[4] Would not any proofs
have to include the experience of millions of people in the very human
endeavour of seeking to combine sex, love and the procreation of new
life in the midst of the turbulence and whirlpool of human sexuality
and the complexities of human life? Is an ideal being confused with
a reality?

If it is only an assertion, is there any reason why we should not apply the principle of logic: What is freely asserted may be freely denied?
If it is no more than an assertion, does it really matter who it is who
makes the assertion or how often it is made? I remind again of the
statement from Veritatis Splendor, 'The Church puts herself always
and only at the service of conscience,'[5] and of the principles I drew
from this in the last chapter. In this whole important field of sexuality,
is conscience assisted only by an unproven assertion? If not, where are
the arguments in favour of the assertion that would convince an open
and honest conscience?

An Ethic Based on Persons

If it is difficult to sustain an entire sexual ethic on the basis of direct offences against God, I believe that God cares greatly about human beings and takes a very serious view of any harm done to them, through

sexual desire or any other cause. Should we not look at sexual morality in terms of the good or harm done to persons and the relationships between them rather than in terms of a direct offence against God? Does the world around and within us lead to the same conclusion as the understanding of the Ten Commandments and of the teaching of Jesus that I have given earlier, that is, that our sexual desires must seek to help not hinder the personal relationships that give purpose and meaning to life and help people to grow? If we may assume that Jesus did not avoid the question of sex, but included it under his principles applying to all human activity, is this not the sexual ethic he presented?

Following from this, may we say that sexual pleasure, like all other pleasure, is in itself morally neutral, neither good nor bad? Is it rather the circumstances affecting persons that make this pleasure good or bad, e.g. a good pleasure for a married couple seeking reconciliation after a disagreement, a bad pleasure for a man committing rape?

POSITIVE GOOD

In saying this, am I simply agreeing with those who say that all sex is good as long as it does not harm anyone, or that all sex is good provided both parties consent? No, I would never want to put the matter in those simple terms, even as a question, let alone as a statement, for I have seen far too much harm caused by these attitudes. As everyone knows, sex is a field in which with great ease people can convince themselves that they are doing no harm when in fact they are, or convince themselves that the other is consenting when this is well short of the whole truth.

If I have moved away from some ideas of the church that I now consider extreme, the idea that all sex is good as long as it doesn't harm anyone or as long as both parties consent will in practice be too close to the opposite extreme. Neither attitude adequately expresses the middle ground that I instinctively seek.

The first statement (as long as it does no harm) is expressed in negative terms and inevitably leads to the serious risk of brinkmanship, that is, that one may seek one's own pleasure and, in doing so, go right up to the brink of causing harm to another. In a field as turbulent as this, countless people basing themselves on such a principle will go over that brink. This attitude is at that fourth level of morality I spoke of in the last chapter, where one looks first to one's own interests and sees other people in terms of their usefulness to oneself.

The second attitude (as long as both parties consent) ignores the many ways in which 'consent' can be assumed or be the result of pressure or deceit. Neither attitude does justice to the close relationship between sex and love and the consequent seriousness of sex.

There is no statement of Jesus that stops at saying, 'Do no harm to your neighbour', for Jesus invariably said 'Love your neighbour', and this implies more than the negative fact of not harming. It implies the third and second levels of morality: a genuine respect for the other and positively wanting and seeking the good of the other. 'Do no harm' can put oneself first, while 'Love your neighbour' always puts the neighbour first. A Christian ethic must, at the very least, be expressed in these positive terms. Is it only on this positive basis of putting the good of the neighbour first and doing all in one's power to help that neighbour that we could feel confident of having found a truly Christian ethic? Could we ever feel that confidence as long as the principles remained negative?

Negative Harm

Furthermore, if we are to see sexual morality in terms of its effects on other people, we must take the harm that can be caused by sexual desire very seriously and look carefully at the circumstances that can make morally bad the seeking of sexual pleasure because they involve harm to others, oneself or the community. Some of these factors are discussed below.

Violence
The immorality of physical violence (rape, sexual assault, harassment) is admitted by all. Should we not also ask questions about the morality of some of the forms of psychological pressure that are used to secure the involvement of a less than fully willing person in sexual activity? Is this pressure not saying, 'I've decided that no harm will be caused, so just agree with me rather than make your own free decision'?

Deceit and self-deceit

Can sexual desire lead to mountainous, even Himalayan, levels of deceit that can harm other people? Can it lead to equally high levels of self-deceit?

Emotional harm to others

The immense emotional harm caused by paedophilia has become better known. Serious emotional harm can be caused to adults as well, for a person in a stronger position can manipulate the consent of a weaker person in a similar manner.

Using people

What should we say of the 'using' of another person, the treating of another as an object rather than a person? If the other is seen only as a female body or a male body rather than a true and full person, is it not inevitable that harm is being caused to both persons?

Sex and Love

If sex is separated from love, can it be so trivialised that it loses not only its sacredness, but even its seriousness? Should we be concerned about any use of sex that, either for an individual or for a community, weakens the capacity of sex to express the depths of love? Can the desire for present satisfaction restrict the ability to respond to the deepest longing of the human heart?

Total Commitment

Because love always desires permanence, does commitment to a sexual relationship necessarily involve at least the hope of total commitment forever? Is there a contradiction in terms between loving completely but only for a time?

The Liberation of Women

Many men are reluctant to commit themselves to a permanent relationship, but in the past the promise of a sexual component was a strong part of the enticement to do so. Has sexual liberation weakened this enticement? Has this in turn weakened the position of many women? Has sexual liberation become for many women the new name of sexual exploitation? Is it the weakest women who will be the most exploited in this manner?

Sex and New Life

Can one have a moral attitude towards sex without having a moral attitude towards the new life that can result from the sexual act? A rebellion against restrictions on sex has come at exactly the same time as science has greatly enhanced the opportunity to have the pleasure of sex without the consequence of pregnancy, that is, when it is possible to separate sex from both love and new life in a way that has never been possible before. Is this not, therefore, a time when there is an urgent need to begin a serious conversation about the harm that can be caused through the use of sex without sufficient thought for its possible consequences? Even for those who believe in choice, is it good enough to think in advance that abortion will take care of any problems, so there is no need to think of consequences? Since the good of the child must always be put before the good of the adults concerned, should a couple not be aware of the circumstances they might be creating for a child?

Building a Relationship

If sex becomes part of a relationship from the beginning, is there the danger that it can get in the way of the slow, patient development of a deeper and more mature relationship? Can it overwhelm the relationship and make it difficult to look calmly at all other important factors? On the other hand, can one person all too easily see a sexual relationship as a level of commitment that the other does not?

Harming Commitment

When two people commit themselves totally to each other, they place their whole lives and happiness in each other's hands and make themselves vulnerable to be profoundly hurt by the other. Is there not normally a very serious injustice in harming the other through sexual contact with a third person? Or in invading the union of another person? Does an 'anything goes' mentality make sufficient distinction between having a relationship with a married and an unmarried person?

The Common Good
The common good needs the stability of relationships. Does straying outside one's own relationship or invading the relationship of another person harm this stability and so harm the common good of the whole society? Can children be harmed by these actions?

Harming Oneself
Can a person who takes for granted a variety of sexual partners later find it difficult to be committed to one?

The Concept of 'Obscene'
Most societies base their concept of what is 'obscene' on what the normal or average man considers obscene. Should we not also ask what the normal or average woman considers obscene? Should the concept of 'obscene' be limited to what arouses sexual desire or should it rather be seen in terms of whatever demeans people or encourages others to think of them as objects rather than persons?

The 'Duties' of Marriage
Sex inside marriage can also be morally wrong, in that it is certainly possible to harm a marriage partner through sexual desire. In particular, can the idea that marriage creates sexual 'duties' that must be fulfilled even at the cost of one's own good be sustained?

The Burden of Proof
Having said this, is not harm to another less likely within a committed relationship than in more casual circumstances? In a field so full of strong desires and emotions and in which the deepest longing of the human heart is so intimately involved, may we say that a person who would seek sex in more casual circumstances has a burden of proof to establish that no harm is being caused?

The Major Questions

In relation to heterosexual sex, the questions I am asking are:

> i) Is there a need for a profound revision of the Catholic Church's sexual ethic? Must we work hard to exclude all trace of both the purity and the property ethic?

> ii) Is it possible to base a sexual ethic on the concept of direct offences against God, or should we move to an ethic based on the good or harm done to others, oneself and the community?

> iii) Are we moving towards a genuinely Christian ethic if we place the sixth commandment in the context of the three that surround it and base ourselves on respect for the relationships that give meaning, purpose and direction to human life, and on treating our neighbour as we would want our neighbour to treat us?

> iv) Within this context, may we ask whether a sexual act is morally right when, positively, it is based on a genuine love of neighbour, that is, a genuine desire for all that is good for the other person rather than self-interest, and, negatively, contains no damaging elements such as harm to a third person such as a partner or a baby brought into being by the act, any form of coercion or deceit, or any harm to the ability of sex to express love?

> v) Is the question of when these circumstances might apply, and whether and to what extent they might apply even outside marriage, one for discussion and debate by both the church community and the wider community, and for decision and responsibility before God, other people and one's own deeper self by each individual?

In relation to autoerotic actions such as masturbation, I would have to apply the same criteria, while noting that a fixation on the autoerotic can harm the ability to relate to others and can involve a loss of respect as a whole person for someone who is constantly used as a fantasy object.

In relation to homosexual actions, I acknowledge that affirmative answers to the questions I have asked would lead to conclusions very different from those of the church. Is a new and careful study of biblical texts along the lines mentioned earlier in this chapter a pressing need? I would insist that, if a change in ethic were to occur, the full weight of the criteria just expressed would have to be applied to homosexual actions as well.

PUBLIC LAW AND PRIVATE MORALITY

Would not a sexual ethic based on the good or harm caused be abused, with many people all too easily convincing themselves that whatever they wanted to do 'wouldn't hurt anyone'? Yes, I am sure it would. But is it not true that any sexual ethic will be abused and flouted? Is it not true that the church's current teaching is largely abused and scorned? I called the last chapter 'A Turbulence and a Whirlpool' to make the point that no society, whether civil or ecclesial, is ever going to have a placid lake in this field, with everyone calmly following the same consistent ethic. Under the ethic of always seeking the good of others, would we not at least have a serious basis on which to enter into discussion with those who would want to do whatever they liked? Is it really possible to enter into the same discussion on the basis of the current sexual ethic of the Catholic Church?

It is said that in the field of the legal (law) things are wrong because they are forbidden, while in the field of the moral (morality) things are forbidden because they are wrong. For example, it is wrong to drive on the right side of the road in Britain or on the left side in France because legitimate laws in each country state otherwise (wrong because forbidden), but it is wrong to drive at 80 kph through a crowded market in either country, because this would seriously endanger the lives of others, and so is immoral whether the law permits it or not (forbidden because wrong).

I make this comment because I know that many people would hold that to say that all sex outside marriage is wrong is a better *public rule* than to say that sex should always help others, oneself and the community. They would say that the first rule is clear and simple, while the second is too vague and uncertain.

To this I have a minor and a major response. The minor response is that, because the rule of good or harm to others is rational, would it not be possible over time to develop many particular rules (e.g. children *cannot* consent, any means of coercing consent is wrong etc.) that would eventually build into a more consistent and satisfying ethic? Because we are still in the middle of an emotional reaction against the restrictions of the traditional Christian ethic, it has not been possible to hold the intelligent conversation that would allow this ethic to develop. Can we judge it before we have seriously tried it?

The major response is that the legal and the moral must not be confused. Law is for the common good of the whole community and it is not right to use law to impose private morality. It is legitimate to have a law to protect the community (e.g. it is not lawful to have sexual intercourse in a public place), but it is not lawful to have a law to impose private morality (e.g. it is not lawful for a couple who are not married to have sexual intercourse anywhere). To maintain that the principle that no sex outside marriage is the better *public rule* is to attempt to coerce private morality by public rule. Without sufficient rational basis for saying that sex outside marriage is forbidden because wrong, it is attempting to make it wrong because forbidden.

The task of the church is not to impose what is wrong because forbidden, but to assist people to form their conscience in such a way that the true good of all people concerned will be promoted. In accordance with all that was said in the last chapter, the church's task in the field of sexuality is to present to people an insight into the depth of all that is involved in sex and love, reminding them of the many factors that people ought to bear in mind. It is then individuals who must make their own decisions and take responsibility for them before God, other people and their own deeper selves.

THE NEED TO THINK AGAIN

At its worst, a wedding in church can be seen as a divine permission, because of human weakness, to engage in sexual activity that is in itself bad or at least suspect. Is today's reaction against marriage and the 'piece of paper' that testifies to it to be explained, at least in part, as a reaction against this attitude? Traditional morality has been seen as a defence of marriage, but is it possible that the extremes that morality went to actually harmed marriage?

On the other hand, if we go beneath the particular teachings of the Catholic Church on sex and come to its most foundational beliefs, do we find four matters where the church and modern Western society are still far apart and even moving in opposite directions?

> i) Is the church saying that, because love is the deepest longing of the human heart and because sex is such an important expression of love, people should do all in their power to bring sex and love into harmony in their own lives and in their relationships with others, while modern society has become more and more accepting of casual sexual activity that is not related to love or relationship?

> ii) Is the church saying that sexual activity has an inherent connection to new life that involves responsibilities for the couple, while modern society more and more views the connection between sexual activity and new life as an inconvenience and demands a foolproof means of separating the two?

> iii) Is the church saying that sexual activity is serious, and even sacred, while modern society will have nothing of the sacred and appears to be saying more and more that sexual activity is not in itself serious?

> iv) Does the church see marriage between a man and a woman as fundamental to the health of society itself, while modern society seems to be more and more seeing marriage as nothing more than one among many equally valid options?

Obviously there is much more to be said. In developing its understanding of sexual morality, the Catholic Church will want to make a profound study of the bible, what has been handed on to us and the world around and within us, using all the powers of discernment and collective wisdom available to it. On a question such as this, it will want to enter into dialogue with the whole world.

Meditation

It is in their personal relationships that most people find the deepest and most rewarding sources of love in their lives.

Since love is the deepest longing of the human heart, these personal relationships are as important to us as the air we breathe and the food we eat. Without them our lives would wither and die. They are subtle and fragile, and yet touch profound depths within us.

If we deliberately or carelessly harm the relationships of a person, all of our alleged respect for that person's life, possessions and good name is pretence and deception.

Like the father in the parable of the prodigal son, God is big enough to brush aside most of our direct offences, but cares passionately about what we do to other people, and in a particular way to their relationships.

"Love one another", said Jesus, that is, make sure that your relationships with other persons are based on more than your own self-interest or pleasure. Make sure they are relationships that avoid all harm and do everything positive to help others to grow to become all they are capable of being.

FOOTNOTES

[1] Until the time of the Second Vatican Council there was a hierarchy among these ends, with the procreative purpose being 'primary' and the unitive purpose being 'secondary'. This teaching has never been formally abandoned, but it is not heard anymore.

[2] The most important papal document on sexual morality of the last century expressed the argument thus: 'Such teaching, many times set forth by the teaching office of the church, is founded on the unbreakable connection, which God established and which men and women may not break of their own initiative, between the two meanings of the conjugal act: the unitive meaning and the procreative meaning. Indeed, in its intimate nature, the conjugal act, while it unites the spouses in a most profound bond, also places them in a position (idoneos facit) to generate new life, according to laws inscribed in the very being of man and woman. By protecting both of these essential aspects, the unitive and the procreative, the conjugal act preserves in an integral manner the sense of mutual and true love and its ordering to the exalted vocation of human beings to parenthood.' Pope Paul VI, encyclical letter *Humanae Vitae*, 26th July 1968, no.12.

[3] Lk. 15:11-32

[4] In recent years there has been an appeal to anthropology, but I have not seen a clear statement of how anthropology demands that every act of intercourse include both the unitive and procreative purpose.

[5] No.64

CHAPTER ELEVEN

A Dark Grace, A Severe Mercy[1]

While this chapter is more directly about sexual abuse, it will, in accordance with what was said in the Introduction, concern more general church attitudes involved in the response to abuse.

SPIRITUAL HARM AND SPIRITUAL HEALING

SPIRITUAL HARM

In an earlier chapter I spoke of the search for meaning, and of love in all its forms as being the only answer to that search. The systems of meaning that people build up are always fragile, for they are made up of the many tiny fragments of their lived experience, the many loves, small and great, of their lives. Sexual abuse is a bulldozer gouging a road through this fragile ecosystem of love and meaning that a person has been painfully constructing.

This is, I believe, the major spiritual harm caused by sexual abuse, the destruction of a delicate and elaborate system of meaning. What ought to be positive becomes negative, what ought to be love becomes the using of a person, what ought to be trustworthy can no longer be trusted. Many of the loves that had given meaning in the past are destroyed. The forces that brought all the different facets of life into one whole are no longer capable of doing so. The relationship is broken between sexuality and love, between trust and love, and between meaning and love, so that love is no longer a unifying force. It is in the abuse of minors more than anywhere else that one learns that sex is never trivial, for it impacts on the deepest being of a person, on the very concept of who one is.

In sexual abuse there is always spiritual harm, for the abuse always harms the person's sense of wholeness and connectedness, and hence the person's sense of meaning and identity.

Because we long for perfect and infinite love, religious beliefs are an important part of the making of meaning in the lives of those who accept them. Religious beliefs claim to answer the big questions of life and the answer they give is based on love: we come from love, we are going to love and love is the purpose and meaning of our existence on earth. Sexual abuse by a direct representative of that religious belief destroys the answers that the religious beliefs have given up to that point. The power that has been abused is a spiritual power that allows a person to enter deeply into the secret lives of others. The link between the minister and the god can be impossible to break and it can easily seem as though the very god is the abuser. The abuse shatters the power of the symbols of that belief, e.g. the picture of a priest holding a host aloft becomes a mockery. The search for perfect love within that system of belief can become impossible.

Within a church community it is impossible to separate the victim's relationships with the abuser, with God and with the community. The abuser will invariably be a person of power and will have a far stronger position in the community than the victim. This means that the abuser will be far more important to the meaning-making of the members of the community than the victim is. Making meaning of life is a long and arduous process and people do not like to see it upset. All too frequently their non-verbal, and even verbal, message to the victim will be, 'We were content before you spoke out. You are a threat to our very system of meaning-making. Go away, leave this community and let us go back to our former certainties.' The victim is then left without a community and feels ostracised, even excommunicated.

The harm is compounded if church authorities react badly when informed of the abuse and the loss of meaning is greater. There may be some realisation in the victim that the abuser is an individual who has acted in a manner contrary to every belief of the church community, but when the church authorities themselves appear to condone the offence and reinforce its effects, it seems that the entire community is joining in the rejection. The magnitude of the effect on the victim's world of meaning must be seriously compared with the abuse itself.

SPIRITUAL HEALING

In sexual abuse spiritual harm is the first to occur and the last to be healed, for damage to any one part damages the whole and the whole cannot be fully restored until each part has been restored. Spiritual healing means helping a person to be whole again and to find a new world of meaning, a new set of satisfying answers to the basic questions of life.

The path to healing will be different for each individual and no neat blueprint can be laid down that would be valid for all victims. In all situations we must obviously respect the needs and rights of the victim and assist rather than direct. The sense of meaning that they finally come to may be very different from the one they formerly had. To spell this out, I, a Catholic bishop, have on a number of occasions found myself in the situation of helping a victim who grew up as a Catholic to find a path in life outside that church. If this is the path that a particular victim must follow in order to reach wholeness, then respect for the dignity of the victim demands that I give the assistance I can.

A new world of meaning, a new set of satisfying answers to the basic questions of life, means a new set of persons, objects, activities and ideas that can be loved. Sometimes, when we meet a victim, we will find some enduring loves from a past life before the abuse, sometimes we will see new loves that have arisen since that time, e.g. efforts to trust a fellow victim or someone who has shown kindness. It is important to actively look for, recognise and welcome any loves, great or small, that we find in a victim and to encourage their development. It is important to foster in the victim the idea that, despite the abuse, there are still persons, objects, activities and ideas that can be loved, that are worthy of love, and that can contribute towards a new world of meaning. Whether the person is or is not open to the idea of divine love must be gradually discovered and cannot be taken for granted, let alone imposed.

This process will always be defective as long as it is only individuals and small groups who are seeking to give victims this sense of meaning in life. It cannot be emphasised too strongly how much more helpful it would be for victims if the entire church community were to cooperate in this work. My experience in the field would tell me that there are two things above all others that victims want.

Firstly, they want someone (and the higher the authority the better) to say 'sorry' in the strong sense of that word, that is, they want someone to say that what happened was very wrong and was not their fault. They want an authority of the church to tell them that they had been controlled and manipulated by persons who were more powerful than they were because they were abusing an authority given them by the church.

Secondly, they want a guarantee that the abuse will not happen again. Directly this means a guarantee that the particular abuser will not abuse them again, but more widely it means a solemn promise that everything possible will be done to prevent all future abuse.

I have many times sought to meet these two needs in so far as it was within my power to do so, but I always felt that my weak position made my efforts inadequate. I must confess my profound disappointment that no pope has so far said 'sorry' directly to all victims and no pope has so far made a public promise urgently to study the causes of abuse and ruthlessly to change anything and everything that might contribute to abuse. If it is the Peter-figure alone who can solemnly proclaim the faith of the church, it is the same Peter-figure alone who can make these two statements in the name of the whole church.

FORGIVENESS

Too often victims have been told that they have a Christian duty to forgive their offender. Apart from the fact that this is an obvious attempt to get victims to resolve the problems caused by offenders, there are other difficulties with this idea, reflecting more general attitudes within the church.

Jesus told us to forgive seventy-seven times, and we know that he forgave those who crucified him. So is there a Christian duty to forgive in all circumstances? With minor offences it is easy, but what if a member of your family is brutally murdered? What if you put everything into your marriage for many years only to have your partner suddenly say, 'I've met someone better than you. Goodbye'? What if you have been sexually abused?

When people suffer an offence of this magnitude, they almost invariably seem to find that they don't even know what forgiveness means in their situation. I have found that this sense of confusion concerning the very meaning of forgiveness is almost universal among victims of sexual abuse.

The reason for this confusion is that there is a common mistaken belief that forgiveness is a feeling, that is, that people have forgiven when they feel good towards the offender, and they have not forgiven when they feel bad or angry towards the offender.[2] In fact, however, people have no direct control over their feelings. If victims think of the abuse, they will feel angry and there is nothing that can be done to prevent this anger. To think of the abuse and not feel angry is simply not an option.

When memory of sexual abuse comes to mind, the anger that is spontaneously felt is in fact positively good and contributes to a sense of meaning because it is part of the loving of oneself. The anger is a defensive reaction, an affirmation of oneself and one's own dignity, an instinctive statement that what happened was wrong, that I (the victim) am worth more than that.

STAGES OF FORGIVENESS

FIRST STAGE
The origin of words can tell us much about their meaning. There are two stages to forgiveness and the first is expressed by the Greek word in the gospels which is usually translated as 'to forgive', but which has the more basic meaning of 'to leave behind, to let be'.[3] In relation to

sexual abuse, this does not mean to 'forgive and forget', for it is actually quite essential to true forgiveness that the offence *not* be forgotten. So it does not mean to deny the abuse or the debt it created. It does not mean to forego attempts to have just debts paid. It does not mean to prevent the memory from rising to the conscious mind whenever this happens naturally. It means to come to a point where one is prepared to begin to leave the matter behind, to let it be, that is, to do nothing to deliberately arouse the memories and the angry feelings they evoke.

If people have no direct control over their feelings, they can gradually acquire a greater or lesser control over their thoughts and actions. Thus a victim can eventually choose not to feel angry by choosing not to think about the abuse. At first this will be impossible, but with the passage of a long period of time it can become more and more possible, and how much the abuse is thought about is a choice that a victim must gradually make.

It must be added that there is such a thing as forgiveness given too early and this forgiveness brings no satisfaction. People can expect that the fact that they have in all sincerity decided to forgive will take away their anger and they can be disheartened when they are still constantly overwhelmed by anger. They can start blaming themselves and think that there must be something lacking in their goodness, when all that is wrong is that they have tried to forgive, that is, to leave behind, to let be, before they were in fact ready to do so.

In his book *Further Along the Road Less Travelled*, M. Scott Peck makes an important point about this first stage of forgiveness,

> 'The process of forgiveness - indeed, the chief reason for forgiveness - is selfish. The reason to forgive others is not for their sake.... The reason to forgive is for our own sake. For our own health. Because beyond that point needed for healing, if we hold on to our anger, we stop growing and our souls begin to shrivel.'[4]

Timing is of the greatest importance. Some people have spoken of never having made a decision to 'leave behind, to let be', but of then waking up one day to find that they have in fact done so at some undetermined moment in the past.[5] They can also find that in between rage and hatred on the one hand and forgiveness on the other there exists an arid grey area and that they can exist in this arid grey area for a very long time.[6]

Second Stage

There is then a second stage to forgiveness that does turn towards the offender. It is easier if the offender has taken responsibility for the offence and acknowledged the harm done, but it is possible even if the offender is unrepentant.

In this second stage of forgiveness the question that a victim must ask is, 'Do I want only punishment for the offender or do I also want to see change and growth?' Victims have forgiven when they are able to answer that, even though they may still see punishment as necessary and desirable, they also want growth and change in the offender. The offence has changed the relationship between the offender and the victim forever, and the victim needs to accept that the former relationship can never be regained. So it is a new relationship that must now be created, even if the two of them never meet or communicate. And the victim must eventually choose whether the new relationship is to be based solely on a desire for further punishment or also on a desire for change and growth.

If the Greek word in the gospels translated as 'to forgive' means 'to leave behind, to let be', in a number of Western languages the word 'to forgive' is made up of the two words 'give' and 'for'.[7] And it is a remarkable fact that, when victims reach the stage of wanting growth and change in the offender, many, even most, seem to want in some manner to give of themselves to help bring about this growth, and their 'giving for' becomes their 'forgiving'.

I said 'in some manner', for among human beings it rarely happens as neatly as in the gospels. There is a woman in the USA whose daughter was brutally raped and murdered, with the murderer now on death row. Years after the event she still cannot think of this man without feelings of deep anger and loathing, but she has started writing regularly to another man on death row convicted of another murder. She speaks of herself as being in the arid grey area, but it appears obvious that she has travelled some distance along the road of 'giving for' the man who murdered her daughter, for she is attempting to understand how there can be a human being behind the face of a murderer and through her letters she would like to help one such human being to grow. Her actions rather than her feelings are the true indicators of where she has come to on the road to forgiveness.[8] She is following her own personal path towards meaning-making and spiritual healing, and no one may take it away from her.

It follows that no-one is ever justified in telling victims that they have a religious obligation to forgive the offender. Indeed, that language can be very harmful, hindering the entire process of recovery. The effects of abuse last throughout life and frequently the offender has expressed no remorse or sorrow. There can be nothing whatsoever in the external circumstances that would lead a person to 'leave behind, to let be', far less to give of oneself to help someone grow who sees no need for growth. For forgiveness to have any meaning at all, it must be the free personal choice of the victim, not an imposed religious obligation. Provided the timing is right, however, one may suggest that to move towards the first stage of forgiveness could be good for themselves. The most basic reason for this is that it can enable love and meaning to enter more easily into their lives.

I have recently seen a documentary film about a couple whose three daughters were murdered in a fit of violent rage by a schizophrenic man who believed he was in love with the eldest daughter and felt rejected by her.[9] Sixteen years later the father has come to the first stage of forgiveness, in that he has made a clear decision to 'leave behind, to let be'. He has also visited the murderer in prison and spoken with him. He does not wish to see the man released, for he believes there would always be a serious risk of another crime, but he is seeking in some manner to give of himself to help the man grow. On the other hand, his former wife, the mother of the three girls, disagrees strongly with his attitudes and actions, believing that he is being disloyal to his murdered daughters and is putting the murderer before them. What outsider could dare to take sides between these two devastated parents or tell either of them what to do? They must each find their own way to healing.

In another case a woman whose husband, a headmaster, was killed when he went to the aid of a student who was being attacked, writes:

> 'I don't want to see Chindamo suffer. There is too much suffering already in the world. I want him to understand, and to be able to change and to come back into society and lead a valuable and valued life. If I thought I could do anything to help that process, I would….. As for my own forgiveness, I just don't know any more. When a fundamental crime against humanity has been committed, I'm not sure I know what forgiveness means. It's too profound for my human understanding. Perhaps only God knows that.'[10]

She struggles to understand forgiveness, and in the process shows that through her struggle, and despite her fears that she doesn't understand, she has moved unerringly to a profound understanding.

There is another forgiveness that is essential. Communities must forgive, in the literal sense of 'give themselves for', victims who have disturbed their comfort and meaning-making by speaking out about their abuse. Within the Catholic Church I must accept that, if no victims had come forward, nothing would have changed. We must learn to be positively grateful to victims for disturbing us. If we feel that we have lost some meaning, it was a false meaning, and their revelation has opened the way to a fuller and more rewarding meaning.

Listening to victims of sexual abuse is the most profound spiritual gift I have received in the last twelve years. They have showed me how to find love in the most unexpected places and they have greatly widened my spiritual horizons. If a better church one day emerges from this crisis, it is they alone who must take the credit for creating it.

When the word 'spiritual' is understood in the broad sense in which I have used it in this book, spiritual healing provides the goal towards which all forms of healing tend. Spiritual healing has made true progress in a victim when the world begins to make some sense again, when there is once again some basic sense of loving and being loved, and when there is hope that the future will bring more, not less, of these qualities to life.

A New Assignment to Ministry?

The question of a possible new assignment to ministry after a sexual offence must be considered here, for one of the major complaints concerning the past was that offenders were simply moved to another place where they abused other minors. As well as the 'mystique' of being 'taken up' and the need to cover up anything that was shameful, profound attitudes towards forgiveness and redemption have been involved here.

Forgiveness and a New Assignment

When the question of a new assignment is raised within the Catholic

Church, an appeal is often made to the essential Christian virtues of forgiveness and compassion. Forgiveness and a new assignment to ministry, however, are two quite different things, to be judged by quite different criteria. Forgiveness is given on the basis of a person's repentance for *past* wrong, while the question of a new assignment must be based on the *future* good of the whole community, especially of potential victims. Every human being knows that it is entirely possible to be genuinely sorry for a past sin without being able to give any guarantee that the sin will not be committed again.

I indicated earlier that this confusion between forgiveness and reinstatement to ministry was caused in large part by seeing the offence as primarily a sexual sin against God, to be responded to according to the normal rules governing all sexual sins. I indicated that we must break away from this and see the sin as primarily a terrible harm caused to a vulnerable young person and God's powerful reaction to this harm. Seen in this light, we have a much better chance of separating forgiveness for past wrong and prevention of future harm.

A new assignment is far from being the only form of forgiveness and is not essential to forgiveness. A person can be forgiven by God and the community for past wrong, even repeatedly, but not given a new assignment because of the danger this would pose to innocent potential victims. A superior who refuses a new assignment is not, for that reason alone, unforgiving or lacking in compassion.

I quoted earlier the parable of the prodigal son. The son was forgiven, but that did not mean that he would receive a new inheritance. The father loved him in the circumstances he had created for himself, and sexual offenders can only be forgiven and loved by God and the community of the church in the circumstances they have created for themselves.

ASSESSING EACH CASE

There is a wide variety of *types* of sexual misbehaviour and, within each type, many variations of *degree*, so each case must be assessed individually.

There is a wide variety of *non-criminal* actions of a sexual nature that a priest/religious can perform. There will be cases where a bishop or religious superior would not even think of removing the person from ministry (e.g. placing a hand once on another person's hand, or telling a slightly inappropriate joke once). And there will be cases where, even though no crime has been committed, the superior would have to remove the priest or religious permanently from all ministries (e.g. the constant and predatory seeking of adult sexual partners in a parish).

There are also *criminal* actions. In the main, these concern sexual activity with a minor and non-consensual activity with an adult, and for serious offences a priest or religious would be permanently removed from ministry. We should remember, however, that it is also a criminal offence e.g. for a person to swim naked at a public beach after a late night party.

Thus there are crimes for which a person would not be permanently disqualified from ministry and there are non-crimes for which a person would be permanently excluded, so whether an action was a crime or not is not a sufficient criterion of judgement. Each case must be studied on its individual merits.

No question of a new pastoral assignment for a priest or religious, however, should ever be based on minimising the seriousness of the offence. Some of the factors to consider are the following.

THE LIKELIHOOD OF OTHER OFFENCES

It is well known that many forms of sexual offence are rarely committed only once, for a number of powerful taboos have to be broken before the first offence occurs, and a second offence is far easier. It is also well known that many sexual offenders will vehemently deny the existence of any offence other than the one that has been proved against them. So the first factor the superior would have to consider is whether, if one offence has been proven, there might be further offences from the past waiting to be discovered. Experience would tell us that this is the case far more often than not, and a superior should be very slow to believe that only one single offence has occurred. Furthermore, repeated offences can turn even a more minor offence into a more serious one, e.g. repeatedly, despite warnings, placing one's hands on children's shoulders in a way that makes them feel uncomfortable.

The rates of re-offending in sexual crimes are very high, especially in crimes against minors. There were too many cases in the past where a bishop or religious leader was moved by the tears of repentance of an offender and re-appointed, only to see a further offence soon after. Because of this long history, the church must today give crystal clear evidence that it has decisively broken away from this practice.

Supervision can give no guarantees. It is possible to put such a person in a job where there is good supervision while at work, but it is virtually impossible to provide supervision at night time and weekends.

Indeed, the problem does not ultimately lie in the work the person does, but in being able to dress as a priest or religious and use titles such as 'Father', 'Brother' or 'Reverend'. If one compares two people with an equal inclination to offend against minors, a priest or religious and another person, the priest or religious is more likely to offend because of three things the other person does not have: the priest or religious will have greater *access* to potential victims; the potential victim will have a greater *trust* in the priest or religious than in the other person; and the priest or religious will have a *spiritual authority* over the potential victim that the other person does not have.

In brief, the priest or religious has a *privileged access* to victims that the other does not, and this privileged access comes from the clerical or religious clothes worn and the titles of 'Reverend' etc. These factors are far more important than the particular work the person carries out. It is this privileged access that must be taken away from a serious offender.

THE NEEDS OF VICTIMS

The church must realise that, if it reappoints *any* serious offender to a position of trust in ministry, *all* victims, and not just the victim in the particular case, can feel that their pain is not being taken seriously, and can feel abused all over again.

THE NATURE OF TRUST

It is a special and sacred trust that is given to priests and religious. If it is abused in a serious manner and then given back to the same person, the trust given to *all* priests and religious is lessened and harmed. I believe that priests and religious must accept that there can be only one chance at a trust as sacred as that given to them. They cannot seriously demand a second granting of trust when, through abuse of that trust, they have harmed a victim, every other priest and religious, the whole church community and the message of Jesus Christ himself.

Sexual abuse would always cause serious damage to the church. But if, when the very first cases came to light, the church had responded decisively, compassionately and openly, the damage done would have been far less. The main complaints were of cover-up, denial, placing priests and religious above victims and moving them from one assignment to another. If trust in *all* priests and religious is to be restored, then it is precisely in these areas that the church must now clearly and openly change its ways.

USEFUL MINISTRY

All ministry must be useful to the community. Canon 1740 of the Code of Canon Law provides that 'When the ministry of any parish priest has for some reason become harmful or at least ineffective, even though this occurs without any serious fault on his part, he can be removed from the parish by the diocesan bishop.' It surely follows, with even stronger force, that a ministry should be taken away when it is through serious fault that it has become harmful or at least ineffective. There can be no doubt about the fact that these conditions apply after any sexual offence against a minor, even a 'one-off' offence. Parents will always react strongly against a person known to have offended against a minor, so it is impossible to see how such a priest or religious could ever exercise an effective ministry, no matter how reformed the person may be.

While the abuse of a pastoral relationship with an adult might not arouse the same level of passion, the community would still consider it unacceptable.

STATE LAW

In most countries a person with a criminal conviction for a sexual crime against a minor is a 'prohibited person' for any form of employment that involves children and will be considered in law to be an 'unacceptable risk'. Leaving aside all other considerations mentioned above, this fact alone means that priests and religious with a criminal conviction cannot be given positions that involve access to children. Indeed, even when there is no criminal conviction but the bishop or religious superior knows that an offence has occurred, the same rule must apply.

A person with a criminal conviction for smuggling drugs across national boundaries will not be able to travel to most countries again, even though the offence was a relatively small one and the person is now a reformed and model citizen. A person with a criminal conviction, no matter how minor, cannot stand for parliament, even though now the most upright of persons. A police officer who is convicted of a crime, no matter how minor, must leave the force and no amount of repentance or good behaviour will set this aside. These laws may be 'blunt instruments' that can be harsh for particular cases, but the community sees the wisdom in them. It surely follows that a person guilty of serious non-consensual sex cannot be given back any form of privileged access to potential victims.

If a bishop or religious leader appoints such a person to a position of ministry, no matter how overwhelming the proofs may be of change and reform, and the priest or religious offends again, the superior may well end up in prison, there will be massive punitive damages and the whole church will be harmed.

It was for all these reasons that the bishops and religious leaders of Australia made the promise that 'Serious offenders will not be given back the power they have abused'.[11]

These criteria will still leave a number of cases to which the answer is not certain. The acid test I suggest to any bishop or religious superior is this: 'Would I be prepared to stand up in front of the congregation, tell them, honestly and fully, the facts of the case and then ask them whether they are willing to accept this priest.' If the bishop or superior is not prepared to do this, the priest should not be appointed.

Meditation

Sexual abuse is a bulldozer gouging a road through the fragile ecosystem of love and meaning that a person has been painfully constructing.

It is in the abuse of minors more than anywhere else that one learns that sex is never trivial, for it impacts on the deepest being of a person, on the very concept of who one is.

In sexual abuse there is always spiritual harm, for the abuse always harms the person's sense of wholeness and connectedness, and hence the person's sense of meaning and identity.

Sexual abuse by a direct representative of a religious belief destroys the answers that the belief has given up to that point. The link between the minister and the god can be impossible to break and it can easily seem as though the very god is the abuser. The search for perfect love within that system of belief can become impossible.

Spiritual healing means helping a person to be whole again and to find a new world of meaning, a new set of satisfying answers to the basic questions of life, and this means a new set of persons, objects, activities and ideas that can be loved.

The journey will be slow and the path followed by individuals will be very personal. We must seek to assist each of them along the path they have chosen, no matter how different it is from our own path.

We must never try to impose a duty to forgive but, if the time is right, we can assist people to leave behind, to let be, and even to seek change and growth in the offender.

In all its horror, sexual abuse can actually become the catalyst that produces a better church, the only force in the church powerful enough to bring about necessary change. If we are willing, it can be for us a "dark grace, a severe mercy".

FOOTNOTES

[1] The phrase comes from the psychologist Robert Grant, who ten years ago helped me greatly in my own response to abuse and to whom I owe a serious debt of gratitude. He is the author of the books *Healing the Soul of the Church, Ministers Facing their own Childhood Abuse and Trauma,* and *The Way of the Wound, A Spirituality of Trauma and Transformation.*

[2] This is one of the meanings of 'to forgive' given by dictionaries, e.g. 'cease to feel resentment against'.

[3] See the entry *aphiemi* in *Theological Dictionary of the New Testament,* Ed. Gerhard Kittel and Gerhard Friedrich, abridged in one volume by Geoffrey W Bromley, The Paternoster Press, Exeter, UK, 1985, p.88.

[4] Simon and Shuster, New York, 1993, p.46.

[5] This was a statement made to me by a victim and published here with permission.

[6] *The Tablet,* 27 June 1998, pp.841-842.

[7] French *perdonner,* Italian *perdonare,* Spanish *perdonar,* German *vergeben.* While these languages owe much to Greek and Latin, in this word they reflect Christian history more than their usual Greek and Latin origins. While Latin has the word *condonare,* the more usual word for 'to forgive' is *veniam dare,* meaning 'to grant a mercy or favour'.

[8] *The Tablet,* loc. cit.

[9] *An Australian Story: Sandy Macgregor,* shown on the ABC channel 2 on Thursday 19th July 2001.

[10] Frances Lawrence, *What does* forgiveness mean?, The Tablet, 14 July 2001, p.1016.

[11] *Towards Healing, Principles and procedures in responding to complaints of abuse against personnel of the Catholic Church in Australia,* December 1996, revised in December 2000, no.27.

Chapter Twelve

The Prison
of the Past

After four chapters concerning teaching on moral questions (what we should do), I now turn to teaching on the beliefs of the church (what we should believe).

The Freedom to be Wrong

In this field I believe that the Catholic Church is in a prison. It was not evil people who put it in this prison. No, it constructed the prison for itself, locked itself in and threw away the key. That prison is the prison of not being able to be wrong.

One of the rights I treasure most greatly in my life is my right to be wrong. I absolutely demand this right. I demand the right to be wrong one hundred times a day, in big things and small things. I demand the right to say, 'Sorry, I was mistaken. Sorry, I did not understand. Sorry, I acted without sufficient thought. Sorry, I was insensitive.' I could surrender many other rights and still live a satisfying life, but I could not survive a single day without the right to be wrong.

Far too often the Catholic Church has believed that it had such a level of divine guidance that it did not need the right to be wrong. As a result, both theologically and psychologically it can be bound to decisions of the past. It can be unable to move forwards, even when clear evidence emerges that earlier decisions were conditioned by their own time and that the arguments for them are not as strong as they were once thought to be. It has not been able to face the idea that on important issues and for centuries of time it might have been wrong.

I have been re-reading some statements of earlier centuries that, for either theological or psychological reasons, the Catholic Church does not believe it can change. Among them I find some that interpret the bible in too literal or too legal a manner. I find interpretations of the bible that I believe should be revised in the light of more recent knowledge of biblical meaning. I find statements that take a text of the bible out of its context in a manner that is not legitimate. I find statements that canonise a particular system of philosophy in a way that is not possible. I find statements that are not sufficiently aware that human words are inadequate carriers of divine truth. I find in places a psychological inability to admit ignorance or error.

In addition, there is the whole mixed history of the Catholic Church over two thousand years. I have long had a difficulty with the idea that I must give 'submission of mind and will' to the *words* of a pope, even non-infallible ones, but *deeds* throughout history that were far from the mind of Jesus Christ seem to be brushed aside. Surely we cannot separate words and deeds in this manner. Surely deeds speak more powerfully than words. Is it not the entire history of the church that we must look at and ask ourselves whether we are once again locking ourselves in a prison of the past if we say that this past must determine our future?

This need to be right at all times and in all matters, or at least to seem to be right, has been a major cause of the poor response to abuse within the church, so it cannot be left out of this book. I strongly believe that the future health of the church depends upon its being set free from the prison of the past. Only then can the church as a whole have the freedom to grow.

The question must be asked: can the Catholic Church definitively leave behind the prison of the past unless two changes are made:

1. Should binding statements be limited strictly to those truths that are essential to the identity of the church?
2. Should a later church authority, including a later universal church council, have the power to change the teachings of an earlier and equal church authority, including an earlier universal church council.?

Truths Essential to Identity

I have already mentioned the ancient saying that in necessary matters there must be unity, in doubtful matters there must be freedom and in all matters there must be love.[1]

In the Catholic Church there are necessary matters, that is, truths that are essential to the identity of the Christian church, e.g. 'Jesus was a real person who lived on this earth.' A person who does not believe that someone called Jesus once lived on this earth can hardly be called a member of the church. If a church community did not have even this belief in common, it would not be a community. If the members of a church could believe whatever they wished to believe, the church would lose all coherence and identity and would no longer be able to help people.

On the other hand, every truth declared necessary creates a serious obligation and such obligations should not be multiplied without very good cause.

The history of Creeds within the church shows both sides of this dilemma. On the one hand, they were seen as necessary so that the church would have a clear identity and would be a true community of people who shared common beliefs and values. On the other hand, bitter battles occurred in their formulation, wars were later fought over them and, rather than a means of building community, they sometimes became a means of excluding people from the church, persecuting them and even burning them at the stake.

In reading again some of the history of the fourth and fifth centuries, I have found myself constantly asking, 'How could mere human beings claim such certainty concerning the inner life of God or the exact manner in which Jesus was both human and divine? Did the bitter conflicts that occurred cause them to turn questions into answers, speculation about the divine into dogmas? Is there not a point, quite early in this speculation, at which we should bow before the mystery of God rather than attempt to spell it out in poor human words?'

The overriding principle must surely be that freedom should prevail, so the necessary statements should be strictly limited to those truths that are quite essential to the identity of the church.

In other words, freedom should prevail, not just in doubtful matters, but in all matters that, whether they are doubtful or certain, are not essential to the identity of the church. One of the problems of the past was that, whenever a truth was considered certain, it was automatically considered to be essential, and this must be queried. The ancient saying I have quoted could be revised to read, 'In essential matters unity, in non-essential matters freedom and in all matters love.'

The question then becomes one of finding the balance between the necessity of having clear statements of the beliefs that are essential to the identity of the church and the need not to place more obligations on individuals than is absolutely essential. It would take the collective wisdom of the entire church, working closely with the Spirit, to find this balance. All I can do here is give an example of each of the two types of question that can arise: a) a belief that is not essential to the identity of the Christian church; b) a belief that is essential in its core, but some non-core details are not essential.

A BELIEF THAT IS NOT ESSENTIAL

On 1st November 1950 Pope Pius XII declared infallibly that, at the end of her life, Mary, the mother of Jesus, was assumed bodily into heaven.[2] One must surely ask whether it was wise and prudent to make an authoritative statement on this matter. Does it belong in the category of essential matters on which unity is necessary? The authoritative nature of the papal statement certainly placed it in this category. For a Catholic, a denial of the Assumption became a denial of the Catholic faith, so it became a very real and powerful obligation. If any persons believed everything else in the Catholic faith but denied the truth of the Assumption, they were considered as outside the Catholic Church, no longer part of it.[3]

If Jesus Christ never existed, the Christian faith would cease to exist. But if Mary was not assumed bodily into heaven, the essentials of the Christian faith would appear to remain intact. So was it wise and prudent to create such a serious obligation concerning it? Should people be perfectly free to believe in the Assumption, but not bound to do so under pain of being excluded from the church?

There are many statements in the teachings of the church that come into this category of teachings 'not essential to the identity of the church', and one must ask whether so many obligations should be created concerning them without strict necessity.

DETAILS THAT ARE NOT ESSENTIAL

The Nicene Creed includes the words 'he ascended into heaven' and this has always been part of the faith of the church. The gospel of Luke (24:51) and the Acts of the Apostles (1:9-11), written by the same author, give a description of this event. There might seem to be nothing more to discuss.

Nevertheless, we must make a distinction. At the end of his time on earth, Jesus returned to his Father. This is an essential part of Christian faith, for, if Jesus did not return to his Father, we would have to query whether he had come from his Father in the first place, and this would place many essential truths in jeopardy. However, did he return to his Father by means of his physical body ascending in a vertical direction from the earth up into the heavens? This is not nearly as certain and is not essential to the Christian faith. If Jesus returned to his Father by some less spectacular means, the Christian faith would appear to remain intact.

There is only one writer (Luke) who speaks of the body of Jesus being seen to ascend from the earth towards the heavens. Neither Mark nor Matthew nor John speaks of this. The writers of the bible preferred concrete rather than abstract language and their concrete language was often pictorial (they 'talked in pictures'). If Luke were alive today, he might be surprised to hear that many modern people took his image so literally.

Hence it would seem more prudent to place this question of the exact manner in which Jesus returned to his father in the category where freedom reigns. People would be free to believe that Jesus ascended bodily from the earth in a vertical direction, but would not be bound to do so, as long as they believed that he returned to his Father.

There are many other statements in the Christian faith where we must distinguish between those parts that express essential religious truths and those parts that do not. Indeed, this is a question we need to ask concerning every religious statement.

A Hierarchy of Non-essential Beliefs

If the church decided to base itself on a system of statements 'essential to the identity of the Christian faith', there would still be a need for many statements that commented on non-essential aspects of the Christian faith in order to inform, explain, educate or edify.

Whether one wished it or not, there would in fact be a hierarchy of authority in such statements. For example, the statement of a universal church council would have more authority than the statement of a local bishop or priest. This would, however, refer only to the attitude of mind with which an individual should approach the document. It would not change the fact that, while the statement represented the particular authority's best endeavour to express religious truth, it was not a statement of essential beliefs and the individual was free to accept its contents or not.

There are two opposing dangers in this situation. For church authorities there is always the danger of having so intense a desire to see the entire church sharing the same beliefs that some binding authority is claimed for the statement. If a church gives in to this temptation, it opens the door to multitudinous levels of authority of documents and to the constant desire to upgrade the authority of each level.

The danger for individuals is that of thinking that, apart from the essential beliefs, they are free to believe whatever they wish, to pick and choose the non-essential truths that suit them. However, one of the truly essential beliefs of the Christian faith is surely that in all matters and at all times we must seek God's truth and goodness. We are never free to believe whatever we wish, for we must always be seeking God's truth. This means that I will read the documents of church authorities with respect and openness, seeking to understand and accept any truths that I find there. The higher the authority, e.g. a universal church council, the greater the respect I will give to its documents. A document may have no authority to coerce my consent, but it can have the authority to demand my respect.

One Authority Changing Another

The second question that must be asked is whether, in order to leave behind the prison of the past, a later church authority, including a later universal church council, should have the power to change the teachings of an earlier and equal church authority, including an earlier universal church council.

Some Precedents

I am not without company in raising this question. I have already noted that in the fifth century, when Pope Leo the Great developed his theory of papal primacy, his ideas were accepted in the West, but there were serious reservations in the East and in Africa. Writing a few years before Leo, St. Augustine from Africa had said,

> 'The writings of bishops may be refuted both by the perhaps wiser words of anyone more experienced in the matter and by the weightier authority and more scholarly prudence of other bishops, and also by councils, if something in them perhaps has deviated from the truth; even councils held in particular regions or provinces must without quibbling give way to the authority of plenary councils of the whole Christian world; and even the earlier plenary councils are often corrected by later ones, if as a result of practical experience something that was closed is opened, something that was hidden becomes known.'[4]

One hundred and fifty years later Pope Pelagius II made a statement that had been drafted by a deacon of his household who, on his death, became Pope Gregory the Great. The document said:

> 'Dear brethren, do you think that when Peter was reversing his position, one should have replied: We refuse to hear what you are saying since you previously taught the opposite? In the matter [now under discussion] one position was held while truth was being sought, and a different position was adopted after truth had been found. Why should a change of position be thought a crime....? For what is reprehensible is not changing one's mind, but being fickle in one's views. If the mind remains unwavering in seeking to know what is right, why should you object when it abandons its ignorance and reformulates its views?'[5]

I have already noted that, in the eleventh century, the Eastern half of the church objected to the introduction of the *filioque* clause into the Creed on the grounds that the Western half of the church alone had changed a creed determined by a council of the universal church. In saying this, they accepted that a later universal council could change a creed determined by an earlier universal council.

At the time of the Reformation, the reformers felt the need to go back to the idea of teaching that could be revised and amended in the light of developing knowledge of the sources of our religious knowledge.

Taken together, these are authorities that must be treated with respect.

PASTOR AETERNUS

In 1870 the First Vatican Council proclaimed the primacy of jurisdiction and infallible teaching function of the pope in a document entitled *Pastor Aeternus*.

As mentioned earlier, the document relied heavily on the statement of Jesus to Peter in Mt.16:17-19 ('You are Peter and on this rock...'), though without referring to the closely connected failure of Peter in the following verses (21-23) or to the giving of the power to bind and loose to 'the disciples' in Mt.18:18.

It also gave great doctrinal and legal weight to two other gospel sayings of Jesus:

> 'And after his resurrection, Jesus conferred upon Peter alone the jurisdiction of supreme shepherd and ruler over His whole flock in the words: 'Feed my lambs.... Feed my sheep.' (Jn.21:15,17).[6]

> 'Indeed it was this apostolic doctrine that all the Fathers held, and the holy orthodox Doctors reverenced and followed, fully realising that this See of Saint Peter always remains untainted by any error, according to the divine promise of our Lord and Saviour made to the Prince of His disciples: 'But I have prayed for you that your faith may not fail; and when you have turned again, strengthen your brethren'.' (Lk.22:32).[7]

It must surely be queried whether these two gospel sayings can be made to bear so heavy a doctrinal and legal weight, that is, whether, in and of themselves alone, the two sayings prove the conclusions drawn from them.

The argument the council derived from the world around and within us was simply that of the need to preserve the faith 'genuine and pure', and hence of the need to have a mechanism to ensure unity of faith. In itself, however, this says nothing about what that mechanism should be.

For the rest, the document relies on an appeal to tradition. A major problem with the arguments on this ground is contained in the introduction to the section on infallibility.

> 'Moreover, this Holy See has always held, the perpetual practice of the Church confirms, and the Ecumenical Councils, *especially those in which the Western and Eastern Churches were united in faith and love*, have declared that the supreme power of teaching is also included in this apostolic primacy...'[8]

One must go so far as to say that it is quite disingenuous to claim that the Eastern Churches ever affirmed papal infallibility. This is simply not true, and the three councils quoted by *Pastor Aeternus* demonstrate this.

THE FOURTH COUNCIL OF CONSTANTINOPLE

The Fourth Council of Constantinople (869-870) is controversial to this day because it is claimed to be ecumenical by the West but not by the East. In the time before the council the pope and the patriarch of Constantinople, Photius, were in dispute over whether the missionary territory of Bulgaria should be subject to Rome or Constantinople. The pope sent bishops to Bulgaria and this so incensed Photius that he called his own council in 867 and actually excommunicated the pope and called on the emperor of the West to depose him. The pope reacted by convoking a new council, Constantinople IV. When the papal legates arrived for this council they presented three papal demands: that the council limit itself to confirming the decision already made in Rome that Photius be deposed, that no bishop consecrated by Photius be allowed to be part of the council, and that all other bishops be allowed to take their seat only if they signed a profession of faith prepared by the pope. It is from this profession of faith imposed by

the pope that the First Vatican Council quotes, not from any delibera-
tions of the council itself. A new patriarch, Ignatius, was appointed
and he was ordered by the pope not to send missionaries to Bulgaria,
but he consecrated ten bishops for that territory soon after the papal
legates had left. The pope threatened him over a period of time and
eventually sent two legates with power to depose him, but they arrived
to find that Ignatius had been dead for a year and his place re-taken
by none other than Photius himself! In this whole story there is little
that is edifying and there was much use of vituperative language on
both sides. To call the Fourth Council of Constantinople a council
'in which the Western and Eastern Churches were united in faith and
love' is hardly accurate.[9]

THE SECOND COUNCIL OF LYONS

The second council quoted, the Second Council of Lyons (1274), is
equally problematic. *Pastor Aeternus* says that 'with the approval of
the Second Council of Lyons, the Greeks professed that.....' In fact,
however, the quotation that follows comes neither from the council
nor from 'the Greeks', but from one individual. It is usually called 'The
Profession of Faith of Michael Palaeologus'. The Byzantine emperor,
Michael VIII, had retaken the city of Constantinople after the Fourth
Crusade, but faced many enemies. For political rather than religious
reasons, he wanted an alliance with the pope and was prepared to make
any concession to obtain it. He wrote a letter to the council in which
he incorporated a profession of faith written by Pope Clement IV. The
letter was not 'approved' by the council, nor even discussed, but simply
read out. That it was not the faith of 'the Greeks' was quickly shown
by the serious troubles the emperor experienced from his own subjects
when he tried to enforce the letter. The elderly patriarch Joseph declared that he would prefer death and the ruin of the Greek Church to
union with the Latins. Michael VIII was refused Christian burial by
his own subjects, and his son Andronic formally repudiated the letter
as soon as he came to power. Once again, talk of 'unity in faith and
love' is misplaced.[10]

THE COUNCIL OF FLORENCE

The third council quoted, the Council of Florence (1441-45), is the council that began its life as the Council of Basel (1431-37). At this council a serious attempt was made at reunion between East and West. At least on this occasion the document quoted in *Pastor Aeternus* was produced by the council itself. More pragmatic considerations , however, were also present, for Constantinople had by this time become a Christian island in a Muslim sea, and the emperor, patriarch and people of that city were desperate to have the support of the entire Western world in their battle against the powerful forces of Islam. Historians are divided on the question of how genuine and free the members of the Eastern Church were at this council. In the period immediately after the council there were serious divisions among its members and union did not survive the fall of Constantinople to the Turkish forces in 1453, a mere eight years after the council ended. In the West the council served to confirm the superiority of pope over council.[11]

Furthermore, none of the quotations attributed to the three councils can be said to affirm the personal infallibility of the bishop of Rome, for they were documents about primacy rather than about infallibility. There is no basis whatsoever for claiming that 'the Greeks', the members of the Eastern Churches, would have accepted infallibility if this question had been specifically raised.

THE SOURCES AND THE TOOL

It must always be remembered that councils are *tools*, not *sources*. So even a far clearer and more consistent tradition than that quoted in *Pastor Aeternus* would not add up to proof of papal infallibility unless it showed a far more substantial grounding in scripture and the world around us. Indeed, the First Vatican Council itself denied that papal infallibility involves a direct revelation to the pope.

> 'For the Holy Spirit was not promised to the successors of Peter that they might disclose a new doctrine by His revelation, but rather, that, with His assistance, they might jealously guard and faithfully explain the revelation or deposit of faith that was handed down through the apostles.'[12]

I understand this to imply the claim that the pope is not divinely inspired to reveal a new truth, and hence is not a third *source* of our knowledge of God, but is assisted by God not to make mistakes in applying the *tool* of discernment to the two sources of the bible and the world around us.

If this is so, one would expect that the arguments based on the sources would prove the conclusion that was drawn from them. One might further expect that nowhere would we find more cogent arguments in favour of papal infallibility than in the document which solemnly proclaimed it. The lack of cogency in the arguments given in *Pastor Aeternus* is, therefore, quite startling. The argument from scripture places too much doctrinal and legal weight on a few gospel texts and assumes perfect knowledge in Jesus. The argument from the world around us proves only the need to have a mechanism to ensure agreement on essential matters, but says nothing about what that mechanism should be. The arguments from tradition have an inadequate basis in scripture, do not affirm a constant and universal belief of East and West, and stop short of personal infallibility.

Despite its statement that infallibility involves no new revelation, it appears obvious that the First Vatican Council, in drawing its conclusions concerning papal infallibility, relied above all on the solemnity of the pronouncement of the council itself. But at this point the tool has become the source.

ASSUMING WHAT IS PROCLAIMED

Reliance on the solemn pronouncement of a council, in the absence of cogent arguments from the two sources, also seems to assume the truth it proclaims. How can a pope infallibly proclaim papal infallibility unless we assume in advance that the pope is infallible? To answer that it was not the pope who proclaimed this, but a solemn council, seems to do no more than move the question one step sideways, for how can a council infallibly declare the infallibility of the pope unless we assume in advance that the council was infallible?

The First Vatican Council was acting out of a very particular situation that had arisen in Europe in general (the Enlightenment, the French Revolution, liberalism) and Italy in particular (Italian unity and the abolition of the papal states in central Italy) in the nineteenth century, and out of the reaction of church leaders to these events. In the long development of papal power, was infallibility the step too far that created a crisis for the church? In the time since then, has the church been living through that crisis? Is there now a need to reassess what happened in 1870?

DISCERNMENT AND INFALLIBILITY

THE TIME OF WRITING

Each of the books of the bible reflects the time and place in which it was written and the personal traits of the writers. In studying any part of the bible, we must go back to the history of the times, the laws and customs of the age and the literary form in which the book was written. In the same way, it is impossible to conduct a church council in a vacuum. Any council will reflect the problems and address the issues of its own age. It will do so according to prevailing philosophies, social values and needs. It will use words according to the meanings they have at the time the council is held. It will work from the knowledge of the bible, what has been handed on and the world around and within us that people have at that time. With the passage of time the problems, issues, philosophies and social values will change and the meaning of words will change. Knowledge of the bible, what has been handed on and the world around us will develop, such that a later generation can clearly see that an earlier generation based itself on quite inadequate understandings of the bible and the world around it. For these reasons alone, is there not an obvious danger of a church putting itself into a prison if it claims an eternal validity for the statements of a pope or council?

HUMAN AND DIVINE IN A COUNCIL

There is both human and divine in the bible and we are never excused from the serious and difficult work of separating the two. Should we not expect the same confusion and conflict between the human and the divine in the church today? Both the bible and church history are the story of a journey as people struggled towards truth. Is it likely that God would now adopt a quite different plan by giving certain answers to most questions through church authorities? Both in the bible and in church history God placed the emphasis on search and responsibility leading to growth. Is it likely that God would now place the accent on certainty and obedience?

CLAIMS OF DIVINE GUIDANCE

Claiming an eternal validity for statements means to claim a level of divine guidance for each single statement that cannot be assumed but must be proven. It appears to be based on the attitude that God could not allow the church to be mistaken on matters seen to be important. Surely we must query whether we really have this level of knowledge of how God operates. Is it not possible that God has permitted church authorities to err in order to break down the trust in human beings that would always be a temptation to the church?

THE KNOWLEDGE OF JESUS

At a time when we are coming to realise that Jesus himself might have given up the privilege of perfect knowledge and have had to struggle through his life and mission with only limited knowledge, should we not be looking again at claims which imply that the church has access to a level of knowledge that even Jesus might not have had access to?

BALANCING THE BIBLE, THE WORLD AND THE TRADITIONS

In an earlier chapter I said that there are two sources of religious knowledge, the bible and the world around and within us, and there is a body of statements that comes from the history of the attempts to understand and apply these two sources. I said that we must test each of these three against the other two. One must ask whether the claim that the statements of a council are unchangeable frustrates this process, allowing of no development in our understanding of the bible or of the world around and within us. Does it, in practice, place the *tool* above the two *sources*? Can this ever be justified? Whenever the statements of authority go beyond the arguments that can be adduced to prove them, is that authority going too close to setting itself up as a third *source*?

DISCONTINUITIES

To think that the people of past generations were ignorant and that we are vastly superior to them is arrogance. But to think that the past was always right is surely just as dangerous, for we have a far better knowledge of the *sources* of our knowledge of God than the people of the past had available to them.

In an earlier chapter I quoted a list of 'discontinuities for the sake of a greater continuity'. When all of these are taken together, it seems logical to conclude that the Second Vatican Council believed that it could change teachings that, though never solemnly defined in a council, had been almost universally held for more than a thousand years.

A Pastoral Council

Of course councils produce truth, but is it eternal and unchangeable truth, or is it, even with divine assistance, the best possible truth a particular council is capable of within the limits that surround any human endeavour?

The Second Vatican Council

I wonder if the Catholic Church realised something of this truth at the time of the Second Vatican Council (1962-65), for it determined that this would be a 'pastoral' and not a 'dogmatic' council. I believe that this gave a freedom to the discussions that the council might otherwise not have had. At the time it was held, its wisdom was the best possible wisdom of the present, at least within the time limits imposed on it. To what extent this wisdom will later come to be seen as an authentic expression of the wisdom of the past, time alone will tell. A later council may quote some passages of Vatican II with approval, rewrite others and abandon others.[13] It is good that this freedom will exist and it does not mean that this council was lacking in wisdom or that it should have less authority than other councils.

Christian Unity

There is a further consideration. In discussions between different churches in recent decades it has become evident that there are many people belonging to other Christian churches who would seriously consider the idea of a Peter-figure in a future united church, but categorically reject the full claims of the Catholic Church on this matter. Is it not clear that the church has a choice between Christian unity and these claims, but it cannot have both, not now and, with overwhelming probability, not at any time in the future?

Thus we may ask whether the idea that a later council should be able to change the statements of an earlier council is a safer basis on which to face the third millennium. Does it better reflect the humility we should always have in approaching the divine?

Particular Issues

Are there a number of important issues where serious questions have been raised, but the prison of the past makes it difficult or even impossible to have an open and intelligent discussion? Do the following matters come into this category?

N.B. In what follows the examples given (original sin, the assumption etc.) are the occasions for the question, but the real question in each case concerns the authority behind the statements. They are different occasions for looking at the authority of a pope or council.

Original Sin

The Catholic Church teaches that the first human beings existed in a state 'of holiness and justice'.

> 'The Church, interpreting the symbolism of biblical language in an authoritative way, in the light of the New Testament and Tradition, teaches that our first parents, Adam and Eve, were constituted in an original `state of holiness and justice'. This grace of original holiness was `to share in... divine life'.'

> 'By the radiance of this grace all dimensions of man's life were confirmed. As long as he remained in the divine intimacy, man would not have to suffer or die. The inner harmony of the human person, the harmony between man and woman, and finally the harmony between the first couple and all creation, comprised the state called `original justice'.'[14]

The Catholic Church then teaches that human beings fell from this original state of holiness and justice through the sin of Adam and Eve. The Council of Trent says,

> 'If anyone does not profess that Adam, the first man, by transgressing God's commandment in paradise, at once lost the

holiness and justice in which he had been constituted; and that...
he drew upon himself.... death with which God had threatened
him.... let him be anathema.

'If anyone asserts that Adam's sin harmed only him and not his
descendants, and that the holiness and justice received from God
which he lost was lost only for him and not for us also; or that....
he transmitted to all mankind only death and the sufferings of the
body but not sin as well...... let him be anathema.

'If anyone asserts that this sin of Adam, which is one in origin and
is transmitted by propagation, not by imitation.... can be taken
away by the powers of human nature..... let him be anathema.[15]

Two things have happened since the Council of Trent made these
statements. The first is that we have come to realise that what we know
about Adam and Eve comes from a *story*, not an eyewitness account of
what happened. The Catechism of the Catholic Church makes allowance for this by saying that the account uses figurative language.

'The account of the fall in Genesis 3 uses figurative language, but
affirms a primeval event, a deed that took place *at the beginning of
the history of man*. Revelation gives us the certainty of faith that
the whole of human history is marked by the original fault freely
committed by our first parents'[16].

The second thing that has happened is that through scientific discov-
ery we have been made aware that the development of the human race
was slower and more complicated than the biblical story of Adam and
Eve allows for. Pope John Paul II has said:

'Taking into account the state of scientific research at the time, as
well as the requirements of theology, the Encyclical *Humani Generis*
considered the doctrine of 'evolutionism' a serious hypothesis,
worthy of investigation and in-depth study equal to that of the
opposite hypothesis.... Today, almost half a century after the
publication of the Encyclical, new knowledge has led to the
recognition in the theory of evolution of more than a hypothesis.
It is indeed remarkable that this theory has been progressively
accepted by researchers, following a series of discoveries in
various fields of knowledge. The convergence, neither sought nor
fabricated, of the results of work that was conducted independently
is in itself a significant argument in favour of this theory.'[17]

Without wishing to go further than Pope John Paul and turn something 'more than a hypothesis' into proven fact, it can still surely be said that it does not seem wise to base religious belief on the idea that a state of original justice and innocence once existed and that the whole human race fell from this state through the actions of the first hominoids to possess some beginnings of a sense of self-consciousness and moral responsibility, whatever their names (if they had any). There is an obvious problem in claiming that death did not exist until this fall had occurred.

The question of the origin of evil in the world is a profound one, deserving of lengthy and serious consideration, but there have always been problems with the story of Adam and Eve as an adequate explanation of this problem.[18]

The story of Adam and Eve is part of a longer story of human beings making progress in technology and culture, but not always making the same progress in morality[19]. The *stories* of creation, Adam and Eve, Cain and Abel, the Flood and the Tower of Babel must be seen as parts of the one story. The answer of God to this story was not final punishment and destruction, but the call of Abram and the beginning of salvation history.[20]

Surely some questions can be asked:

i) Is it proven fact that the account of the fall in Genesis 3, while using figurative language, affirms 'a primeval event, a deed that took place *at the beginning of the history of man*'? What is the proof and where does it come from?

ii) In the light of all we have learned about the origins of human beings, is it safe to base religious belief on such an affirmation?

iii) Does revelation give us 'the certainty of faith that the whole of human history is marked by the original fault freely committed by our first parents'?

iv) Is it a safe opinion to believe that death did not exist before the fall of our first parents?

v) Do the statements in no.390 of the Catechism of the Catholic Church destroy the balance between the bible, what has been handed on and the world around us? In that catechism does what has been handed on both determine what the bible is saying and deny the relevance of what we have learned from the world around us?

vi) Can the concept of original sin be retained without a complete revision of our understanding?

There are many and serious questions here for the church to talk about, but do they not need the freedom of life outside of a prison in order to do so?

A 'Tradition' Outside The Bible

I have already mentioned the idea of truths handed down from Jesus himself outside the bible. The Council of Trent was less than crystal clear on this topic.[21] The Second Vatican Council did much to raise the profile of the bible within the Catholic Church and there is universal agreement that it made lasting changes to the *balance* between the bible and what has been handed on within that church. And yet this is one more example of where that council moved away from the past but did not find a clear statement to replace older statements, leaving us with compromise and even contradiction.

The basic questions are:

i) Are there truths handed down from Jesus himself to the church outside the bible?

ii) What are they?

iii) Do they meet the three tests of antiquity, universality and consensus applied with the same stringency as these tests were applied to many so-called 'gospels' in the first four centuries of the church's history?

iv) Can the statement of the Council of Trent on this subject be allowed to stand?

The Ordination of Women

I have not been impressed by the arguments put forward to claim that women cannot be ordained to the priesthood, so whenever I mention bishops or priests in this book, I do not assume that they will be exclusively male forever, and I hope that the language I use reflects this.

This is particularly true if one again asks whether it is proven fact that Jesus acted with perfect knowledge and authority at the Last Supper, laying down eternal and divine rules for the church. Nevertheless, my direct concern here is solely with the power of popes and councils to make statements that can never be changed.

On 22 May 1994 Pope John Paul II published a document in which he said that 'the Church has no authority whatsoever to confer priestly ordination on women.' He added that 'this judgment is to be definitively held by all Christ's faithful', but did not use the word 'infallible'. However, a subsequent 'Reply to a Doubt' from the Prefect of the Congregation for the Doctrine of the Faith, Cardinal Joseph Ratzinger, did claim that the question had been decided 'infallibly'. As a consequence it was said that Catholics were not free to discuss a question that had been infallibly decided once and for all.

These statements raise many questions concerning the requirements for infallibility. In particular, does a teaching become infallible simply because it has been repeated over a long time? The cardinal quoted the constant teaching of the bishops over the centuries, but the bishops of today were not consulted on this matter, either by the pope or by the cardinal.

The fundamental questions appear to be:

i) In appealing to tradition, is it enough to quote the fact of a continuous teaching of the past, or is it also essential to carry out a rigorous analysis of that tradition in order to understand exactly what was being said and why?

ii) Before any statement is declared to be essential to the identity of the church, should we always look again at what the bible and the world around and within us have to say on the subject?

iii) If a pope can acquiesce in the calling of a statement infallible without reference to the college of bishops, what does it mean to say that the college of bishops is co-holder of supreme power within the church?

iv) Does the teaching on the ordination of women meet the essential requirements for an infallible statement?

THE ASSUMPTION

Earlier in this chapter I asked the question whether it had been *prudent* to make an infallible declaration on the Assumption of Mary. Here I ask the question whether it was *possible* to make an infallible declaration. The declaration of Pope Pius XII in 1950 expressly invoked infallibility and certainly fulfilled all the technical requirements for an infallible statement. [22]

The problem is that there is no evidence from the bible for the Assumption, the tradition does not go back to the event itself, and the arguments from the world around and within us are weak. These latter arguments are known as *decet* or 'it is fitting' arguments, and theologians know that they are the weakest of all arguments, for they presuppose that human beings know exactly what God would find fitting.

If someone were to ask me whether I believe in the Assumption, I would answer 'Yes'. If I were asked why, I would answer 'Because that is what my mother told me as a child and I have always believed it.' If I were asked whether I could prove that she was assumed into heaven, I would answer, 'Can you prove that she was not? I have an ancient tradition and the common faith of the Catholic and Orthodox Churches behind my belief. What do you have behind your denial?'

In other words, I am free to believe in the Assumption and no one may forbid me to, for *faith* does not require binding proof. However, an *infallible declaration* is in a totally different category, for it does require overwhelming proof. Thus the question is not whether it is lawful to have *faith* that Mary was assumed into heaven, but whether the pope could *infallibly declare* that she was assumed into heaven. In short, the question concerns papal authority, not Mary.

The fundamental questions appear to be:

i) How strong are the arguments from the bible, what has been handed on and the world around and within us in favour of the Assumption of Mary?

ii) If the proofs are less than overwhelming, may a pope base an infallible statement on them?

BIRTH CONTROL

In fact and in practice, there has been no discussion of the morality of birth control since July 1968 when Pope Paul VI published his encyclical *Humanae Vitae*. Since that time all discussion has been about papal authority. To make progress on this question, do we need to turn the discussion back from authority to birth control and look at the arguments again in the light of both the First and Second Testament teaching on sex?

The fundamental questions appear to be:

i) Can questions of sexual morality be resolved on the basis of direct offences against God?

ii) There is both a unitive and a procreative element in marriage. But do both of these elements essentially belong, not just to marriage as an institution of the human race, but also to every marriage, no matter what the circumstances, and, indeed, to each and every act of intercourse within every marriage?

iii) Is the statement that both elements must be present in every act of intercourse more than an assertion? If so, what are the arguments that prove it?

THE SACRAMENT OF RECONCILIATION

In recent years there has been much discussion of the possibility of a general absolution of sins rather than individual confession. Some authorities in the church have said that this desire comes from a loss of the sense of sin by Catholic people, but surely we can argue that the extraordinarily large numbers of people who have attended ceremonies of general absolution show two things with crystal clarity: there is a widespread and strong sense of sin and of the need for forgiveness; and people want this forgiveness through the church. In their own way, the crowds have been a profound affirmation of the essentials of the church's tradition in this field, for they have been examples of people voting with their feet. To find out why fewer people are using individual confession today, we should look more closely at past defects of individual reconciliation.

The answer given by church authority to the request for general absolution is that the matter was decided once and for all by the Council of Trent when, interpreting John 20:22-23, it said that the priest in confession had the role of a judge and judges can not make a decision unless all the facts are placed before them, so only individual confession is lawful.[23] To a number of people this is too legal an interpretation of a non-legal text and they believe that the matter needs to be looked at again. In other words, they question the authority even of a solemn council.

It seems best to present the question in a broad form:

    i) Is the church's penitential tradition and discipline in harmony with the gospels in general and John 20:22-23 in particular?

INFALLIBILITY

I have already made comments on this question in discussing the First Vatican Council. Several questions arise:

    i) If we must assume infallibility in order to proclaim it infallibly, can it ever be a question that has been finally resolved and is beyond review?

    ii) If we stand outside the prison of the past and look again at the bible, what has been handed on and the world around us, is there convincing proof of infallibility?

    iii) Is infallibility a matter that is 'essential to the identity of the church'?

DIVORCE AND REMARRIAGE

Many Catholic bishops express a real uneasiness about the present teaching of their church on the subject of divorce and remarriage. They want to be faithful to the teaching of Jesus Christ, but after many years of pastoral practice, after much thought and prayer, they are not convinced that the current teachings of the Catholic Church on this subject fully reflect the mind of Jesus. Their conviction is not based on some novel interpretation of the words of the gospels, but on a lifetime of prayerful reflection concerning the kind of person Jesus was, the way he acted towards people and the manner in which he combined challenge and compassion.

However, the Council of Trent pronounced on this question and the official response is always that the question has been settled for all time and cannot even be discussed again.[24]

Some questions can be asked:

i) Is the teaching of the Catholic Church on divorce fully in harmony with the person of Jesus as revealed in the gospels? Is the particular tradition on divorce fully in harmony with the Great Tradition?

ii) Did Jesus replace one divine law on this subject with another divine law, or did he rather speak the language of moral imperative, that is, did he speak of what justice and love demand of people in the diverse situations that can arise when serious problems occur in a marriage?

iii) If it is maintained that Jesus replaced one law with another law, are there other cases of Jesus acting in this legal manner, or is this a unique case?

iv) Is remarriage after divorce a sin against God because one is disobeying a law laid down by Jesus, or is it to be seen in terms of whether the action constitutes an injustice against a partner and children and an offence against the good of the whole community?

v) Is the teaching of the Council of Trent so certain that the word 'infallible' can safely be attached to it?

vi) Is there a need for renewed discussion of these serious matters?

THE CERTAINTY OF FAITH

A provision that a later authority could overturn an earlier authority would not throw all Christian teaching into chaos and would not mean that all certainty was destroyed. No universal church council is going to change earlier councils without a very good reason for doing so. The idea that all statements of councils could be changed does not mean that all will be changed.

The Nicene Creed would remain basically as it is. There are only a few phrases in that Creed that might be considered in need of change.[25] There are also a few statements that some might consider adding to the creed, e.g. a statement of faith in the dignity of all people and in the goodness of the world God created and redeemed. On the other hand, we would need to be aware of the danger of opening up again something that caused so much controversy in the first place.

I would also see the Creed as too much a list of propositions to which intellectual consent is required and would wish to preface it by something that expresses faith as a response of love to a person and a story. In other words, we should first proclaim the Great Tradition before we proclaim particular traditions.

Meditation

The *Shemah*, the prayer that a good Jewish person says every morning and evening, expresses a response of love to God's invitation. Jesus adapted it by combining the first part of the *Shemah* (Deuteronomy 6:4-5) with Leviticus 19:18 in this fashion:

> Hear, O Israel: The Lord our God, the Lord is one.
> You shall love the Lord your God with all your heart,
> and with all your soul, and with all your mind,
> and with all your strength.
> And you shall love your neighbour as yourself.
> There is no other commandment greater than these.
> *Mk.12:29-31*

In a world in which we must use weak human words in our attempt to express the divine, this prayer is as close as we will ever come to a statement in human words of eternal and unchangeable truth. The thought it expresses should be at the heart of any Christian creed.

The promise of Jesus Christ was not that the church will never make mistakes, but that it will survive its mistakes, for the truth of Jesus Christ will always be present in the church – tarnished and even obscured, but always there to be rediscovered. The promise is that, in spite of many errors in detail, the church will be maintained in the basic truth of the Great Tradition, and that the ugliness in the church will never completely destroy its underlying beauty. The church's faith will often be weak, its love lukewarm, its hope wavering, but that on which its faith is based, its love is rooted and its hope is built will always endure. [26]

There is an absolute certainty of faith, but it is first and foremost a certainty in something that comes before words. It is faith in the person of Jesus Christ and in the love that fills his story.

FOOTNOTES

[1] *In necessariis unitas, in dubiis libertas, in omnibus caritas.*

[2] Pope Pius XII, Apostolic Constitution *Munificentissimus Deus*, 1 November 1950, DB, no.2331-2333.

[3] 'Therefore, if anyone should freely dare (may God prevent it) to deny or call in doubt that which has been defined by Us, let him know that he has completely defected from divine and Catholic faith.' *loc. cit.*, quoted from *The Christian Faith in the Doctrinal Documents of the Catholic Church*, Editors J. Neuner and J. Dupuis, Collins Liturgical Publications, London, 1983,

[4] St. Augustine, *De baptismo contra Donatistas*, Book III, ch.2.

[5] Quoted by Robert Markus, emeritus professor of history at Nottingham University, in a book review of the book *Papal Sin, Structures of Deceit* by Gary Wills, in *The Tablet*, 2nd September 2000.

[6] Neuner-Dupuis, *op.cit.*, no.836, p.233.

[7] *Op.cit.*, no.819, p.228.

[8] *Op.cit.*, no.831, p.232. The underlining is my own.

[9] For a detailed account of events before, during and after this council, see *Histoire des Conciles Oecumeniques*,Vol.IV, *Constantinople IV*, by Daniel Stiernon, Editions de L'Orante, Paris, 1967.

[10] See *Histoire des Conciles Oecumeniques*, Vol.VII, *Lyon I et Lyon II*, by Hans Wolter and Henri Holstein, Editions de L'Orante, Parish, 1966.

[11] See Joseph Gill, *The Council of Florence*, Cambridge University Press, 1959.

[12] *Op.cit.*, no.836, p.233.

[13] The different documents have already had quite different receptions. The document on the media has already been largely left behind, and it is generally recognised that there have been better documents since the council on religious life than the document produced by the council itself.

[14] *Catechism of the Catholic Church*, 1992, nos.375-376.

[15] The General Council of Trent, Fifth Session, Decree on Original Sin (1546), quoted from Neuner-Dupuis, *op.cit.*, pp.137-38.

[16] *Op.cit.*, no.390. The emphasis is from the original.

[17] Address to the members of the Pontifical Academy of Sciences, 22nd October 1996.

[18] To deny the historical reality of the Fall would have profound implications across much of theology, and yet to maintain its historical reality is full of problems. The recent statements of Cardinal Schoenborn raising queries about evolution must be seen in this context. For an overview of the question, see Douglas Farrow, *The Fall*, in *The Oxford Companion to Christian Thought*, edited by Adrian Hastings, Alistair Mason and Hugh Pyper, Oxford University Press, 2000, pp.233-234.

[19] See especially Gen.4:17-24:

[20] Gen.12:1

[21]The Council clearly perceives that this truth and rule are contained in the written books and unwritten traditions which have come down to us, having been received by the apostles from the mouth of Christ Himself or from the apostles by the dictation of the Holy spirit, and have been transmitted as it were from hand to hand."See Neuner-Dupuis, *op.cit.*, p.73. The First Vatican Council (1870) quoted verbatim from Trent.

[22] '... by the authority of Our Lord Jesus Christ, of the blessed apostles Peter and Paul, and by our own authority, we proclaim, declare and define as a dogma revealed by God: the Immaculate Mother of God, Mary ever Virgin, when the course of her earthly life was finished, was taken up body and soul into the glory of heaven. Wherefore, if anyone – which God forbid – should wilfully dare to deny or call in doubt what has been defined by us, let him know that he certainly has abandoned the divine and Catholic faith.' Pope Pius XII, *Munificentissimus Deus*, 1 November 1950, quoted from Neuner-Dupuis, *op.cit.*, p.207.

[23] 'For it is clear that without knowledge of the case priests could not exercise this judgement..... if penitents declared their sins only in general and not specifically and in particular.' The General Council of Trent, Fourteenth Session, Doctrine on the Sacrament of Penance (1551), ch.V, *Confession*, quoted from Neuner-Dupuis, *op. cit.*, p.461.

[24] The General Council of Trent, Twenty-Fourth Session, Doctrine on the Sacrament of Matrimony (1563), Canons 5 and 7, quoted from Neuner-Dupuis, *op.cit.*, p.529.

[25] Mk.12:29-31

[26] Hans Kung, *Infallible?*, Collins Fontana Library, 1970, p.153.

CHAPTER THIRTEEN

A Government in which All Participate

In this chapter I come to practical issues that must be addressed if we are to avoid in the future the problems we have encountered in responding to abuse. It concerns a new understanding of how the church would operate in such a way that unhealthy ideas would find it much more difficult to become entrenched.

It is also the chapter in which I seek to set out some of the concrete structures without which the authority of the college of bishops and the authority of the *sensus fidei* of the entire church would remain ideas without any practical importance or reality in the church.

THREE LEVELS OF GOVERNMENT

I have suggested that the church should have the same three levels of government as almost all other organisations: the whole people, a middle level (e.g. a council or synod or 'parliament') and a leader. Despite this, there are serious differences between the ideal form of government for the country of which I am a citizen and the church of which I am a member, so I cannot take forms of government from my own or any other country and apply them without further thought to the church.

I am a citizen of the country I was born in and, for as long as I live there, I cannot cease to be a citizen. I am bound by its laws and I must accept its government, whether I voted for that government or not and whether I like its policies or not. A church, on the other hand, is a voluntary society. I am free to join it and, if I do not like the decisions made there, I am free to leave it. History would say that, when people do not like a church, they simply stop attending it, or they join another church, or they even found another church. In a necessary society such as a country the 51% can impose its will on the 49%, while in a voluntary society such as a church it cannot do so without running the serious risk of breaking up the society. A church must always seek to work by consensus.

It is quite impossible to resolve matters of belief by means of a popular vote. It would be nonsense for a church to say that God existed last week because 51% said so, doesn't exist this week because the vote has gone down to 49%, but might exist again next week if the vote returns to its earlier level. All belief must be based on a search for God's truth, and in practice belief requires a high level of consensus.

I have said that the authority of a papal document depends first and foremost on the power of the arguments it contains rather than the authority of the person signing it. To replace papal authority with the popular will would still mean paying attention only to the authority behind the document rather than the force of the arguments in it. The only difference is that the authority would be the popular will rather than the pope.

If I have reservations about papal infallibility, history warns me to have even greater reservations about the infallibility of popular opinion.

In most countries people vote for the members of parliament only once every four or five years. In an election there can be many issues and a voter may have different opinions on different issues, but must summarise everything in one vote for one person. It is true that today a politician will listen to opinion polls as expressions of the popular will, and yet the people despise one who seems to have no firm beliefs and merely follows the polls. Furthermore, in most countries people do not vote for judges, chiefs of the armed forces or police, the heads of the civil service, the chief officers of banks and major commercial enterprises, or the proprietors and editors of media outlets, though collectively these unelected people have immense power and a huge influence on how a society thinks and acts. The ordinary people have no direct vote on many major issues that come before the parliament. So there must be reservations about the extent to which governments of today truly reflect the will of the people. Within the church in recent years, on the other hand, some people have demanded to have a formal vote on most issues that arise, that is, they can demand a far higher level of popular participation and consultation than they receive in civil society. Talk of consulting the will of the people within the church must bear this in mind and be realistic in its demands.

Most countries have elections in which candidates put themselves forward for election. They campaign hard and make many promises. Large sums of money are spent and the contest can become bitter. I do not believe that anyone would wish to see this happen within the church. Where elections are required within the church, we must think carefully about how they should be conducted.

There are also three considerations of a more spiritual nature. Sociologists tell us that in any society people will always vote in favour of anything that gives them more power or more freedom, and they will always vote against anything that takes away from them any power or freedom. They tell us that this tendency is so strong that it is pointless, a waste of time and money, to put such a matter to the vote, for the outcome can be known with certainty in advance. And yet the Christian religion is about someone who died on a cross out of love. It is about following and imitating someone who freely voted a complete powerlessness and a total lack of freedom to himself.

We live in a world where many people ask the question 'What is good for me?' rather than 'What is good for everyone?' This is less than a true Christian attitude and a church must do its best to ensure that it does not become a dominant attitude in deciding either belief or practice within the church community.

In most countries today the vote of a person who has thought carefully about all issues facing the country and the vote of a person who has not spent one second on these matters are equal in value. I have described the *sensus fidei* as a 'sensitivity and power of discernment ', and this is far more than an uninformed vote. Where religious beliefs and practice are at stake, a church would want to do all in its power to have a system in which the rights of all would be respected, but a different value would be given to different contributions according to their worth.

On the other hand, there can also be similarities between a country and a church that some church people would not wish to admit. In particular, there are always parties within a large church. They may not call themselves political parties, but they can act in a very similar manner. There can be church politics that are as bitter as secular politics. There can be the same hunger for power. The major parties in the church today are those of the proclaimers of certainties and the seekers after truth. Since such parties exist, it is better to bring them out into the open where they can be dealt with in an open and honest manner rather than pretend that they do not exist.

Even if we cannot simply take ideas from the secular field and apply them without further thought to the church, there is still plenty of room within the church for three levels of government. The best way to explain this, I believe, is to give examples of what can happen.

At this point I must come down to concrete suggestions, and this always creates the problem that, if people do not like the concrete details, they will reject the bigger idea that the details seek to implement. But the idea of a church with three levels of government – the Peter-figure, the middle level/parliament, and the will of the whole church - remains important whether people like the details I propose or not. Because we will be dealing with the practical, I can do no more than offer ideas for discussion, but I believe it is important that the discussion take place.

The First Level: the Peter-Figure

I have already explained why I believe that this level is important and I have stressed that the Peter-figure must not be reduced to a mere figurehead. I have indicated some details of the important role I see for the Peter-figure. On the other hand, I have also suggested legislation concerning what should happen in the event of

i) a schism, with more than one claimant to be the Peter-figure;

ii) a Peter-figure becoming, through physical or mental illness, incapable of carrying out essential duties;

iii) a Peter-figure being prevented from carrying out essential duties by an external force;

iv) a Peter-figure falling into formal heresy by denying a truth essential to the identity of the Christian faith;

v) a Peter-figure acting in such a non-Christian manner as to cause serious harm to the church.

I further believe that there should be legislation that clearly sets the Peter-figure within the church and accountable to the church, just as Peter was. Among other matters, it should set out when the Peter-figure must have the consent of, or at least consult with, the bishops and/or the whole church.

The above legislation would have to be legislation of 'the church', the only human power to which the Peter-figure is subject. I suggest that the legislation should acquire the force of law when it has the agreement of the Peter-figure, a consensus of the bishops and a consensus of the members of the church.

Just as such legislation could be given the force of law only by 'the church', so it could be changed or repealed only by 'the church' and the legislation would have to cover how this would happen. It would be essential that it could not be repealed by a single pope withdrawing consent from the legislation.

It would be possible today to know the mind of all the members of the church by means of a process of preparation and education that ended in a vote taken at the Masses on a given Sunday.

THE ROMAN CURIA

The Roman Curia must serve the whole church, that is, the pope, the bishops and all members of the church. The idea that it already does this by its service of the pope needs to be revised, for too much of its energy is devoted to protecting papal power and privileges, and to exercising that power itself. This will involve a change of mind and heart as much as a change of structures.

In order to assist this change, I suggest that the members of the Roman Curia not be bishops or cardinals. I do not make this suggestion out of any desire to downgrade their importance, but solely because it would clarify roles.

For more than a thousand years it was said that a bishop's powers of governance came from a direct grant by the pope. Under this system, the powers of governance granted directly to the members of the Roman Curia were considerable. Because of the special powers given them by the pope, they were more powerful than other bishops and held a special place. Since the Second Vatican Council it has been understood that this is no longer true and that a bishop's powers of governance come from ordination.

What we have now is an unsatisfactory alliance of the old and the new, and the older ideas of a superior power of governance for the members of the Curia have not gone away. Unquestionably, the bishops of the Curia are a powerful force within the worldwide church. The fact that they are often seen as 'superior' bishops is a cause of confusion, for there are no superior members of the college of bishops. If they were not bishops, they would be clearly seen as what they are, the 'civil service' at this level of church government, and they would be esteemed for the service they gave.

I do not like the idea of bishops who are not attached to a local church, and I do not subscribe to the idea that all people who are important to the church must be bishops.

The transition would have to be managed sensitively, for I have no desire to reverse roles between the Curia and the bishops, with the bishops then giving orders to the Curia. That would merely replace one set of problems with another, for any government that is not working in co-operation with its civil service is in serious difficulties. I have no desire to hurt the present members of the Curia or to downgrade the important service they can give to the church, but I believe that, if they were not bishops, there would be a greater clarity of roles and a better basis for cooperative work. As long as the old and the new try to live and work side by side, we will have problems.

The Second Level: The Bishops
The Synod of Bishops

I believe that synods are full of potential, but that this potential is not being realised as well as it might be.

Limitations

There are too many papal appointees, especially from the Roman Curia, so the perception is that the synod is not truly representative of the bishops.

There is the perception that through the secretariat there is too much curial control of what happens at a synod, especially concerning which ideas are allowed to go forward and which are not. The bishops can be left feeling that they are being manipulated.

The synod lasts for four weeks and the first two weeks are taken up entirely with speeches from each of the more than three hundred people present.[1] While the speeches can powerfully show the diversity of the church, they take up so much time that the last two weeks become a rush to draw some sense out of this diversity. In this format, there is inadequate time for the synod to do its work properly.

Because the large majority of the bishops are not professional theologians, synods are not good at resolving theological questions. They are much better at discussing practical ideas and pastoral strategies. This would not be a problem if there were another forum in which serious theological questions could be given the consideration they deserve.

Towards the end the bishops vote on a number of propositions, but I found that each proposition was a paragraph containing several ideas. There were times when I would have preferred a separate vote on each idea put forward in a paragraph.

The decisions of the bishops are not published. Instead the entire material of the synod is handed over to the pope, who later produces a *papal* document that represents the official outcome of the synod. I do not accuse any pope of being deliberately unfaithful to the mind of the bishops, but it is obvious that there is considerable latitude in choosing the ideas to include and where to place the emphases.

Because only about one in twenty of the bishops of the world is present at a synod, it has not been seen as expressing the mind of the whole world-wide body of bishops.

The danger arising from all the factors I have mentioned is the perception that the final result is a papal document rather than a truly collegial one.

More fundamentally, the synod is not seen as an adequate embodiment of the principle of collegiality.

Potential

In order to make the synod a true embodiment of collegiality I suggest the following ideas.

That it be accepted that synods are for the discussion of practical matters and pastoral strategies, and that another forum be provided for the resolution of matters of faith and morals.

That all members be elected by the bishops of the world, with the Roman Curia electing three of their members to represent them and with no other papal appointees.

That the staff of the secretariat be appointed by the bishops rather than simply be drawn from the Curia.

That, twelve months before the synod, each bishop member forward a two-page written submission on the selected topic. That these submissions be published in book form to the whole church at least six months prior to the synod. That these submissions take the place of the speeches normally given at the synod, so that there will be four (or at least three) rather than two weeks to coordinate the material and prepare resolutions.

That, before votes are taken, the pope address the assembly concerning the matters proposed, not to tell the bishops how they must vote, but to exercise a role of leadership. This could be done in much the same way as an impartial judge might summarise the evidence for the jury and highlight certain aspects, while still fully respecting the jury's right to determine the verdict.

That the fruit of the synod be, not a papal document, but a series of resolutions, each containing one idea, voted on by the synod.

That the propositions favoured by a majority be submitted in written form to all the bishops of the world and they be invited to send a written reply confirming or rejecting each proposition.

That the propositions favoured by the bishops of the world, with the results of the voting attached to each proposition, be made public by the pope as the final result of the synod.

Since the meeting with other bishops from around the world is one of the best aspects of the synod, consideration be given to the possibility of all the bishops living at the one place during the time of the synod.

A COUNCIL OF THE CHURCH

While synods deal with practical and pastoral matters, it would seem advisable to hold a council to deal with matters of faith and morals.

The last three ecumenical councils of the Catholic Church (Trent, Vatican I and Vatican II) have treated of most aspects of the church. They have been rare events, for Trent took place in 1545-1563, Vatican I in 1869-1870 and Vatican II in 1962-65. The principle of collegiality is hardly a reality in the church if it is exercised in relation to matters of faith and morals only on occasions as rare as these.

In earlier Christian history, on the other hand, there were examples of councils called to discuss specific questions. Today it would be possible to hold councils that:

i) responded to a specific question;

ii) could use the modern means of communication to the full in the preparatory stages in order to minimise both the number of occasions and the length of time when very large numbers of people would need to be brought together;

iii) in this same manner could overcome the serious problem, experienced at Vatican II, of trying to deal with difficult and complex topics in too brief a period of time.

There are precedents in church history for people other than bishops attending a council and having a vote.[2] There is no reason why others, including a significant body of laypersons, could not be members of the Council. However unpalatable it may be to some, it must be recognised that a council consisting exclusively of men would lack credibility in many quarters today, and not just among women, before it even met.

There are many different forms such a council could take, according to the nature of the questions being discussed. In all cases I would envisage a lengthy period of preparation in which the best material on both sides of the question was gathered and shared with the whole church. I would envisage this process continuing until all concerned felt that they had a good and balanced understanding of the issues involved and of the arguments on both sides.

When the time for decision finally arrived, in some cases it might be enough to have the members vote by post. In other cases, in a fashion similar to a synod, elected representatives could come together, formulate proposals and submit them to all the members of the council throughout the world for their acceptance or rejection by means of a postal vote. In other cases it might be necessary to bring all the members together.

The force of a decision of a council would depend on whether the council saw a particular statement as essential to the identity of the church. A statement seen as essential would surely require a consensus of the bishops that was considerably higher than a mere 51% majority. The council would need to determine what percentage constituted such a consensus. I believe that even this would not be enough and will return to the question when discussing the role of the whole church.

In relation to statements not seen as essential to the very identity of the church, I suggest that, rather than have an artificial pass mark of 50%, it would be more informative and useful to the church to give the results of the vote for each statement approved. if would surely help people if they knew that 99% of bishops approved of one statement, while only 57% approved of the next one, rather than simply put the two statements side by side without any indication of the support they received.

PRESIDENTS OF REGIONS

In this section I shall propose a system of government for the Latin Church based on that of the Eastern patriarchs. If this were adopted, however, there would be a need for a change of name, for the term 'patriarch' has strong negative overtones for many women in the West. Pending a better title, I shall here speak of the 'patriarch-president'.

I have already noted that, in the early centuries of the Christian religion, there were five patriarchs, one in the West (Rome) and four in the East (Constantinople, Antioch, Alexandria and Jerusalem). Later, as Christianity spread, other Eastern patriarchs were added. Today there are patriarchs in the Orthodox Churches and there are patriarchs within the Catholic Church. Within the Catholic Church the patriarchs are the heads of Eastern communities such as the Copts, Melkites, Maronites, Syrians, Chaldeans and Armenians. These are parts of the Catholic Church, and so they acknowledge the pope as head of the church, but they have always had their own liturgy, language and customs and have enjoyed a measure of self rule within the church.

Although these patriarchs are the heads of their whole community, they can exercise their authority only together with the other bishops of that community. They may perform certain less important matters alone, and both the presidency and a certain power of initiative in all matters are in their hands, but in important matters they require the consent of the permanent synod of the patriarchate. Considerable detail concerning the role of a patriarch is already contained in canons 55-150 of the Code of Canons of the Eastern Churches.[3]

Even when taken together, these descendants of the four Eastern patriarchates make up only a small part of the Catholic Church. All of the rest of the church descends from the one Western patriarchate (Rome) and constitutes the so-called Latin Church, in which for many centuries Latin was the official language of the liturgy. In this greater part of the Catholic Church the pope is not only pope but also patriarch of the Latin Church. However, the roles of pope and patriarch of the Latin Church are two quite distinct roles and there is no necessity that they both be held by the one person. There is no reason why another person could not be appointed to the office of patriarch of the Latin Church in exactly the same manner as a person other than the pope is appointed as patriarch of the Copts or Melkites. Just as the original four Eastern patriarchates were expanded and new patriarchates added, so there is no reason why the Latin Church could not be divided into a number of different areas, with each of these areas having its own patriarch-president. There is no reason why each continent or, indeed, each nation could not have its own patriarch-president and the same level of autonomy in running its own affairs as the Eastern patriarchs have. In other words, there is no reason why a system of government that is already highly respected within the Catholic

Church could not be extended to the whole church. There could be another 'discontinuity for the sake of a greater continuity'. The canons of the Eastern code could easily be adapted to the Latin Church.

In any case, it is only by stretching the word beyond breaking point that we could today refer to the churches of Asia, Africa, South America and Oceania as 'Latin'. It is time that the special character of different cultures should be respected.

In all circumstances I would see the patriarch-president being elected by the bishops of that region and then appointed by the pope. There would be no necessity for the person to be elected for life rather than for a fixed term.

In their origins, the patriarchs were the heads of dioceses in major cities, but there is no absolute reason why patriarchs-presidents must have a diocese of their own,[4] and there is nothing to be gained by giving two full-time jobs to the one person. However it is managed, they must have the time to attend to matters concerning the whole region. They must also be free to visit Rome at regular intervals together with all other patriarchs-presidents and ensure that the greater autonomy and diversity brought about by this system did not endanger the unity of the church. This regular meeting between the pope and the patriarchs-presidents of national churches would be another form of collegial governance of the church.

As can be seen, within the Catholic Church itself there are already models of more participatory forms of government.

THE NATIONAL CHURCH

The introduction of a system of patriarchs-presidents for each nation could help to overcome another difficulty.

One of the many problems that arose when revelations of sexual abuse began to appear came from the system of governance within the Catholic Church. The pope is at the head of the universal church and a bishop is at the head of each diocese, and in the Latin Church there is no real or effective level of government between the two. There is a Bishops' Conference in every country large enough to have several dioceses, but it has no power to pass laws binding the whole country.

The only way to have a law binding the whole nation is for the Bishops' Conference, by a two-thirds majority, to request the pope to make such a law for the nation.[5] This is a cumbersome process and in practice does not work, especially in a matter where authorities in the Vatican have little knowledge of a subject or of local conditions, as was certainly the case in relation to sexual abuse.

To complicate matters further, each religious congregation of religious nuns, brothers or priests also has a large degree of autonomy from the local bishop and guards this autonomy jealously.

All of this meant that in a country like Australia, with a population of twenty million, a nationally binding response to sexual abuse required the *unanimous* consent of about 180 people – about 30 bishops and 150 religious superiors. Our measure of success was that only two refused to join (one bishop and one religious superior). We still had problems with bishops and superiors dispensing themselves from various provisions of the agreed procedures and there was still no means of insisting that these individuals should change their ways, but coming so close to a national system did help us considerably.

In some larger countries, on the other hand, there were so many dioceses and so many religious congregations that unanimous consent was seen as impossible and no serious attempt was made to have a nationally binding response. As a result, each diocese and each religious congregation followed its own procedures. Wrong actions by an individual bishop or religious leader reflected on the entire country, and yet the national church had no power and no mechanism to ensure that individual bishops or religious leaders acted in a proper and accountable manner. This made it quite inevitable that in those countries the entire church would end up being judged by its worst cases, and this is what happened.

I use this example because it powerfully makes the point that there are occasions when the whole church of a particular nation *must* speak and act together. It is essential to the concept of participatory government that decisions be made at the *appropriate* level, for it is only when decisions are made at the appropriate level that they will be effective.

To any request for a national legislative body the usual response given is that it was Jesus himself who established Peter and the apostles, and hence the pope and the bishops, and gave them power to rule the church, so a system of government with the pope in charge of the universal church and a bishop in charge of each diocese cannot be changed. I have already indicated that I have serious problems with the idea of a Jesus with perfect knowledge giving permanent and detailed structures to the church. To this I would add that it would surely be quite wrong to put the blame on Jesus himself for any part of the church's poor response to sexual abuse!!!

To this one can add that the problem does not exist in the same way in those parts of the church where there is a patriarch, so a universal system of patriarchs-presidents would solve many problems. There are occasions when there is a powerful and urgent need for the church of a whole nation to act as one, and a system of government reflecting this need must be put in place.

THE ELECTION OF A POPE

The election of a pope is always seen as the election of the bishop of the diocese of Rome, who automatically takes on the role of pope. For a thousand years this was seen as the responsibility of the clergy and people of Rome.[6] Then, around the turn of the millennium, the College of Cardinals developed from various offices that assisted the pope. There were the bishops of the seven dioceses surrounding Rome, and these became the cardinal bishops. There were the parish priests of certain designated parishes in Rome and these became the cardinal priests. There were the seven deacons who looked after the poor in the seven districts into which Rome was divided and these became the cardinal deacons. In 1059 these three groups were united and became the electors of the bishop of Rome. Later on, bishops from dioceses far from Rome were appointed cardinals, so that the whole church would be better represented in the election of a pope. The idea of the diocese of Rome electing its new bishop was maintained by having each of the cardinals appointed as nominal parish priest of one of the Roman churches.

The Second Vatican Council (1962-65) introduced a new college alongside the College of Cardinals. This was the College of Bishops, made up of all the bishops of the church with the pope as head of the college. This introduced a new element into the election of a pope, for it could also be seen as the College of Bishops seeking a new head. This fact has been in part recognised in the requirement that, if persons appointed as cardinals are not bishops, they must immediately be ordained as bishops.[7] In this way the College of Cardinals is presented as in some manner a representative body of the College of Bishops.

The cardinals, however, are handpicked by the pope and so cannot really be said to speak in the name of the College of Bishops. Furthermore, because the cardinals are carefully chosen, the pope has a large say in the choice of a successor. This goes against the wisdom of the world around us, which says that no one in any field should choose their own successor, for there is too much danger that they will choose the person who most closely resembles themselves. It is also true that, under the present system, the whole church has no part in the process of electing a new pope and so has no sense of ownership of the choice made.

One solution would be to determine the number of electors (e.g. 100) and then divide this number among the Bishops' Conferences of the world, with the bishops then electing their representative(s) to this college of electors on a three-yearly renewable basis. One day it might be possible for the whole church of a nation to elect the representatives, but I believe that we would have to work towards this goal gradually. One could combine past and present by naming as cardinals on a temporary basis the bishops chosen, on condition that they would retain the title only for the term of their election and would wear no special robes or use any titles beyond that of 'cardinal'.

The link with the Church of Rome electing its new bishop would be exactly the same as it is now, and this system would better represent the College of Bishops.

In my proposal, the patriarchs-presidents would have a role of governance together with the pope, while the cardinals would be limited strictly to the one role of electing a new pope. Needless to say, the two roles could be combined, but this would require further thought.

THE APPOINTMENT OF BISHOPS

Over the centuries there have been different methods of choosing and appointing bishops. In the case of St. Ambrose the choice took place by public acclamation in the cathedral church (374 A.D.). During the worst times of church history a prince or other secular power named the bishop (and often gave the office to a member of his family). Various church groups have also had this right at different times, e.g. the chapter of canons in some older dioceses or the Council of Bishops or the clergy in the Eastern Catholic churches. With widely differing degrees of success, for some eighteen hundred years the local church had at least some say in the choice of a bishop.

Coinciding with the rise of papal power in the nineteenth century, however, the pope more and more reserved the right both to choose and to appoint bishops. Currently, the bishops of a region have a right to submit names and express their views and preferences, but their views can be ignored, for all power belongs to the Congregation for Bishops and to the pope. Controlling the appointment of bishops is obviously a powerful means of controlling the church.

The present method has the advantages that unity with the rock of Peter is ensured and that the pope can introduce a fresh person from outside into a diocese when this is greatly needed. It has the serious disadvantages that bishops can be chosen for 'political' reasons (e.g. proclaimers of certainties before seekers after truth) and that the local church has no sense of ownership of the appointment, and this can lead to a lesser commitment both to the bishop appointed and to the work of the church at the diocesan level.

There is a moment in the ordination ceremony of a bishop when the candidate is presented to the people and they accept by acclamation. This acclamation is always given, for the appointment cannot be changed, so there is little to be gained by refusing to accept the person named. Nevertheless, there are times when the acclamation is something less than a heartfelt acceptance of the new bishop.

There is a tension between the needs of the universal and the local church in relation to the appointment of bishops, and this tension must not be resolved by crushing either side. The two should be kept in balance and the needs on both sides satisfied. The present system fully protects the rights of the pope, but it crushes the legitimate desire of the local church to have a voice in the choice of its bishop.

I believe that union with the rock of Peter is so important that the actual appointment should always come from the pope, but I believe that three criteria should be observed in choosing the candidate:

The first and overriding criterion is that the method adopted must be one that produces the best candidate for the task. Essential to this is that the candidate should have not merely priestly qualities, but also an abundance of human qualities and virtues, including a real ability to relate to people. In church history there have been too many examples of bishops who were perfect 'churchmen' and theologically most safe, but who lacked basic human qualities.

The local church should have such a voice in the process that it will feel a sense of ownership of the choice made. The people should not later say, 'An outside power placed this person over us; it is up to them to make it work.' They should rather say, 'We made this choice and it is up to us to make it work.'

The pope and the bishops of the region should also have a voice in the process. This should be done in order to ensure that the people of the diocese are not simply looking inwards, but are aware of the greater good of the whole church and are open to the new spirit that a person from outside the diocese might bring.

Neither the Orthodox nor any of the Protestant churches seem to have found the perfect means of choosing their leaders, so we must approach the question carefully.

Given the difficulties involved in choosing the best candidate, groups of people sometimes meet, not to choose a candidate, but to describe the kind of person they want and the qualities their new bishop should possess. This process, however, often produces a description, not of any mere mortal, but of 'Jesus Christ on one of his better days'. One must query how useful this process is, for in the real world the choice must eventually be made from among a number of very limited human beings.

A popular vote would be pointless unless people knew the candidates, but I doubt that anyone would wish to see candidates putting themselves forward and waging expensive political campaigns inviting people to vote for them.

It would seem that one or more methods must be found of choosing a select number of candidates and then giving sufficient detail about them for people to be able to make an informed choice. One method would be that the bishops of the country put forward three candidates, at least one from outside the diocese.

There should be room for a questioning of the candidates and a making public of their views. If an informed choice were to be made, then both strengths and weaknesses would have to be mentioned. This has its dangers, especially if a certain heat enters into the process.

If factions developed and the process produced more heat than light, a higher authority (e.g. a patriarch-president or pope) should have the power to step in to resolve the situation, even, in an extreme case, by making the appointment.

It is not necessary that one single method be followed in all dioceses throughout the world. It would be wise to allow each Bishops' Conference to develop its own system and then, over time, select those methods that best produce the desired outcomes.

In these suggestions I believe that I am proposing a discontinuity with the last two hundred years for the sake of a greater continuity with the previous eighteen hundred and, indeed, with the Great Tradition itself.

The Third Level: The Mind of the Whole Church

There are obvious difficulties in consulting with a body of more than a billion members, but the mind, the *sensus fidei*, of the whole church is something so powerful that it cannot be ignored.

A Council of the Church

In any council the aim should always be to have an ongoing *dialogue* between the pope, the bishops and the whole church, with all invited to play an active part. It could legitimately be expected, therefore, that, in preparing for a council, the members of the council would consult with those around them, so that the outcome of the council truly expressed the faith of the church. The level and method of consultation would depend on the topic of the council, so it is not possible here to do more than insist on the fact of consultation.

I have already proposed the idea that a significant number of laypersons could be members of the council. In virtually all countries today there are numbers of laypersons with degrees in theology, and, indeed, the level of expertise in theology of many of them can be higher than that of many of the bishops.

Councils often produce discursive documents containing no truths 'essential to the identity of the Christian church'. When this happens, the documents could be published as the best truth the council was capable of reaching on the topic, and one would sincerely hope that all members of the church would treat such documents with the respect they deserved.

If, on the other hand, a council did seek to determine a truth 'essential to the identity of the Christian church', I suggest that we would be faithful to both Mt.16:19 and Mt.18:18 if we insisted that it be solemnly proclaimed by the rock only when it had been clearly established that the statement was the faith of the pope, the faith of the bishops, and the faith of the whole church.

This idea is essential if we are to do more than pay lip service to the idea of the mind of the whole church, the *sensus fidei*. In any nation, the whole people vote on the basic constitution of the society and the nation would be on a weak foundation if they did not. In a similar way, truths 'essential to the identity of the church' must have this level of support. Think, too, of the power of a statement when a pope, the rock, proclaimed a truth so affirmed.

It would, of course, be the pope alone, the rock, who would finally proclaim a truth 'essential to the identity of the Christian church.' Needless to say, a pope could not be bound to proclaim something that violated the pope's own conscience, but would have no right to publish as an essential truth a personal opinion that had not been shown to be 'the faith of the church'.

OTHER SYNODS

The Synod of Bishops is perceived by many people as a powerful body, indeed, as possessing far more power than it in fact has. There has, therefore, always been considerable pressure to have other people present at these synods. Over the years a significant number of people other than bishops have been invited to these synods, with a right to speak and take part in discussions, but not with the right to vote. I question whether this is a move in the right direction.

In a parliament, only the elected members have the right to be present, to speak and to vote. Others, no matter how great their competence on a particular topic, must make their contribution by advising elected members, preparing speeches for them to deliver and assisting in answering questions outside the parliament. In accordance with this analogy, I have no problem with synods of bishops consisting solely of bishops.

A synod, however, is not a parliament and there is no reason why synods should be limited to synods of bishops. There could be synods of laypersons or women or young people or religious or priests or school principals or any other group within the church. Rather than invite a limited number of people to attend a synod of bishops, with a right to speak but not to vote, I would prefer to see different groups holding their own synods with the right to both speak and vote.

The value of any such synod would depend on the quality of the work produced by the synod, the perception of its importance by the members of the church, the recognition given to it by authorities and the practical consequences that flowed from it. There is no reason why such bodies could not become as influential as I would like to see the synod of bishops become. In the simplest terms, they would be as important as we wanted them to be.

The regular meeting of the Synod of Bishops is held every three years. Why could we not have a synod every two years, alternating between a synod of bishops and a synod of some other group? As for the bishops, so for these other groups the discussions would not concern dogmatic matters but practical and pastoral issues, and they could make a significant contribution to the church.

A LEGISLATIVE COUNCIL OF THE CHURCH

Law is a particularly sensitive subject within the Catholic Church, for there is the perception that there are far too many 'rules', and yet a large society cannot exist without some structure and practical rules.

A solution to this dilemma would be to have a Legislative Council of the church, with all new legislation from any source purporting to bind the whole church requiring the approval of this body. Its major role would be that of being the voice of the whole church.

I suggest three conditions:
> i) It must not seek to resolve matters of belief or to canonise one among several legitimate theological opinions, under pain of the invalidity of its decisions;
> ii) All members must be free to vote according to their conscience before God alone, so there must be no requirement to vote along party lines, under pain of any decisions involving such parties being made null and void.

iii) It must make every effort to work by consensus rather than a simple majority.

The members of this Legislative Council should be elected from around the world.

Participation at the Diocesan Level

I would see the necessity for a structure similar to that of the Legislative Council in each diocese before any diocesan laws were passed. Parish priests have no legislative power, but a similar structure would be necessary in each parish, too, before any major decisions were made.

The Selection of a Parish Priest

In most countries in the Western world there is an acute shortage of priests. In many areas bishops have had to suppress parishes or give two or more parishes to the care of one priest. Many bishops would, therefore, resist the introduction of more rules concerning the appointment of parish priests. They would say that they already have very little choice. I have been involved in the appointment of parish priests for twenty years and I know the difficulties that arise.

Despite this, I believe that some further requirements need to be introduced. There are still countries where there is an abundance of priests. Even in areas of shortage, there are still occasions when several priests apply for the same parish. Because of the shortage, there can at times be the temptation to appoint a priest who is not suitable but who is the only person available. I believe that in this last case, the people should at least have the choice between having this priest or having no priest.

The major innovation I would like to see is a dialogue between the members of the parish and the priest or priests being considered for the parish. A method of dialogue that was fair to all concerned could be developed, with the parishioners then informing the bishop of their thoughts and feelings. If the people reject a particular priest, the bishop may at times need to respond that there is no other priest to offer.

There may well be much argument about the particular forms of government I have put forward in this chapter. But if these forms are rejected, I suggest that others must be found, for a genuinely participatory government is a safer and richer basis for the life of the church as it enters the third millennium.

Meditation

I will be your God and you shall be my people." This idea, expressed time and again in the First Testament, expresses the essence of the Covenant, the great bond that united God and the people of Israel.

No people, however, can live its life with only a vast idea to guide it. People demand concrete expressions of the larger idea, homely, down-to-earth things with which they can identify. So the Covenant was made concrete in priest, prophet, king, law and land.

In the same way, beautiful ideas concerning participatory government, service of the reign of God within the hearts and minds of all people and the *sensus fidei* of the entire church will remain nothing but beautiful ideas unless they are given concrete expression in the daily life of the church.

It is, unfortunately, all too possible to accept the beautiful ideas, but reject all proposals for their concrete expression.

And yet a denial of imperfect and contingent expressions quickly becomes a denial of the beautiful ideas themselves.

FOOTNOTES

[1] At the most recent synod (October 2005), the first under Pope Benedict XVI, the speeches were reduced to one week and the whole synod to three weeks. This does not resolve the problems I refer to and may downgrade even further the importance of synods.

[2] At the Fourth Lateran Council (1215) eight hundred abbots and priors attended together with four hundred bishops. At the Council of Florence (1435-42) three estates were present – bishops, abbots and religious, and 'lower clergy' – and a motion required a two-thirds majority from each of the estates.

[3] Published by Pope John Paul II on 18th October 1990.

[4] I said earlier that I am not in favour of bishops who are not attached to a particular church, but I see no reason why that church cannot be a national church rather than a diocese. In a moment I shall also advocate the necessity of a national church in many matters.

[5] See canon 455 of the Code of Canon Law.

[6] And this had its serious problems, for at times the papacy became the plaything of powerful Roman families. See, for example, the truly extraordinary story of Marozia (c.892-c.937), who may have given rise to the Pope Joan legend.

[7] Canon 351 para.1.

CHAPTER FOURTEEN

A Change
of Heart
and Mind

In the gospel of Mark, Jesus began his ministry with a call to a change of heart and mind,[1] implying that, if people were to accept him, they would need to be ready to put aside old values and see the world in a new way. The need for this change of heart and mind is a permanent one, both for individuals and for the whole church. No changes in external structures will of themselves alone bring about the better church I dream of, and there will always be a need for this more internal change of heart and mind in relation to all exercise of power within the church.

At the heart of this change is the idea that it is very hard indeed to serve a community by exercising a near absolute power over it. I have already referred to this, and to ideas such as that of priests being 'taken up' out of the world. Here I can do no more than give a few examples of the changes that I see as necessary.

Accountability and Professionalism
Accountability

It is not enough that people should have a voice in such matters as determining the essential beliefs of the church, passing laws and electing officials. It is also necessary that those who serve the community in positions of authority should at all times think of themselves as accountable to the people they serve.

The pope is answerable to no human being. The members of the Roman Curia are answerable to the pope, but a pope cannot possibly know every detail of all that happens in the Curia, so in most matters they answer to no one. The bishops are answerable to Roman authorities, but an appeal to Rome against a bishop is often a painfully slow way of achieving very little. Priests are answerable to their bishops, but it is often difficult to know what is happening in a parish if the parish priest does not want the bishop to know.

I believe that the present quite inadequate accountability towards superiors must be complemented by accountability towards the community one serves. I shall give one example of what I mean but, while the details might differ, I apply the principle behind this example to every level in the church.

Parish priests are normally appointed for a period of six years, with the appointment renewable at the end of that period. During the fifth year of the appointment I would like to see a formal *appraisal* of the work of the priest. The priest would first be asked to write out, as it were, a 'job description', that is, an account of what the priest sees as the essential elements of the work, and then a self-appraisal of perceived performance against this job description. An independent panel would be established, and the members of this panel would interview the priest and then a significant number of representatives of the parish. The panel would then report to the priest on their findings. The purpose of this appraisal is emphatically not to limit itself to passing judgement on the priest by listing negatives.[2] On the contrary, the panel would be expected both to affirm the priest for all the positives it found and to suggest helpful and practical ways to respond to any negatives that became apparent. In briefest summary, the task of the panel is to see whether the priest's job description is adequate and whether the self-appraisal is affirmed or contradicted by the parish representatives. It follows that the best way for the priest to ensure a positive outcome is by being totally honest in the self-appraisal.

If I may add a personal note, in appraising a priest during a visit I have always asked whether the priest gets a regular day off each week and a regular annual holiday, whether there are good and true friends outside the parish, whether the priest makes sure there is adequate time for prayer and reading, and whether there is a satisfying amount of *eros*, love and emotional satisfaction in the priest's life. I believe these matters are just as important as any duties.

I would then like to see the bishop carry out a formal visitation of the parish shortly after this appraisal. A copy of the report would be made available to the bishop, who could then affirm the positives and give support in relation to the negatives. On the basis of the appraisal, the bishop would be in a better position to affirm the whole parish. There could then be a further check on progress towards the end of the sixth year, and then both priest and bishop would be ready to consider the request for a renewal of the appointment for a further six years.

By my own choice, I arranged a few years ago for this form of appraisal of myself and my own work, and I found it to be a most rewarding and affirming experience. It had its unpleasant moments and its fears, and there were negatives to point out to me, but it is one of the best things I have done in my professional life.

Bishops are not appointed for six-year periods, but I believe that they should have the same appraisal every six years. To introduce this requirement for priests but not have it for bishops would be massively counter-productive. If a system of patriarchs-presidents were introduced, the president could arrange for the appraisal of each bishop. I also believe that every member of the Roman Curia should have the same periodic appraisal. Indeed, it would be a supremely good example if the pope did the same thing. The pope does not have a superior judge,[3] but is accountable to the church, as Peter was.[4]

This form of appraisal is now a commonplace in most professions and most workplaces. If ministers of the church do not adopt it, they will have only themselves to blame when people do not take them seriously. I know of nothing that can so help priests to feel good about themselves and their work.

Professionalism

I believe that, as well as a *spiritual director*, all bishops and priests should have a *supervisor*, someone with whom they can discuss the many incidents that arise in their professional life and the manner in which they have handled them. There should also be *in-service training* to keep bishops and priests up to date with developments in ministry, and this should be obligatory if they wish to have a new appointment or a renewal of their present appointment. In particular, bishops and priests need to be given assistance in learning the many skills required to be part of a truly *collaborative ministry* with the people of the diocese or parish.

There should be a *code of conduct*, so that bishops and priests might know what is expected of them in all ordinary circumstances and there should be a means of enforcing this code. If bishops or priests are given genuine assistance as soon as they begin to depart from what is proper, there is surely less chance of their offending in serious matters.

Other Factors

Dress

During the second millennium many bishops adopted clothes and ornaments that spoke of power and riches. I do not believe we have yet gone far enough in abandoning this trend. The church could start by consigning the mitre to the dustbin of history. The world around and within us has taught us the truth that only a small part of communication is verbal and that body language is of great importance. Wearing a hat that makes one far taller than any other person present is strong body language, conveying the message, 'I am more powerful and important than anyone else here.' Is this the message that Jesus wished to convey? After the mitre I would want bishops to look at pectoral crosses, pastoral staffs and rings made of expensive materials.

On the other hand, many priests have reacted against the black suit or cassock of the past by going to the opposite extreme of wearing nothing that would identify them as priests. There is a need for neat and distinctive but modern attire, e.g. a tie that identifies a priest.

Radical Suitability

There is also a need for a way of *dismissing a priest* from the priesthood. At present this can be done for certain specific crimes, but allowance has to be made for the person who, after every concession and assistance has been given, has shown a radical unsuitability for the priesthood. Certainly, every proper safeguard against arbitrary or unjust dismissal should be put in place, but keeping totally unsuitable persons in the priesthood for life helps no one and can be a source of serious scandal. It has been part of the scandal caused by sexual abuse.[5] It is quite unhealthy that any priests should think that, no matter what they do, they have a secure position for life.

The Laity: Citizens or Civilians?

The Greek word *laos* (people) expresses the common element shared by all members of the church. The Latin term *laici* (laypersons) was derived from the term *laos*, but in the process came to refer only to those who were not clerics.[6] *Laos* expresses a positive concept (people), *laici* expresses a negative concept (those who are not clerics).

As an analogy, we can say that all people are citizens of their own country. Most are also civilians, but this latter term is both negative and relative. It is negative because it really means 'non-military', and it is relative because it has a meaning only in relation to the military. Some rights and obligations flow from being a civilian, but the major rights and duties of any individual flow from being a citizen, and the negative and relative term 'civilian' cannot express the whole reality of citizenship. In a similar way, the term 'laypersons', which is also negative and relative, cannot express the whole reality of the vast majority of the members of the church, and their major rights and duties cannot come from this term.

It must always be remembered that the first meaning of the word 'laypersons' is 'non-clerics'. The full effect of the word would become apparent if we went through Vatican documents substituting 'non-clerics' every time we found the words 'laypersons' or 'laity'. It would become evident that the basic perspective of the document was often a clerical one, just as we would immediately be aware that a document had a military perspective if it continually referred to the vast majority of citizens as civilians. In such documents the clergy or the military are the basic point of reference for everything in the document, and everything revolves around them.

There are times when it is legitimate for the military to refer to civilians, or for doctors or lawyers to refer to laypersons (i.e. non-doctors or non-lawyers), and there will be times when it is legitimate for clerics to refer to laypersons (non-clerics), but if the term is used constantly, if it is the normal term, we know that we are meeting a military or medical or legal or clerical outlook on life.

Furthermore, the terms tend to be elitist and discriminatory, denying the essential contribution of e.g. army reservists in relation to the military, nurses in relation to doctors, law clerks in relation to lawyers and religious and laity in relation to clerics. The terms also deny such things as the citizen's concern for the defence of the country, first aid and care of the sick in the home, the concern of people to know the law and obey it in driving a car or filling in a tax form, and the marvellous variety of charisms that exists within the church. In such perspectives, 'laypersons' become an amorphous mass, their special talents and possible contributions are not recognised and, inevitably, their full potential will never be realised.

To see this more clearly, take the perspective of another sacrament, that of marriage[7]. From this perspective we may refer to the married and the unmarried in the church. Almost all clerics would come under the heading of the unmarried, but would rightly object if this became the dominant perspective and the normal language, for they would say that to class them simply as unmarried does not do justice to their role in the life of the church and does not allow their full potential to be realised.

Against the vision of church that I have given in this book, the sacrament that should determine the dominant perspective must surely be neither marriage nor orders, but baptism. Here, however, we encounter the problem that, while we have a church equivalent of the term 'civilians' (i.e. laity), we have no adequate equivalent of the more important term 'citizens'. Recent documents written in Latin speak of

Christifideles (usually translated as 'Christ's faithful'), but the term has never become popular, and the term 'the faithful' definitely refers only to non-clerics. One could speak of 'Christians' or 'Catholics' but these words have other connotations. There is no easily accessible word that refers equally and impartially to the pope and a baby christened this morning in a village in the highlands of Papua New Guinea. In the absence of such a term, church documents frequently use the negative term 'laity' when they really intend the positive equivalent of the word 'citizens'. But in doing this, they are once again giving a clerical tone to the document.

The sacrament of orders creates three categories of action in the Church: there are actions that require the sacrament of orders and are reserved to clerical members of Christ's faithful (e.g. celebrating Mass); there are actions that are forbidden to clerics and are performed only by those members of Christ's faithful who are not clerics (e.g. standing for election to parliament); and there are actions that are neither reserved nor forbidden to clerics and are performed equally by all Christ's faithful.

This last category is a rich one, containing much of the work of the church but, because it is neither specifically lay nor specifically clerical, there is the danger that it can at times be forgotten. A church document should never use the term 'laypersons' when it is referring to an activity that is common to all members of the church and is neither reserved nor forbidden to clerics.[8]

The synod of 1987 attempted to resolve this problem by giving a positive meaning to the word 'laity', defining laypersons by means of their 'secularity' or involvement 'in the world'[9], as though laypersons were in the world but clerics were not. This must be called a misguided attempt to give a positive meaning to an essentially negative term. It has led to many anomalies, e.g. contemplative nuns would have to be considered as 'in the world' because they are not clerics, but married deacons who work in a factory throughout the week would have to be considered as not 'in the world' because they are clerics. At best this is an unusual and forced understanding of the word 'world', and it appears to be a dangerous basis on which to build a theology. It is not possible to give a positive definition to an essentially negative term. It is the perspective, not the definition that must change.

Assigning the sacred to clerics and the secular to the laity comes too close to identifying the sacred with actions reserved to clerics and the secular with actions forbidden to clerics, while leaving out altogether the actions common to both. While it is sometimes legitimate to speak of sacred and secular things, a complete separation between the two must be avoided. Spiritual and temporal, sacred and secular, church and world, faith and life all constitute the one reality created by God, and they interpenetrate and complement each other. If Catholic people are to integrate their faith into their lives, a dualism between sacred and secular must be avoided, for all members of the church without exception live 'in the world', that is, in a world that is both sacred and secular. As Pope Paul V1 said, 'The whole Church has an authentic secular dimension'[10]. This approach is necessary if the church is to fulfil its role of offering life to the full to the whole cosmos.

Since it would assist the 'change of mind and heart', I suggest that the term 'citizens' be adopted by the church. The term appears to be compatible with the New Testament.

'So then you are no longer strangers and aliens, but you are citizens with the saints and also members of the house of God, built upon the foundation of the apostles and prophets, with Jesus Christ himself as the cornerstone.' (Eph.2:19-20)

RENEWING THE THEOLOGICAL CONVERSATION

In earlier centuries an error by a theologian was corrected by other theologians through a 'theological conversation' in which one author published an article criticising some aspect of the work of another author. There were rules governing the conversation and it was important that it was always carried out in a courteous and respectful manner. e.g. 'My esteemed colleague has contributed greatly to our understanding of the sacrament of baptism, but on one point I find that I see things from a different perspective, and I respectfully present my arguments.'

With the developments of the last two centuries within the Vatican, the role of correcting theological error has been taken over by the

Congregation for the Doctrine of the Faith. There are constant complaints that its procedures are shrouded in secrecy and can even deny fundamental tenets of natural justice.

Because of this, we have the undesirable situation that theologians will all come together to defend one of 'their own' against the perceived 'enemy' of the Congregation in Rome and what are seen as its heavy-handed procedures. Because of their felt need to support each other against this powerful congregation, they can sometimes do this even when they are aware that there are problems with what the particular theologian is saying.

Taking on the role of watchdog of orthodoxy is an obvious outcome of recent developments in the papacy described in earlier chapters, but it is not a positive step. Peter was told to 'confirm' his brothers and sisters, a positive action, not simply correct their errors and keep them in line. If infallible statements were abandoned in favour of statements of those truths 'essential to the identity and unity of the Christian church', and if theologians were consequently given as much freedom as possible, the 'theological conversation' would be a far better way to guard against dangers to the church. Under such a system the pope would be the rock that no theologian would ever wish to abandon by denying an essential truth and would have the far more positive role of confirming all that was good and true. It would be another 'discontinuity for the sake of a greater continuity'.

This change may not be the most important change facing the church, but it is a symptom of the change of mind and heart that I see as necessary.

Putting our Own House in Order

The weight of history is so heavy that there is no form of pastoral outreach by the Catholic Church towards today's world that can be truly effective unless the church is seen to be definitively putting a number of aspects of the past behind it. There must be an open acknowledgement of the fact that the rejection of much the church did in the second millennium has considerable justification. The change can never take place through words alone, and only a truly radical reform can give the church credibility again. There are some further elements of this reform that deserve mention here, and they involve the change of heart and mind of which this chapter speaks.

Wealth

The Catholic Church is seen as immensely wealthy. There is much that is mistaken in the accusations made, for the wealth is largely in the land on which churches, schools and hospitals are built, and there is more often a debt on the land and its buildings than there is any spare money. Nevertheless, over a period of two thousand years the church has gradually acquired an enormous amount of property. It is time for the church to look honestly at this phenomenon and ask itself where a church that models itself on Jesus should go in the next millennium. It is simple fact that the wealth of the church is a significant factor in preventing people from seeing the person of Jesus.

I believe that for a church material assets are always spiritual liabilities. Often a church must incur the spiritual liability of some material asset in order to do its work, but it should never for a moment forget the fact that for a church material assets cannot help being spiritual liabilities. The church must ask itself just how heavy a spiritual liability it can afford to carry around with it at all times.

Justice Within the Church

Over the last century the Catholic Church has developed a considerable body of social teaching. There are nine principles in particular that deserve serious attention by all people who care about this world:

    i) The essential and equal dignity of all human beings;

    ii) The right to individual freedom balanced by the common good;

    iii) The universal destination of all created goods, that is, that while we must respect an individual's right to the acquired use of private property, it remains true that all created goods ultimately belong to the whole world and all people in it;

    iv) The priority of labour over capital;

    v) The solidarity of the whole human race, that is, what

happens to the poorest people in the world happens to me;

vi) The preferential option for the poor;

vii) Stewardship of the earth's resources in sustainable development;

viii) The principle of subsidiarity, that is, decisions that can best be taken at a lower level should not be reserved to a higher level;

ix) The principle of participation, that is, that all people should have some share in their own governance, some say in what happens in a society.

Sadly, this concern for social justice has too often been weakened by a lack of justice within the church itself. Bishops and priests often have few restrictions on their power, while groups such as women or victims of abuse are powerless. There are too many cases of unfair and unjust actions. Laypersons have very little say in the governance of their church. If it were only a matter of this or that individual behaving badly, one might not be concerned, but much injustice is seen as endemic and institutional, and few are convinced that problems such as sexual abuse have yet been faced with total honesty and genuine courage by the whole world-wide church. As long as the church fails in these areas, few people will be listening to the many good things the church has to say about how human affairs in the whole world should be ordered.

INSTITUTIONAL HYPOCRISY

As long as the church is made up of human beings, there will always be hypocrisy in it, as in every other institution in the world. But a religious community must have a special concern in this regard. It must be particularly careful of any form of hypocrisy that appears to be institutional, the hypocrisy that a person is prey to simply by being a member of that institution or by holding a particular office. I speak solely for myself, but the sight of a large group of bishops on a sanctuary, all wearing mitres, is for me too close to a vision of institutional hypocrisy, for it seems such a long way from the human weakness of the same bishops and from the simplicity and sincerity of Jesus.

PRACTICAL WORK

The Catholic Church must be part of the work to overcome the rock-hard problems of today's world. A vast number of both individuals and groups within the church have in fact been deeply involved, but there is always more to do. Example will always be more important than words. As a global institution itself, the church is ideally placed to model the kind of global institution the world is in need of in the economic and political spheres, but the centralisation of all power in the pope means that this example is not being given in the way it could be.

The church's agencies have done much work for the poor over many centuries, but in the past they were frequently identified with the idea of the 'hand-out', and there is further work to do in changing this. Justice can never be based on the haves giving something from their surplus to the have-nots (the 'hand-out'). True justice must involve the haves sitting down with the have-nots on a basis of equality to discuss together the very values on which the society must be built.

A CHURCH IN THE WORLD

Paradoxically, in speaking about attitudes towards power in the church, it seems necessary to add some comments about attitudes towards the church's lack of power in many fields.

Many people in the church speak as though everything that happens in the church must be explained solely in terms of the church. Thus, if people do not attend church as often as they once did, the only explanations given are e.g. that they are not taught their faith in school as they once were or that the modern liturgy is inferior to the older liturgy. They fail to understand that the church exists in the world and is influenced by all the currents that flow in that world. Catholic people have been influenced, for example, by the conflict between reason and faith over five centuries and the modern reaction of feelings against both. They have been influenced by the effects of the Industrial Revolution and the reaction against the sense of alienation that it caused. In our own day, they have been influenced in a thousand different ways by the New Age movement. This movement is not 'out there' somewhere; it is also alive and well within the church.

It is not only individuals but also communities and institutions that have been affected by forces in the world around us. In my childhood people went to church for religious reasons, but they also went because it was a chance to meet people and socialise. In other words, the parish served both a religious and a social need. Indeed, for two thousand years the parish was greatly helped in its spiritual role by the fact that it was also the most powerful social centre in the town or village. As a social centre it brought together people of all ages and this made it far easier to exercise a spiritual role towards them.

In a few brief years the parish, at least in the developed world, has ceased to be the social centre it once was and this has made it far more difficult to exercise a spiritual role. Parishes throughout the developed world are struggling to adapt to being a spiritual centre without the assistance of being a social centre. What caused this seismic change? I don't believe it was the Second Vatican Council, but the far more pragmatic forces of the car, the television set and the telephone, for the car freed people to move beyond their local area for their social life, television entertained them at home and the telephone became a prime means of making and maintaining connections between people, that is, of building one's own community.

In a similar way, it is possible to think of several non-religious reasons to explain why fewer candidates present themselves for the priesthood today.

> i) In my childhood there were many larger families while today families tend to be smaller, and this alone will mean less candidates for priesthood.
>
> ii) In my youth it was possible to inspire young people to permanent commitments, while today there is a fear of such commitments.
>
> iii) In a similar manner, there was a sense of community and of willingness to give oneself for the common good, while today there is a greater sense of individualism.
>
> iv) Those who hold strongly to feelings and subjective truth are unlikely to choose priesthood.
>
> v) For those for whom the self rather than God has become the centre of life, priesthood will not be an option.

Needless to say, there are also religious reasons for the changes in parish life and the smaller number of candidates for the priesthood, and they must be given their full weight. But it is a serious mistake to think that all changes in the church must be explained solely in terms of church, for this takes the church out of the world. In every single aspect of the church's life we must look to see both the religious and the non-religious causes of change.

Looking solely within the church for all explanations of change has also contributed greatly to the angers that have arisen. Within the church it is easy, for example, to blame bishops for all perceived problems, and yet they did not create the Industrial Revolution or the New Age movement, and they did not create a movement away from faith and reason and towards subjective feelings. They did not invent the car, the television set and the mobile phone. They did not decree that families should be smaller or that people should fear permanent commitments or that individualism should replace a sense of community. They have negligible power to undo these massive forces and return the world to its former state. And yet these forces are affecting every aspect of the church's life.

We must accept that there are powerful forces in the world, forces that may take centuries to work themselves through. We must learn to live in the world we have been given and must try to do what we can to be a leaven in that world.

CONCLUSION

At the beginning of this book I stated my belief that there must be profound change in the Catholic Church on the two subjects of power and sex. Throughout the book I have tried to indicate a number of areas in which attitudes and beliefs in the church have contributed, either to the abuse itself or to the poor response by many authorities to that abuse. What is needed is an open and honest discussion of such matters by the whole church.

When I see this open and honest discussion taking place, I will believe that the church is serious about confronting abuse. Until that happens, I cannot have this conviction.

Changes in external structures can help, but they cannot of themselves produce a new church. The more important change is the change of heart and mind.

> "You know that among the Gentiles their seeming rulers lord it over them, and their great ones are tyrants over them. But it is not so among you; but whoever wishes to become great among you must be your servant, and whoever wishes to be first among you must be slave of all. For the Son of Man came not to be served but to serve, and to give his life a ransom for many."[11]

Meditation

The most fundamental change of heart and mind required of us is that of a constant return to the Great Tradition, the person and story of Jesus Christ, and the song that he sang.

For in everything he did and in everything he said, Jesus Christ sang a song. Sometimes, when he cured a sick person, he sang softly and gently, a song full of love. Sometimes, when he told one of his beautiful stories, he sang a haunting melody, the kind of melody that, once heard, is never forgotten, the sort of melody you hum throughout the day without even knowing that you are doing it. Sometimes, when he defended the rights of the poor, his voice grew strong and powerful, until finally, from the cross, he sang so powerfully that his voice filled the universe.

The disciples who heard him thought that this was the most beautiful song they had ever heard, and they began to sing it to others. They didn't sing as well as Jesus had – they forgot some of the words, their voices sometimes went flat –but they sang to the best of their ability, and the people who heard them thought in their turn that this was the most beautiful song they had ever heard.

And so the song of Jesus gradually spread out from Jerusalem to other lands. Parents sang it to their children and it began to be passed down through the generations and through the centuries.

Sometimes, in the lives of great saints, the song was sung with exquisite beauty. At other times and by other people it was sung very badly indeed, for the song was so beautiful that there was power in possessing it, and people used the power of the song to march to war and to oppress and dominate others. Despite this, the song was always greater than the singers and its ancient beauty could never be destroyed.

And so the song continued through the centuries, sung in many languages and forms, argued about, fought over, treated as a possession, distorted, covered by many layers of human accretions, but always captivating people by its sheer simplicity and aching beauty.

At last the song came down to us and, like so many people before us, we too were captured by the song, and wanted to sing it with our whole being. The song must not stop with us, and we in our turn must hand on its beauty to those who come after us. We must always remember that this song has two special characteristics.

The first is that we, too, sing it badly, but if we sing it to the best of our ability, people do not hear only our voices. Behind us and through us they hear a stronger and surer voice, the voice of Jesus.

The second is that we always sing it better when we learn to sing it together – not one voice here, another there, each singing different words to different melodies, but all singing the one song in harmony, for it is still the most beautiful song the world has ever known.

Compared to this song, there is little else that is of great importance. In the atmosphere created by this song, abuse cannot flourish.

FOOTNOTES

[1] 1:15. The usual translation given is 'repent', but the Greek word is *metanoia*, and 'change of mind and heart' is a more accurate translation.

[2] If a serious problem exists in a parish, it should be confronted directly. An appraisal is not the way to handle such a problem.

[3] Canon 1404, 'The First See is judged by no one.'

[4] Acts 11:1-18

[5] I do not advocate casting all sexual abusers out into the street, for this would almost ensure that they would offend again. The church must adopt the far more responsible role of seeking competent treatment for them that will address both their psychological problems and their ideas concerning power and sex, and then trying to ensure that they live in a healthy environment that will assist them to avoid new offences.

[6] *Lumen Gentium, no.31.*

[7] cf. Teresa Pirola, *Laity - A Block to the Mission of the Church*, Australasian Catholic Record, October 1989, p.425.

[8] cf. e.g. Post-Synodal Apostolic Exhortation *Christifideles Laici* on the Vocation and mission of the Lay Faithful in the Church and in the World, 30 December 1988. n.42: 'The lay faithful cannot remain indifferent... in the face of all that denies and compromises peace ... On the contrary ... the lay faithful ought to take upon themselves the task of being 'peacemakers'. And yet surely all Christians, lay or clerical, should take on the task of peacemakers.

[9] ibid., n.15.

[10] Pope Paul VI, Talk to the Members of Secular Institutes, 2 February 1972, AAS 64 (1972), 208.

[11] Mk.10:42-45.

Claws of Fire
Seeking the Whispering Friend

Terry Monagle
9781920721367   PB $34.95

'This book epitomises, I hope, how, in contemporary times,
the spiritual quest takes its form. We are each hooded falcons
desperate for light and fight.'

With a mix of the humorous, the poetic and the profound, Terry
Monagle offers up his experience of faith and joy in life in the scru-
tiny of proximate and terminal cancer. He unsentimentally shares
the questioning his love of life engenders when faced with the
problem of having to let go all that he loves in the physical world,
from the beauty he finds in the natural environment to his relationships with family, friends and the Church. As he does so he finds
comfort whispering to him, and makes sense of his fate through its
service to others.

Also from Terry Monagle:

Fragments
Moments of Intimacy

9781920721037   PB $32.95

You will smile, you will pray, your heart will grow as you read
this book.

Daniel O'Leary, author *Travelling Light*

THE LIVING VOICE OF THE GOSPEL
THE GOSPELS TODAY

FRANK MOLONEY SDB
9781920721336   PB $34.95

A completely rewritten edition of a previous bestseller.

How do we reach into the Gospels today, and how do the Gospels reach back out to us? In the light of all that has been written over the ages, is there a fresh approach that speaks to the 21st century Christian?

Fr Francis J. Moloney offers his experience and scholarship to lead the lay person through such a guide. The reader is brought up to date about how a Gospel is read as 'theological narrative' today, a markedly different understanding from the past. Each Gospel is reviewed as a whole, followed by a focused study of a particular section in which Moloney demonstrates how each Gospel author works the text to his own theological purposes. The final chapter outlines the general intellectual and academic history which forms the background to this position before Moloney makes his own case about the nature of Jesus, the Son of God and the Son of Man and the role of our discipleship today.

This book is a thought-provoking yet readily accessible invitation to study the Gospels at an intermediate level. It is highly suitable for personal or group work.

Freeing Celibacy

Donald Cozzens
9781920721305 PB $19.95

Donald Cozzens explores priestly celibacy as source of power and burden of obligation, as spiritual calling and gift of the Spirit. Putting mandatory celibacy in historical perspective, he examines the ancient and contemporary experience of married clergy in the Eastern churches and the Roman rite church. In his signature calmness and his talent for distilling the spiritual truth, he concludes that it is time to set celibacy free from canonical mandate to become what it is meant to be: a graced way of life for some but not for all of the church's ordained ministers.

Also by Donald Cozzens:

Faith That Dares to Speak

9781920721145 PB $29.95

Sacred Silence

9781875938940 PB $32.95

AND THE DANCE GOES ON
AN ANTHOLOGY OF
AUSTRALIAN CATHOLIC WOMEN'S STORIES

COMMISSION FOR AUSTRALIAN CATHOLIC WOMEN
9781920721244 PB $32.95

'This is a love story, and like all love stories it is the stuff of
life. What makes it different is that it is the love story of
contemporary Australian women and the Eternal Lover.
Here you will find stories of loving and laughing, longing and
sometimes languishing. The stories tell something of what it
means to be a Catholic woman today. They grapple with the
question of the relevance of Catholicism as women continue to
seek meaning and growth in Love's embrace.'

Therese Vassarotti, Executive Officer,
Commission for Australian Catholic Women

THE SPIRIT OF GENERATION Y
YOUNG PEOPLE'S SPIRITUALITY
IN A CHANGING AUSTRALIA

MICHAEL MASON, ANDREW SINGLETON, RUTH WEBBER
9781920721466   PB $45

The current generation of youth, Generation Y (born 1981-95), are growing up in a world vastly different from that of their Baby-Boomer parents, featuring the cultural pluralism of late modernity, increased anxiety about personal and environmental risk, precarious employment, rampant consumerism, the information deluge, greater individualisation and increased instability in families.

Much has been written about the decline of the mainstream church and the place of organised religion in these rapidly changing times. Despite the prominence in the mass media of alternative spiritualities, reincarnation, horoscopes and Buddhism, this book argues that for the most part, young people are not active spiritual seekers, but instead have a highly individualistic and relativistic approach to life and spirituality, and are hardly familiar with religious traditions. Only a small percentage of Generation Y is actively religious. The religion of those young people who do belong to a denomination, is for the most part 'low temperature'.

The Spirit of Generation Y describes young people's spirituality, values, worldviews and community engagement. Drawing on data from a large scale national study of youth values, spirituality and citizenship, it describes the patterns and 'types' of spirituality in Generation Y, and discusses the possible influences shaping these forms of spirituality. It further considers the consequences of these forms of spirituality for the way in which members of this generation participate in society.